# Landscape and Utopia

This book examines three landmark utopian visions central to 20th-century landscape architectural, planning, and architectural theory.

The period between the 1890s and the 1940s was a fertile time for utopian thinking. Significant geographic shifts of large populations; radically altered relations between capital and labor; rapid technological developments; large investments in transportation and energy infrastructure; and repetitive economic disruptions motivated many individuals to wholly reimagine society – including the connections between social relations and the built environment. *Landscape and Utopia* examines the role of landscapes in the political imaginations of the Garden City, the Radiant City, and Broadacre City. Each project uses landscapes to propose a reconstruction of the relationships between land, labor, and capital but – while the projects are well-known – the role played by landscapes has been largely left unexamined. Similarly, the radical anti-capitalism that underpinned each project has similarly been, for the most part, left out of contemporary discussions. This book sets these projects within a historical and philosophical context and opens a discussion on the role of landscapes in society today.

This book will be a must-read for instructors, students, and researchers of the history and theory of landscape architecture, planning, and architecture as well as utopian studies, cultural and social history, and environmental theory.

**Jody Beck** is an associate professor in the Department of Landscape Architecture at the University of Colorado Denver, USA. His research interests center around the political content of landscape. His first book, *John Nolen and the Metropolitan Landscape*, covers the political underpinnings of a figure significant to the development of the modern professions of both landscape architecture and city planning. He has also published several works on the importance of food and agricultural production to the politics of landscape.

# Routledge Research in Landscape and Environmental Design

Routledge Research in Landscape and Environmental Design is series of academic monographs for scholars working in these disciplines and the overlaps between them. Building on Routledge's history of academic rigour and cutting-edge research, the series contributes to the rapidly expanding literature in all areas of landscape and environmental design.

**Landscape Performance**
Ian McHarg's Ecological Planning in The Woodlands, Texas
*Bo Yang*

**Desert Paradises**
Surveying the Landscapes of Dubai's Urban Model
*Julian Bolleter*

**Ian McHarg and the Search for Ideal Order**
*Kathleen John-Alder*

**Walking, Landscape and Environment**
*David Borthwick, Pippa Marland, Anna Stenning*

**Climate-Adaptive Design in High Mountain Villages**
Ladakh in Transition
*Carey Clouse*

**Waste and Urban Regeneration**
An Urban Ecology of Seoul's Nanjido Post-Landfill Park
*Jeong Hye Kim*

**Landscape and Utopia**
*Jody Beck*

For more information about this series, please visit: www.routledge.com/ Routledge-Research-in-Landscape-and-Environmental-Design/book-series/ RRLAND

# Landscape and Utopia

Jody Beck

LONDON AND NEW YORK

Designed cover image: Jody Beck

First published 2023
by Routledge
4 Park Square, Milton Park, Abingdon, Oxon OX14 4RN

and by Routledge
605 Third Avenue, New York, NY 10158

*Routledge is an imprint of the Taylor & Francis Group, an informa business*

© 2023 Jody Beck

The right of Jody Beck to be identified as author of this work has been asserted in accordance with sections 77 and 78 of the Copyright, Designs and Patents Act 1988.

All rights reserved. No part of this book may be reprinted or reproduced or utilised in any form or by any electronic, mechanical, or other means, now known or hereafter invented, including photocopying and recording, or in any information storage or retrieval system, without permission in writing from the publishers.

*Trademark notice*: Product or corporate names may be trademarks or registered trademarks, and are used only for identification and explanation without intent to infringe.

*British Library Cataloguing-in-Publication Data*
A catalogue record for this book is available from the British Library

*Library of Congress Cataloging-in-Publication Data*
Names: Beck, Jody, author.
Title: Landscape and utopia / Jody Beck.
Description: Abingdon, Oxon : Routledge, 2023. |
Includes bibliographical references and index.
Identifiers: LCCN 2022031182 (print) | LCCN 2022031183 (ebook) |
ISBN 9781138483866 (hardback) | ISBN 9781032405445 (paperback) |
ISBN 9781351053730 (ebook)
Subjects: LCSH: City planning–History–20th century. | Urban landscape architecture–History–20th century. | Howard, Ebenezer, Sir, 1850–1928. Tomorrow. | Le Corbusier, 1887–1965. Ville radieuse. |
Wright, Frank Lloyd, 1867–1959. Living city.
Classification: LCC NA9050 .B395 2023 (print) |
LCC NA9050 (ebook) | DDC 711/.4–dc23/eng/20220720
LC record available at https://lccn.loc.gov/2022031182
LC ebook record available at https://lccn.loc.gov/2022031183

ISBN: 978-1-138-48386-6 (hbk)
ISBN: 978-1-032-40544-5 (pbk)
ISBN: 978-1-351-05373-0 (ebk)

DOI: 10.4324/9781351053730

Typeset in Bembo
by Newgen Publishing UK

# Contents

| | | |
|---|---|---|
| | *Preface: How to Read This Book* | vii |
| | *Acknowledgments* | xii |
| 1 | Why Utopia? Why Landscape? | 1 |
| 2 | Landscapes as Political Media | 17 |
| 3 | When the Social Order Was a Public Question | 41 |
| 4 | Land, Capital, and Labor | 62 |
| 5 | Technology | 84 |
| 6 | Food and Agriculture | 100 |
| 7 | Leisure | 116 |
| 8 | Freedom, Cooperation, and Authority | 130 |
| 9 | History, Nature, Agency; and So, What Next? | 148 |
| | Afterword | 168 |
| | *Index* | 170 |

# Preface

## How to Read This Book

While I would be thrilled if everyone sat down with this book and read it cover to cover as one would a novel or a history, I realize that most academic reading is more strategic. This book is, hopefully, designed such that reading the entire book from start to finish is a rewarding and enlightening experience, but it was also my intention to design the book such that each chapter can stand alone — particularly in courses that focus on only one or another of the topics covered in the broader frame of this book. Reading Chapter 4 on capital, labor, and land will certainly bring more depth to reading Chapter 7 on leisure for instance, but it is my intention that reading the latter chapter by itself will have value as well. Similarly, reading Chapter 3, which uses the writings of Marx, George, Bellamy, and Kropotkin to provide intellectual context for the times in which Howard, Corbusier, and Wright thought about the world and show that they were not the intellectual outliers that they might appear to a modern reader, gives much more depth to the understanding of the relations between capital, labor, and land that underlie each of the proposals as described in Chapter 4 — but also may be more political theory than some readers need or desire. Similar things can be said about each chapter of this book. This attempt to have it both ways admittedly leads to some repetition, but that is hopefully managed in a productive manner.

It should also be stated up front that I am more interested in the books than in their authors. I have not tried to figure out what any of the authors *really* meant when they wrote these books by forensically examining the rest of their work or by performing an armchair post-mortem evaluation of their childhoods, apparent morals, the politics implicit in their associations during different periods of youth or old age, or other life events. The book you are now reading is ultimately, and rather simply, about three other books and the utopian proposals they contain for a better and more just society. I propose that we benefit in our thinking about the contemporary world by letting the ideas they contain stand or fall on their own merits. To that end, I am also not interested in telling readers *how* or *what* to think about the Garden City, the Radiant City, or Broadacre City. That said, I am admittedly and quite explicitly pulling viii *Preface*

forward a critique of capitalism shared by all three writers which organizes their projections for a better world but which has been largely overlooked by most histories of theory about cities and landscapes. Their significant reliance on landscapes to ground the political imaginations of their proposals for better worlds is intimately related to this shared critique and has also been largely overlooked.

I use many of their words not only because it is *their* words and *not* mine that interest me, but also as a device to insert what is perhaps an unusual number of footnote references. This is intended to give readers quick access back into the primary texts I am working with, and I hope that many readers will use this book as a guide to explore them further. Attempting to allow the texts to speak for themselves along a particular narrative line and arguing neither for nor against any of their positions has also led me to choose to leave out discussions of secondary literature – much of which is trying to tell readers what the original authors *really* meant or how to think *correctly* about what they wrote. While I value and see a place for such secondary literature, I chose not to clutter this presentation of the original ideas with interpretive and often tendential accounts of those ideas.

My ultimate intention is to prompt readers to use the shared critique and subsequent proposals by Howard, Corbusier, and Wright as a tool to think about change in the contemporary world. Thus, I urge readers to engage this book alongside current news about politics, legislation, policy, social and economic inequality, environmental concerns, and other pressing issues of their day. And while reading this book, I ask them to consider whether – if the political will could be summoned to implement the proposals described – our world would be a better place for it.

To that end, it is important to note the book you are about to read was substantially completed in the United States during 2021 following the broadening awareness of institutionalized and persistent racism in our society brought forward by the murder of George Floyd, who, it must be tragically noted is one of many, many victims of the racist and violent acts by police and others which – horrifically – continue apace. While people of color, and particularly men of color, are subject to higher rates of police violence than others, we must also acknowledge the long history and continued disproportionate use of violence by police against poor and working-class people of all backgrounds. This growing awareness appears to be leading to a growing willingness to acknowledge and hopefully begin to redress the evils rooted in institutionalized racism and other forms of systemic inequality. While there is a glimmer of hope, there is much work to be done and many injustices to correct.

This book was also written during the middle of the global Covid pandemic, which continues to not only take many lives around the world but also leave many more injured in ways that we do not yet understand. These negative impacts are not equally distributed across populations either globally or within nations. Within nations, the inequities fall along familiar racial and socioeconomic lines that are closely correlated to household wealth and income.

Preface    ix

The pandemic has, tragically, served to expand the gap between the wealthy and the poor. Between nations, the inequities of Covid's impact both highlight and exacerbate the extreme levels of inequity that are among the legacies of colonialism and other forms of oppressive appropriation.

Against this background, there is a growing, and much needed, reconsideration of the texts we teach and an attempt to be more inclusive in how we teach history, theory, design, policy, and all other aspects of our work. And yet, this is a book written about three books written long ago by white men who, while not wealthy, certainly held the privileges that came with their gender and race. While all of them spent considerable effort addressing social inequities in both the critiques and the subsequent proposals they put forward, none of them acknowledged or addressed racism per se. While each was an adamant critic of global capitalist structures of trade, none of them acknowledged or addressed colonialism and its legacies. What are we to make of this? What value do these works hold for us today? While it is productive to hold these issues and challenges in mind while reading, I would also propose that we would do well to not reject their works out of hand given their blindspots or their identities.

Instead, I would ask readers to think through each of their proposals and ask to what degree the impacts of institutionalized racism and class inequality would have been undercut if their proposals had been carried out in full. For example, what would our societies look like today with regard to racially motivated violence and other characteristics of racial inequality if there had been no racial disparities between groups with regard to household income and security of housing tenure for the last 80 to 100 years? While material equality is not the same as genuine equality before the law and does not erase histories of racism or deep-seated racial prejudices, collective wealth ultimately can buy collective political and social power to address these issues. It is undeniable that the inequalities in wealth which Howard, Corbusier, and Wright thought should be overturned, having been let stand, have allowed certain classes in society to maintain financial, political, legal, and social power at the expense of others – and the resulting differential of privilege has consistently tracked with racial disparities.

Similarly, each of these authors argued strenuously against the precedents to the highly capitalized global trade that characterizes our economies today. While they did not discuss colonialism and how it was related to exploitative patterns of trade and industrialization, we ought to ask ourselves whether the impacts of Covid, for instance, would have had the reach or the depth had their vision been realized and societies established which were not based on exploitative global capitalism. To go further, if one imagined the world they proposed in its fulfillment, would the legacy of colonialism be as destructive as it still is? Could the disparities in wealth and health exist between nations if all societies were grounded in primarily local economies focused on equality between people and the care of land?

On a similar note, each writer imagined a world in which an effective and deeply collaborative citizenship could develop largely as a result of the financial

x   *Preface*

security and political power which their proposals gave to the laboring class – though the content of that collaboration varied widely between them as will be discussed. Could the politics of fear, hatred, and division that have, at least in the United States, amplified the duration and tragedy of the pandemic flourished in the societies they imagined? Furthermore, could those politics have grown to the point that they threaten democracy itself as they now do? This author finds it hard to imagine that they could.

This book is also written as the impacts of climate change are becoming ever more apparent and the environmental damage that has been wrought by how we generate and use energy as well as the highly toxic externalities and rapidly accelerating waste produced by our consumerism is becoming unavoidably clear. While they did not argue against consumerism from the standpoint of environmental damage, reigning in the overproduction of goods and redirecting machine power to support quality of life (as each saw it, of course) was a key theoretical move for at least Corbusier and Wright. It could be debated whether the energy demands of the societies they envisioned would have been enough lower due to reorganized and more efficient production and transportation networks and reduced consumerism that we would not be facing the same climate crises we now face. However, it seems clear – at least to this author – that the politics they envisioned as integral to their vision for cities and their relationships to landscapes would have provided a path for at least more productive responses to the dilemmas we have before us.

Lastly, all three books contain gendered phrases and ideas that rightfully make modern readers cringe, though perhaps a little self-righteously if we honestly imagine the prejudices we would have held had we lived in their time. In some places, I have paraphrased their ideas with language that embodies a radical equality between people regardless of how they identify themselves. In cases where this would have led to much awkwardness in the language and not allowed me to use their words where they were most apt, I kept the gendered words they used. I ask readers to challenge each gendered assumption, most of which are left to be discovered in the original texts, and particularly those around issues of privilege and authority, and ask if the problem of gendered inequality as stated or implied in their language can be resolved by simply replacing the pronoun. In some cases, this simple fix is an adequate conceptual resolution. In some cases, it is not and the assumption of differential privilege remains. But the distinction between instances in which assumed differential privilege is inseparable from a core idea and the situations in which it can be easily separated will not only help us critically glean what is valuable from these texts but, I propose, provide a model for how to re-approach many texts that are overdue a critical, productive examination to separate the value they continue to offer our thinking from the prejudices they contain which we should consciously seek to remove from *our* thinking and *our* proposals for a better world.

There is no question that there are theoretical if not practical problems with the Garden City, the Radiant City, and Broadacre City. None would be a perfect world, and none would have fully resolved all the issues we face today.

*Preface*  xi

However, this should not forestall asking whether the societies they propose and the landscapes that embody them are not in some ways better than our own, and if so – in what ways. More importantly, it should not forestall our use of these ideas to challenge our own world and offer improvements to it where the comparison illustrates that such as are warranted. To that end, I propose that readers hold two opposing frames of mind in productive tension while they read this book and consider the utopian proposals it presents. First, there are many valid reasons to be of a skeptical mind with regard to the utopias of Howard, Le Corbusier, and Wright. I propose that readers keep those in hand, but also simultaneously balance that skepticism with giving the proposals the benefit of the doubt. Being merely skeptical will lead one to abandon what may be valuable, and enjoyable, avenues for thought before their length is fully surveyed. Simply giving these proposals the benefit of the doubt will not lead to the creative and constructive critique they make available. The critical but generously curious frame of mind that will result from this proposed tension will allow the reader to most productively use this work and its subject matter as a foil by which to enhance their own thinking about proposals to improve the world.

# Acknowledgments

I would like to thank Robert Fishman for writing his book *Urban Utopias in the Twentieth Century*, which I first read as an undergraduate student over 30 years ago and which has stayed with me ever since. While I do not make use of secondary literature in this volume, this has been an invaluable and influential text. Approximately half-way between then and now, David Leatherbarrow entertained many valuable discussions about these utopian proposals with good humor, wisdom, and patience – all of which I value to this day. Following these words of appreciation, my first acknowledgement of contribution to my thinking must go to the many students who have directly and indirectly engaged the topic of utopia with me in studios and seminars over last many years and enriched my thinking while they tolerated, with both good humor and enthusiasm, being given unsolvable problems and unanswerable questions. Second, my family must be thanked for their constant support, understanding, and patience. Four colleagues in particular at the University of Colorado Denver have read chapters or portions of chapters and contributed valuable insights and challenges – Sasha Breger Bush, Jeremy Németh, Jesse Kuroiwa, and Joern Langhorst. Hillary Quarles provided invaluable editing support and her work has made this book not only more clear but also, I think, a far more valuable and enjoyable experience for the reader. The editorial staff at Routledge who have worked with me since the project started have been not only supportive as this project changed shape significantly early in 2021 but have also been encouraging and amazingly, thankfully, patient. Most importantly, I must especially acknowledge John Dixon Hunt who not only read drafts of key portions of this text and asked pointed questions which helped me first reframe and then sharpen my thinking on several crucial arguments but has also provided years of valuable discourse, encouragement and support critical to my thinking about landscapes as well as critical to my career as a whole. Of course, any remaining flaws in the text remain my sole responsibility and are more than likely an indication of good advice I was given but did not take.

# 1  Why Utopia? Why Landscape?

The time is once again ripe for Utopian thinking. Inequality by any measure continues to increase. The foundational systems of society that satisfy the needs for food, for shelter, and for the capacity to thrive are damaged, challenged, and under attack as is the very earth itself. The world and its productive capacity have been appropriated by the few and the wealthy at the expense of the many – leaving them insecure and impoverished. Landscapes across the planet bear the scars of this appropriation as do the people who live with them. Anyone who attempts to tackle the large problems societies face finds that the contributing factors run both deep and broad, from the centuries-old philosophical foundations of our legal systems to the finest digital tendrils of global trade. It has become obvious that all genuine proposals to address problems such as inequality, poverty, hunger, obesity, and homelessness as well as the even larger problems of global climate change, pollution of fresh water, depletion of marine resources, and loss of biodiversity must be as systematic as the problem they seek to address. If we take utopian thinking to be that which radically and holistically re-imagines human action to systematically improve the condition of life for all, then it is utopian thinking that we so desperately need.

Ruth Levitas, in the introduction to her book *Utopia as Method*, proposes using utopian thought as a conceptual framework for moving against problems such as those noted above. She proposes that this method involves an imaginative reconstruction of society – exactly what the Garden City, the Radiant City, and Broadacre City offer. Levitas further proposes that a utopian method relevant to our contemporary world

> would provide a critical tool for exposing the limitations of current policy discourses about economic growth and ecological sustainability ..., facilitate genuine holistic thinking about holistic futures, combined with reflexivity, provisionality and democratic engagement with the principles and practices of those futures, ... and require us to think about our conception of human needs and human flourishing in those possible futures.[1]

All three imagined utopian futures which will be examined in this book are based on particular understandings of human needs and human flourishing and

DOI: 10.4324/9781351053730-1

## 2    *Why Utopia? Why Landscape?*

systems of organization intended to achieve those understandings. These visions were put forward as direct critiques of the worlds into which they were given and – I propose – continue to have value as tools to evaluate our world today for its organization and its support of human needs and human flourishing or lack thereof.

It is true that Utopia as a project has been discredited to the point that the word itself is often used to pejoratively describe something which is hopelessly optimistic, naïve and unfeasible. However, recent history and current events have shown that expecting the current systems of governance, culture, laws, and economics to solve any of the systemic societal problems just mentioned is perhaps even more hopelessly optimistic, naïve and unfeasible. While some detractors of utopian projects point to the very real and truly horrific acts that have been committed under the guise of creating a uniformly perfect society, there is reason to argue that these harms had more to do with the megalomania of particular individuals using power to construct and preserve privilege for themselves than they had to do with any sincere attempt at uniformly improving lives for all people. One can also respond to the critics of utopian thinking by pointing to the very real and horrific harms that the current world, organized as it is around the imperatives intrinsic to capitalist modes of production, must perpetuate to preserve the privileges of power and the powers of privilege. Ruth Levitas observes, I would argue accurately, that "this anti-utopian discourse equates utopia with a blueprint producing violence and terror, and gives rise to a politics of quiescent subordination to the dictates of capitalist markets."[2] If we are not willing to engage with systematic thinking that gets to the root of the issues we want to solve, then we are acquiescing to the world as it is and reinforcing obeisance those who currently hold power over it.

What we need, then, is a rehabilitated utopian project in the vein of Levitas' proposal for utopia as method. This project needs to: be unapologetically optimistic yet capable of being implemented at the scale of the problems we face, revere difference while being deeply and broadly systemic, and foster participatory efforts to positively impact the world and increase equity. A proposal which meets these criteria can only be achieved when we begin with the ultimate foundation of any utopian project and of society: the landscapes they inhabit. A landscape is not the backdrop to the actions of society but it is at one time the body of material resources we use, the expanses that separate them, the processes of the non-human world on which we rely and the social, cultural, political, and economic processes of human action. Landscapes are things lived not things lived upon. I propose that landscapes are the foundational political medium, as will be elaborated on in the next chapter.

The three utopian proposals considered herein – The Garden City, The Radiant City, and Broadacre City – each use the design of landscapes as the foundations of their imagined reorganization of political relations. Ebenezer Howard proposed revising the structure of ownership of both productive and residential landscapes in the Garden City to undercut the connection between speculative property ownership and poverty. Le Corbusier's grounded the Radiant City on a rich and freely accessible landscape which was a response to a radical proposal for equitably reorienting the relationship between labor and capital. Frank Lloyd Wright organized his proposal for Broadacre City on the redistribution of land to allow for genuine democracy and freedom facilitated by landscapes of self-determination.

As different as their ideas were, Howard, Corbusier, and Wright shared a similarly critical stance toward the impacts of the industrial revolution and capitalism and their dominance over forms of life and landscape. Their individual critiques of industrialization and materialism led each of these writers to an open criticism of capitalism as the primary organizing force of the built environment and therefore of human life. While their particular criticisms varied, and their proposed resolutions even more so, each saw the private, profit-seeking, ownership of land as the foundation of the problems they were attempting to address. It is therefore not surprising that each one proposed the control of land for the common good as the foundation of a more just distribution of the benefits of industrialization. It is also not surprising that re-imagined social and political relationships intimately embedded in specific forms of landscape are central to the logic of each proposal. While Howard argued for a cooperative model of landownership, Corbusier assumed a technocratic and managerial distribution of access to land, and Wright proclaimed the imperative of universal and unassailable individual land holdings allowing for self-sufficiency at the household level, there is one striking similarity between the three proposals. In each case, forms of life intimately engaged with immediate landscapes organized around an ideal of human flourishing was the proposed antidote for the inequities intrinsic to unchecked capitalism and the impact that industrialization was having on both societies and psychologies. A deeper understanding of the position which landscape forms held in the proposals for the Garden City, the Radiant City, and Broadacre City can inform a reinvigorated and utopian discussion of the role that landscape architecture can play in addressing the inequalities of contemporary society.

## The Garden City

Ebenezer Howard published his concept for garden cities in 1898 as *Tomorrow: A Peaceful Path to Real Reform*. With some revision, it was republished in 1902 with the title *Garden Cities of Tomorrow*. While Howard may not have been unequivocally opposed to capitalism, he was highly critical of what he referred to as 'capitalist oppression' and his formal proposal is inseparable from his emphasis on dedicating the benefits of owning land to the common good. He included several measures in his proposal which would have severely constrained the practices of capitalism in this way. He wrote that since

> every form of wealth must rest on the earth as its foundation, and must be
> built up out of the constituents found at or near the surface, it follows...

## 4 Why Utopia? Why Landscape?

that the reformer should first consider how best the earth should be used in the service of man.[3]

He repeated J.S. Mill's distinction between the land which subsists and other forms of wealth and productive capacity which do not and was careful to distinguish his proposal from socialist proposals in which both the land and all instruments of production were controlled by some agency of the common good.[4] The denial of private property ownership in the Garden City, and therefore the denial of speculation and exploitative rent, was intended to preserve single family homes with gardens and proximate if not direct access to parks set within a large belt of agricultural land. The agriculturalists who worked this land would be able to make efficient use of the waste from the town as fertilizer and be provided with stable and profitable local markets for their goods. In return, the residents would benefit from inexpensive and high-quality food. It is important to keep in mind that Howard was as committed to improving life in rural areas as he was committed to improving life in towns.

Howard's proposal, which he claimed would lead to "a juster and better system of land tenure and a better and more common-sense view of how towns should be built"[5] rests on three types of relationship to landscapes, all of which are made possible by the common ownership of land; single family homes with gardens, central public gardens and large open spaces throughout the town, and the belt of protected agricultural land that balanced the size of the town. While it may seem banal now, Howard's proposal for a town comprised of private homes each with its own garden was a stark contrast to London of his day – and particularly the part of London that the poor and those recently arrived from the country experienced. However, Howard did not imagine that this emphasis on single family housing would lead to a society of isolated individuals. One of the few comments he makes on the houses themselves is an observation that groups of houses may have common gardens and co-operative kitchens.[6]

The extensive landscapes for public recreation, and their proximity to these dwellings, also provided a striking contrast with the condition of cities that Howard and many others of his time criticized. The very center of the town was to be a well-watered garden of five acres, surrounded by civic institutions including a library, a theatre, a concert hall, a museum and galleries, and a hospital as well as the town hall. Immediately outside the ring of civic buildings was the circular Central Park of 145 acres. Surrounding this was the Crystal Palace, a glassed-in market space which encircled the central park and provided recreational outdoor space during inclement weather. Outside this were two rings of housing and the circular Grand Avenue. Howard noted that this "additional park of one hundred and fifteen acres" was no further than 240 yards from any dwelling – a walk of less than five minutes.[7]

The extensive agricultural green belt surrounding the Garden City is critical to the ideal put forward by Howard. This belt of agricultural land was neither a mere buffer of vegetated space nor a recreational area. The relationships that it allowed between people, and between people and the landscapes they inhabited, was a conceptual foundation of his entire vision. Howard's critique of life in the country and his desire to improve life for those in agricultural areas held weight equal to as his critique of life in the city and his desire to improve life for those who dwelled in towns. This fact is often forgotten or neglected in discussions of Howard's proposal, and it was particularly forgotten in most of the attempts at implementing his ideas. The town, Howard proposed, would raise the incomes of the farmers by generating a market of 30,000 people within short distance of their farm. This proximity would allow them to grow higher-value crops of vegetables as well as compete more successfully with the grain producers of the United States and Russia. Not only does the agricultural estate contribute a significant portion of the funds which makes the Garden City feasible according to Howard's calculations, but it forms a symbiotic relationship with the town estate by using the sewage from the town as fertilizer to grow quality produce for the city's residents.

Even more importantly, however, the proximity of the agricultural estate and the small scale manufacturing facilities achieved one of the goals that Howard set out for his project; to overcome the fallacy that the "present form of industry, in which sharp lines divide agricultural from industrial pursuits" was the only possible arrangement of economic activity and patterns of settlement.[8] This portion of his proposal was clearly influenced by the writing of Peter Kropotkin, a Russian born anarchist to which Howard referred to in his text. This combination of economic pursuits was intended to avoid the negative physical and mental impacts of highly repetitive work central to the industrial production as well as help insulate people from potential weather induced crop failures and market-based price collapses for agricultural goods on one hand and from the abuses of industrial managers on the other.

## The Radiant City

Like Howard, Le Corbusier perceived that the control of land for the common good was central to any systematic proposal to address the depth of problems faced by society and cities at his time. The first declaration of *The Radiant City* published in 1933, was "Decision: Mobilization of the Land for the Common Good. We must undertake the redistribution of the land in the country and in the cities."[9] He argued that the only thing needed to realize a new type of city which would be healthy for human bodies, human minds, and human society was "to put the ground to use" and claimed that he had been forced by the barrier that "unproductive property" placed in the way of his professional proposals to discuss politics and economics against his inclination.[10] In the chapter titled 'Mobilization of the Land,' Le Corbusier's first resolution of principle was that "the city should provide liberty for the individual and the benefits of collective action on both the material and the spiritual plane."[11] In order to achieve this, Le Corbusier argued, "contemporary society must have the entire land surface of the country at its disposal" because the "mobilization of private property, whether built on or not" was a "fundamental condition of any planned

## 6  Why Utopia? Why Landscape?

development of cities."[12] Whereas Howard offered precise calculations defining how his proposed Garden City would acquire control of land, Corbusier avoided the issue of land acquisition with a simple claim that mobilization did not mean nationalization but merely solidarity, without making any projections of how that solidarity was to come about.[13]

Le Corbusier's critique of capitalism was foundational to his critique of the city. While he wrote that "we must *concern ourselves with man*, not with capitalism or with communism; with *man's happiness*, not with company dividends; with *the satisfaction of man's deepest instincts,* not with the race for success being run between the managements of two companies or corporations," he clearly did not align himself with capitalism and often railed against money, calling it a disease and worse.[14] He claimed that the emphasis on money had blackened and deflowered modern society and made the peasant's life barren and sooty. He described free competition in the market as a form of slavery in which every effort was countered by opposite effort. "We have become merely a flock of rams," he claimed, "horns locked together, all trying to push one another backwards. The flock's strength is drained away, yet it is not moving, it remains always in the same place: we can make no progress!"[15] Le Corbusier called for replacing this

> violent, savage, cruel and ruthless civilization of *money* with another based on *harmony and collaboration*; one in which each member of society will feel himself a vital agent in this enterprise that will *restore the face of our country,* that will illumine our countryside with those symphonic images that enable the human spirit to draw strength from its active collaboration with the forces and beauties of nature, our indisputable and immutable mother.

In order to do this, he claimed that "we must lay hands on our cities as they stand and destroy their misery, their ugliness and their horror; we must make them human."[16] He repeatedly observed that this would not be possible as long as the private control of small parcels of land stood in the way of making improvements at the scale he felt necessary.

The scale of infrastructure and building proposals that Corbusier put forward was not the only reason that he felt the use of land needed to be reorganized for the common good. This was also driven by the way he imagined time being spent in the equitable society he imagined. One of the central issues of the era, one which directly guided Le Corbusier's proposal, was the number of hours to be spent working for money. As machine production dramatically increased the per capita production in nearly every arena, it seemed obvious to many, including Le Corbusier, that workers should be able to maintain themselves and current levels of production with significantly fewer hours of work. It was this reduced workday which drove the urban form in *The Radiant City.* Le Corbusier claimed that if the economy were properly planned, the hours required for production would be greatly diminished and that this offered a glimpse into the "gaping void awaiting the modern age, that imminent danger: leisure. Every day, there will be a great number of hours unoccupied" and that "we must plan for this leisure time. Cities and countrysides alike must be reconstructed. The sites and buildings necessary for the basic pleasures to be brought into these people's lives must be constructed," and that thus "the idea of the Radiant City was born...from observation of the laws of nature, from a comprehension of simple and true events, from the recognition of natural movements, activities, and even aggressions."[17] In another passage, he wrote that "the leisure time ahead constitutes a threat to those cities that have done nothing towards preparing for it! Eight hours of each day without work to fill them – if we domesticate our machines successfully."[18] He went on to describe the urgent necessity of designing sites that would meet these needs as a "search for an environment to liberate our *basic pleasures*" which would require unearthing "the truth of contemporary life."[19]

Le Corbusier proposed that sport would best fill these extra hours in which people were not working and provide for many of the basic pleasures he described. Sport, he wrote, is "a food as indispensable as bread itself." After thinking through the problem of sport and its accessibility, he came to the formula, "*sports should be a daily matter and* IT SHOULD TAKE PLACE DIRECTLY OUTSIDE THE HOUSES." Based on his studies into this necessity, he claimed that he had "arrived at the idea of the 'Radiant City' type. The sports grounds were directly outside the houses."[20] He described the vast parks at the foot of residential buildings for sport and pleasure walks, the children's playgrounds shaded under the pilotis of the housing blocks, and the beaches for therapy and sunbathing as "the very basis of the residential neighborhoods," claiming that they were "part of the home," and that it was "thanks to them that the city dweller is guaranteed the 'BASIC PLEASURES.'"[21]

While the physical aspects of sport were important to Le Corbusier's use of the city, the psychological aspects of sport were just as important. In addition to its ability to "revivify their lungs, improve their circulation, strengthen their muscles and fill them with joy and optimism," sport would provide for the expression of human values such as aggression, performance, individual contribution combined with teamwork, and freely accepted discipline that were at the center of human nature but which had been trampled on as "the human animal was being crushed, subjugated, torn apart, denatured by its subjection to the machine."[22] Throughout his proposal, Le Corbusier included a large percentage of landscapes dedicated to passive recreation such as strolling and sunbathing in addition to grounds for organized sport. The health of the body was not the end unto itself, however. "To a healthy body," he wrote,

> to a mind kept in a continual state of activity and optimism by daily physical exercise, the city, if the right measures are taken, can also provide healthy mental activity. This would take two forms: first, meditation in a new kind of dwelling, a vessel of silence and lofty solitude; secondly, civic activity, achieved by the harmonious grouping of creative impulses directed toward the public good.[23]

8   *Why Utopia? Why Landscape?*

It is this emphasis on sport and on a landscape available for the free and self-chosen leisure activities as well as the possibilities that it offered for contemplation and cooperation which is foundational to *The Radiant City*. Therefore, when looking at images of his city, one should start with the detail plans and imagine the entire ground plane as the fully inhabited landscape he intended.

## Broadacre City

Like both Howard and Le Corbusier, Frank Lloyd Wright was ultimately interested in the possibility of human life free from domination by the dictates of capital and the imperatives of industrial production. Wright attacked the same components of the city they did – money, capitalism, landlords, the unmodernized form of the city, and the separation of people from natural systems in everyday life. However, his focus on household autonomy as the elemental basis of democracy in combination with his emphasis on agrarian foundations of civilization drove his project to a very different resolution than either the cooperative municipal structure of Howard's proposal or the administered metropolis of Le Corbusier. Democracy, Wright proclaimed, was "civilization of man and ground – really organic agronomy."[24] This conceptualization of society grounded his famously radical form of decentralization in Broadacre City. The core concept of Broadacre City was published in three different books over several decades. The first was *The Disappearing City* published in 1932. This text was significantly revised and published in 1945 as *When Democracy Builds*. Wright's final revision and most complete proposal, *The Living City*, was published in 1958 – the year before his death. It is this last, most complete vision of Broadacre City which is examined in this book.

Wright was as focused on the role of the machine in human society and its impact on society and forms of human settlement as were Howard and Le Corbusier. He explicitly tied the gross inequality he saw around him and the undemocratic power held by the captains of industry to the impact of industrialization. "What a tragic finality," he wrote, "for our industrial revolution to have turned the citizen himself over to the machine as a slave of production – himself made only another kind of machine – all this done in order to concentrate and maintain more money power."[25] Wright envisioned a new form of city that would overcome the inequality of power within society and put an end to the negative impacts of industrialization on the individuality without which Wright felt that democracy could not thrive. Wright was not a crass individualist as often misconstrued. In fact, he writes at considerable length about the distinction between individualism which he called rank and profane and individuality which he claimed led to highly developed people and therefore more highly developed communities. He wrote that the citizen of his new city would be a "true exponent of a man's true relationship to his fellow-men because he *is* a fellow-man" and it was this authentic human relationship, unmediated by the power of capital and bureaucracy and made possible by each individual's relationship to the landscape, which was the actual intent of Wright's work.[26]

## Why Utopia? Why Landscape? 9

In response to the centralizing forces of the rapidly expanding industrialized city which machine production required, Wright proposed a radical decentralization of human settlement and the end of the city as it existed. Centralization was akin to communism or monarchy for Wright and he proposed that every household have a minimum of an acre per person. If access to land were distributed in this way, he wrote, "no man need be a kept or 'Yes' man; if he goes intelligently to his birthright in nature he is now independently a 'No' man, if he so chooses."[27] According to Wright, this form of life on the landscape would provide the basis of a true form of capitalism as well as the basis for a genuine democracy.[28] He repeatedly referred to profit and rent-seeking capitalism as we know it as a false or artificial form of capitalism.

The precariously upside-down pyramid is an image Wright referred to often and illustrated for him the relationship between artificial capitalism and the form of the contemporary city. For Wright, the upside-down pyramid represented much of what he saw wrong with society and the city. He claimed that the broad base of power upon which democratic ideals must rest could only be realized through universal ownership of land which allowed for household self-sufficiency and therefore true individuality and the potential for independent thought and action (a pyramid right-side-up). However, what he saw around him at the time was the opposite – both political and economic power were disproportionally held by the few at the apex of the pyramid who derived their power from massive rents made possible by the centralization and density of the contemporary city. Wright characterized the land market of the city as chronic artificial scarcity and saw that this artificial scarcity was the underlying driver of the rent which Wright found so damaging to society.[29] Wright described the poor as "those citizens most hardened, hindered or damaged by inexorable, multiple *rents*. ... The poor are poor because of the *triple rent*: rent for land, rent for money, rent for ideas."[30] In contrast, the poor man in Broadacre City would have

> the same quality available to him as the rich. He can say his soul is his own because his own ground opportunity has opened to him in natural ways. He has the right *to be*. ... he becomes a gentleman because no longer enslaved to exercise himself as a soulless faculty of some machine-made producing system – probably for export. ...He lives on his own in his own country.[31]

In Broadacre City, the pyramid would rest on its base and the independence brought about by the genuine potential for self-sufficiency and individual choice of social and economic activities would provide for true individuality and therefore a genuine democracy.

## Landscape in *Utopia*

Howard, Le Corbusier, and Wright were certainly not the first to connect utopian proposals to the forms and uses of landscapes. Thomas More, Francis

## 10 Why Utopia? Why Landscape?

Bacon, Tomasso Campanella, and many others imagined reorganizations of society and its laws, customs, and distribution of resources to achieve social ends prior to the early 20th century. Many science fiction writers, including Ursula Le Guin, Stanley Robinson, and Robert Heinlein to name just a few, have put forward similarly useful writings in recent times. These and many other thinkers provide not only a history of utopian political thought but also provide models for understanding the role particular landscape forms played within political and utopian visions. Their proposals included varying degrees of specificity regarding the landscapes of these imagined societies, but all were aware of the close tie between landscape and polity. It is only after the industrial revolution that people could plausibly regard political entities as if they were divorced from landscapes. The contemporary conceptual distance between politics and landscape is an illusion allowed by the prevalence of long-distance transportation supported by state subsidies of the petroleum industry and its subsidiaries, the material and metabolic transformations characteristic of highly mechanized manufacturing processes, and the obfuscatory function of highly developed forms of capitalist trade.

Thomas More's text *Utopia*, with which he coined the term in in 1516, is an ideal place to begin this consideration of the intimate relationship between landscape and utopian thinking even if it is not the first text or proposal to make the connection. It is particularly clarifying to start not with the actual description of Utopia by the character Raphael Hythloday, but rather with the narrative with which he introduced his description of life in Utopia. When Raphael was asked why, given his extensive travel and great learning, he was not in the service of some king offering counsel to the benefit of a people, he responds that the intrigues of the court and the drive of its members to amass wealth, glory, and power to themselves preclude the fruitful giving of giving wise and honest counsel – and especially any counsel that would benefit the people as a whole at even the slightest expense to the king and members of his court. By way of illustration, he tells the story of a dinner with people such as those who held political and social power in England during the middle of the 16th century. During this dinner, one character, an English lawyer, speaks favorably of the fact that justice was so well delivered to thieves that at times up to 20 hung from one gibbet. This same lawyer then proceeds to wonder – given the gruesome severity of the punishment and the very public nature of its execution – why there continue to be thieves. Raphael responds that there is no reason to wonder at this, given that many people are kept in such poverty that they have no option but to steal to eat, choosing the uncertainty of being caught and hung over the predictability of starvation. He tells the lawyer and the rest of the company that "first you make the thieves and then you punish them."[32] Raphael states that there are several ways in which people are impoverished to the point that thievery is their best if not their only option to stay alive. These include the keeping of a standing army by the king and the widespread and merciless use of the

*Why Utopia? Why Landscape?* 11

laboring poor to feed the idle rich. An additional factor, which he claimed was particular to England, was

> the increase of pasturage…by which your sheep, which are naturally mild, and easily kept in order, may be said now to devour men and unpeople, not only villages, but towns; for wherever it is found that the sheep of any soil yield a softer and richer wool than ordinary, there the nobility and gentry, and even those holy men – the abbots! – not contented with the old rents which their farms yielded, nor thinking it enough that they, living at their ease, do no good to the public, resolve to do it hurt instead of good. They stop the course of agriculture, destroying houses and towns, reserving only the churches, and enclose grounds that they may lodge their sheep in them.[33]

He goes on to describe how people are not only removed from their homes and their lands by the powerful classes in their insatiable desire for additional wealth but also denied their previous sources of income. Since the need for agricultural labor was greatly diminished when only one shepherd was required to care for the flock of sheep occupying land formerly worked by many people, the shift in land-use cost many households their livelihood – leaving them without means of sustenance. It is important to highlight that his part of the narrative is not fiction. Thomas More was criticizing, through the narrative offered by his written character Raphael, the actual events of his day. The powerful who would have been at such a dinner were in fact committing exactly the kind of rapacious acts that More called out. In this initiating narrative, the reader can see not only source of the antipathy to conspicuous wealth and the accumulations of power that run through More's description of Utopia – but also the motivation for addressing these issues with a reconsideration of the distribution and control of land.

The fictional polity of Utopia was designed by Thomas More to accomplish two things; first, the production of enough food and basic goods for all members of the society to live healthy and satisfied lives and second, the equal distribution of not only the food and basic goods produces but also the labor necessary for this production. In order to accomplish this, he needed to first do away with money which he saw as the primary culprit in allowing thousands of people to starve to death while the rich hoarded grain. His antipathy toward money as a social institution also forms the foundation of his critique that, other than the government of Utopia, "all other governments that I see or know … are a conspiracy of the rich, who, on pretense of managing the public, only pursue their private ends."[34] As we will see with all the writings considered in this book, money and the ownership of property are closely bound. Raphael states at the beginning of his narrative that, in his opinion, "as long as there is any property, and while money is the standard of all things, I cannot think that a nation can be governed either justly or happily" because, in his analysis,

## 12  Why Utopia? Why Landscape?

a few of the worst people will benefit the most and divide the production of society amongst themselves while the majority of people are "left to be absolutely miserable."[35] One can certainly make the claim that his observation is not far off the mark when looking at the state of massive inequality of wealth and the prevalence of poverty in the current world. Thus, the primary organizing factor behind the landscapes of Utopia is the production and distribution of the necessities of life without the need for money as an intermediate of exchange. This is achieved through four main characteristics; the correlation of the size of cities relative to the productive areas within close proximity, the distribution of population so that all people are engaged in agricultural production to some degree, the design of settlements around the centralized and common distribution of goods, and the organized distribution of access to housing and gardens.

There were 54 cities in Utopia spaced such that no city is closer than 24 miles to another and no city is more than a day's walk from at least one neighboring city. No city can have more than 6,000 families and no family can have less than ten or more than 16 people. While there is no minimum number of families per city, there is a provision that people are moved between cities if the natural increase is too large in one or too small in another. If the population of the whole of Utopia becomes too large, people are moved to settlements on the neighboring continent that follow the same laws as Utopia and if its population drops too low, people are brought back from these settlements. Each city has jurisdiction over an area of at least 20 miles in each direction throughout which they have built farmhouses for those who work the land. No farm family has more than 40 people in it. Every two years 20 people from each farm family move to the city to live and work and are replaced by 20 people who move from the city to the farm. During the harvest, additional people are sent from the town to the country as needed. This arrangement has the benefit of both making sure that all people know how to grow food to support the city and as well as distributing the hard labor of agriculture more evenly throughout society. More food is grown than is needed each year as insurance against future poor harvests and to trade with neighboring societies for gold and silver, which is only used to hire mercenaries in the case of war, which of course the Utopians never start. Concerns regarding hierarchy and control in Utopia, which have been hinted at above and which may be troubling some readers at this point, are quite valid and will be brought forward for consideration momentarily.

The cities are designed in quarters with a market at the center of each. People come to these markets for food and other goods including clothing and whatever else a family may need. There is no payment for the goods selected or requirement that anything else be left in exchange. People are free to take what they need without being questioned. Because there is a guarantee of plenty for all, hoarding goods or taking more than you can use is actually a burden on life and offers no benefit since it provides no more security than only taking what you need and there is no profit to be made from excess. The goods that are found in these markets are produced by people following crafts and trades passed on within families. People who choose to change career and follow

*Why Utopia? Why Landscape?* 13

another trade request to be adopted into a family that works in the trade they would like to follow, with the caveat that all people engage in agricultural work on rotation except those who choose to work in food production full time. These markets also provide food to the great halls that serve 30 families each. While people are free to cook and eat at home, most choose to dine in these public halls because "it is both ridiculous and foolish for any to give themselves the trouble to make ready an ill dinner at home when there is a much more plentiful one ready for him so near hand."[36] A deeply troubling component of this vision is that the most unpleasant work of preparing food and maintaining the hall is done by slaves, while the rest is done by women.

Raphael extols the houses of the Utopians, but even more so the enclosed gardens associated with each house. These gardens of vines, fruits, herbs, and flowers are not only productive but also the basis for competition between streets. The houses are not locked as there is no property in Utopia and therefore no concern about theft – especially since all households can get what they want or need from the market at any time. Furthermore, the houses and gardens are cared for equally across society and have been steadily improved since the founding of the polity by Utopos – developing from low dwellings of timber, mud, and straw into three story dwellings faced with stone or brick. Houses are exchanged between families by lot every ten years, ensuring that there is no generational accumulation of property or wealth and that equality in the conditions of life is maintained between people as much as possible. Utopians, as constructed in More's imagination, see themselves as tenants who are caretakers of property which rightfully benefits all of society rather than as landlords or owners who see the benefits of holding property as a private good.

While these and other arrangements of Utopian society can be imagined as achieving More's goals of a society in which there is no hunger and in which labor is distributed equally, there are several highly disturbing aspects in More's utopia. Utopia was founded through an act of military conquest and domination. It was physically created as an island by the native conquered population who were forced to dig a channel to separate it from the continent. The fact that the conquering army dug the channel alongside the conquered people probably would not have forestalled resentment on the part of the conquered population to quite the degree that More imagined. When the population of Utopia grows beyond what the lands of Utopia can support, colonies are set up on the continent through the same kind of martial conquest if necessary and more justifies the use of violence to take land and conquer people that is not unlike the logic that was used to support colonialism at its height.

Even though the Utopians select the people to be in positions of leadership and power is not hereditary, it is still a highly structured and regimented society. This hierarchy even dictates the seating arrangement and order of being served food in their shared dining halls. One could only travel with a passport from the Prince. Though this restriction on travel – particularly travel by peasants – by those in power was quite common across many societies in More's day, it still probably strikes the contemporary reader as being at odds with the

## 14  Why Utopia? Why Landscape?

more progressive ideals of equality that *Utopia* was intended to forward. This hierarchical bent does not stop at official structures of power, however. More's description of family life and other aspects of Utopia are highly structured in rigid hierarchies in which men dominate women and the old dominate the young. The dominance of social structure also reaches into the structure of the family. Families are maintained between ten and 16 people by moving children between families. The fact that this is mentioned in passing only highlights the presumption of the power of society over individual choices as intimate as having and raising children.

As mentioned above, slavery is a significant aspect of Utopian society. The most bestial tasks of slaughtering animals and such things is reserved to slaves because the Utopians "suffer none of their citizens to kill their cattle, because they think that pity and good-nature, which are among the best of those affections that are born with us, are much impaired by the butchering of animals."[37] People became slaves by being conquered in war, being purchased away from death sentences by travelling Utopian merchants, by volunteering to become slaves because even the life of a slave in Utopia was better than the life they live in their own country, by travelling repeatedly without a passport, or by committing adultery.

### Conclusion

The question at hand is whether the benefits of Utopia – the end of extreme poverty and the equal distribution off work – can be had without the aforementioned obvious and deeply troubling as well as profoundly inequitable drawbacks. In particular, and in relation to the exploration of landscape and utopia herein, can the design of landscape and the distribution of its benefits to benefit society as a whole be separated from the overbearing structures of power that More writes into his critique of the society of his day? While the urban proposals of Howard, Corbusier, and Wright do not include disturbing structures of power of the same intensity as those found in More's work, certainly none of them are devoid of concerning aspects. The question I am leaving to the reader to answer for themselves in the rest of this volume is exactly the same one I leave for the reader in the discussion of More's *Utopia* above. Can we structure society to benefit everyone equally by denying capital its power and its need to enforce gross inequality without accepting in trade structures of power which are unacceptable in other ways? If not, then what is the balance to be struck and what are the trade-offs? Are there ways to have both freedom and equality? What is the role of landscape in answering these questions?

In the next chapter I will present an argument for a claim made earlier in this one, that landscapes are political media. The chapter following that looks at the works of Karl Marx, Henry George, Edward Bellamy, and Peter Kropotkin to establish some of the context in which Howard, Corbusier, and Wright wrote as a way to show that, for their time, their underlying critique of land ownership and capital was not as novel as we may assume it is today. The subsequent chapters each take on an aspect of the social and landscape arrangement proposed. These are topical and each treat of the Garden City, the Radiant City, and Broadacre City. These range from abstract concepts like labor, capital, and freedom to concrete aspects such as technology, agriculture, and food. The book concludes with a discussion of nature, history, and agency – which brings us back to the questions noted above because, in the end, this volume is about *our* potential path toward better societies, as we face many of the same problems as did Howard, Corbusier, and Wright – as well as some they weren't able to foresee.

## Notes

1 Levitas, *Utopia as Method: The Imaginary Reconstitution of Society*, p. xi.
2 Levitas, *Utopia as Method: The Imaginary Reconstitution of Society*, p. xiii.
3 Howard and Osborn, *Garden Cities of To-morrow*, p. 123.
4 Howard and Osborn, *Garden Cities of To-morrow*, pp. 118, 123.
5 Howard and Osborn, *Garden Cities of To-morrow*, p. 106.
6 Howard and Osborn, *Garden Cities of To-morrow*, p. 24.
7 Howard and Osborn, *Garden Cities of To-morrow*, p. 55.
8 Howard and Osborn, *Garden Cities of To-morrow*, p. 15.
9 Le Corbusier, *The Radiant City*, p. 1.
10 Le Corbusier, *The Radiant City*, pp. 9, 43.
11 Le Corbusier, *The Radiant City*, p. 188.
12 Le Corbusier, *The Radiant City*, p. 189.
13 Le Corbusier, *The Radiant City*, p. 189.
14 Le Corbusier, *The Radiant City*, p. 69.
15 Le Corbusier, *The Radiant City*, p. 68.
16 Le Corbusier, *The Radiant City*, p. 70.
17 Le Corbusier, *The Radiant City*, p. 85.
18 Le Corbusier, *The Radiant City*, p. 182.
19 Le Corbusier, *The Radiant City*, p. 182.
20 Le Corbusier, *The Radiant City*, p. 65.
21 Le Corbusier, *The Radiant City*, p. 280.
22 Le Corbusier, *The Radiant City*, pp. 65–66.
23 Le Corbusier, *The Radiant City*, p. 67.
24 Wright, *The Living City*, p. 25.
25 Wright, *The Living City*, p. 203.
26 Wright, *The Living City*, p. 208.
27 Wright, *The Living City*, p. 219.
28 Wright, *The Living City*, p. 219.
29 Wright, *The Living City*, p. 79.
30 Wright, *The Living City*, p. 147.
31 Wright, *The Living City*, p. 153.
32 More, *Utopia*, p. 46.
33 More, *Utopia*, p. 44.
34 More, *Utopia*, p. 157.
35 More, *Utopia*, p. 67.
36 More, *Utopia*, p. 90.
37 More, *Utopia*, p. 88.

16  *Why Utopia? Why Landscape?*

## Bibliography

Howard, E., Osborn, F.J., 2001. Garden Cities of To-morrow, 11th print. ed. MIT Press, Cambridge.

Le Corbusier, 1964. The Radiant City: Elements of a Doctrine of Urbanism to be Used as the Basis of Our Machine-Age Civilization. The Orion Press, New York.

Levitas, R., 2013. Utopia as Method: The Imaginary Reconstitution of Society. Palgrave Macmillan, Basingstoke, Hampshire, New York.

More, T., 2016. Utopia. Verso, London, New York.

Wright, F.L., 1958. The Living City. Horizon Press, New York.

### Suggested Readings

Bacon, F., 1942. New Atlantis. Walter J. Black, New York.

Campanella, T., 2020. The City of the Sun. Independently published.

Dorrian, M., Rose, G. (Eds.), 2003. Deterritorialisations: Revisioning Landscapes and Politics. Black Dog Publishing, London; New York.

Eaton, R., 2001. Ideal Cities: Utopianism and the (Un)built Environment. Mercatorfonds, Anvers.

Fishman, R., 1982. Urban Utopias in the Twentieth Century: Ebenezer Howard, Frank Lloyd Wright, and Le Corbusier, 1st MIT Press pbk ed. MIT Press, Cambridge.

Giesecke, A., Jacobs, N. (Eds.), 2012. Earth Perfect? Nature, Utopia and the Garden. Black Dog Pub, London.

Heinlein, R.A., 2018. The Moon is a Harsh Mistress. Ace, New York.

Le Guin, U.K., 1974. The Dispossessed: an Ambiguous Utopia, 1st ed. Harper & Row, New York.

Manuel, F.E., Manuel, F.P., 1979. Utopian Thought in the Western World. Belknap Press, Cambridge.

Olwig, K., 2002. Landscape, Nature, and the Body Politic: From Britain's Renaissance to America's New World. University of Wisconsin Press, Madison.

Robinson, K.S., 2021. Red Mars. Penguin Random House LLC, New York.

Schaer, R., Claeys, G., Sargent, L.T. (Eds.), 2000. Utopia: The Search for the Ideal Society in the Western World. The New York Public Library; Oxford University Press, New York.

Zamalin, A., 2019. Black Utopia: The History of an Idea from Black Nationalism to Afrofuturism. Columbia University Press, New York.

# 2 Landscapes as Political Media

We now turn to my claim that landscapes are foundational political media which is central to the work at hand of elucidating the role of landscapes in the proposals for the Garden City, the Radiant City, and Broadacre City. The ultimate goal, in turn, of that work is to help us think about what it means to implement landscapes as political media in our present world. It is important to point out that Howard, Corbusier, and Wright put their urban proposals and the attendant landscapes forward to solve problems like class inequality, the industrial revolution's detrimental impacts on mental and physical health, disenfranchisement from social and political life, and above all the domination of forms of life by the imperatives of capital. For each of them, the reorganization of life in cities was a means to those ends and was largely accomplished through the design of landscapes. These landscapes not only generated the pragmatic responses to the problems they intended to solve – but in each case also foregrounded a particular political imagination for their imagined inhabitants and a sensorial and operational frame for what each considered to be a good life. As the first step toward considering what it means for landscapes to be political media, I will present how I'm using the term 'politics' followed by what I mean for something to be a political medium. Then I will put forward an understanding of landscape as used in this text, followed by the three ways that landscapes operate as political media. Lastly, I will connect these three ways to a selection of previous writings about landscapes and cities to set these ideas in the context of the related literature. While by no means a definitive or complete recounting of how this concept can be seen in previous writing about landscapes and cities, this will at least provide enough references to situate our thought for the rest of this volume and hopefully provide a basis for future explorations of this understanding of landscapes and their role in the world, should the reader be so inclined.

## Politics

I find great clarity in Hannah Arendt's definition of politics in her work *The Promise of Politics* as that which "arises in what lies *between men* and is established as relationships."[1] The promise of this understanding of politics is in contradiction

DOI: 10.4324/9781351053730-2

18    *Landscapes as Political Media*

to both rank partisanship in local and national affairs and to statecraft which takes place between countries. If the reader can put aside those conceptions of politics, they will have a better understanding of the optimistic use of the term 'politics' in this work. Many if not most people have developed an aversion to partisanship, often referred to as politics, seeing it as a raw and tawdry struggle for power between parties largely devoid of genuine discourse about matters which impact people's lives in meaningful ways. Partisanship masquerading as politics does not play a role in this text. The overshadowing of politics as Arendt characterizes it by partisanship and the sense held by many that the real stakes in politicians' struggle for power is the use of the force of government to illegitimately benefit a few people — often themselves and their already privileged social circle — or as an act of self-aggrandizement at the expense of the rest of society lies at the heart of the broad and rapidly expanding disillusionment with politicians and political processes. This is certainly not a new observation. In 1971, André Gorz wrote in the preface to *Strategy for Labor: A Radical Proposal* that

> the so-called representatives of the people are picked by parties that, far from expressing any popular will, are bureaucratized machines, bent on exerting power on behalf of the "elite" that actually wields that power, and on winning privileges for those who serve the interest of the elite.[2]

Statecraft which is focused on the chess-board play of economic and military power between nation-states is also not the focus of this book, though there are implications for statecraft in each of the proposals we will examine.

Politics, in Arendt's formulation above and as used in this volume, is concerned with relations between people. These relations are largely about access to and power over resources. This includes decisions regarding how resources are to be used to benefit people as well as how those benefits are distributed amongst them. These resources are both natural — as found in the world before human investment in their transformation or relocation, and social — as generated by the interactions of people and as the output of collaborative or competitive work. It is also important to bring forward the fact that space itself, physical room in the world, is as much a resource as natural and social resources. This includes both land and location given that the value of any particular piece of land is highly contingent on where it is relative to other resources and sites of material or social production. This understanding of politics as the set of relationships between people also extends beyond the pragmatic and material realm. Having bodily access to shared social space is key, but having one's identity legitimated in shared social space is just as critical to living a fulfilled human life. The ability to regularly experience delight in one's daily surrounds is similarly crucial to living such a life. As such, politics framed as the relations between people encompasses not only the raw material facts necessary to bare life but also to such aspects of the world as those related to identity, belonging, and delight.

While excluding statecraft and partisanship from our imagination of politics is a significant shift in mental habit, there is an even more substantive implication awaiting the reader in Arendt's formulation of politics. While partisanship and statecraft are by nature organized around a competition for control over resources and narrative within a zero-sum game, Arendt's conception allows for politics to be cooperative and value-generating. What happens between people can be, and often is, productive and constructive in a way that multiplies rather than divides value. All three utopian proposals to be discussed at length in this book include a political imagination of this kind – one in which people cooperate to increase not only the total value held in society but also in the equity of its distribution – often using landscapes as the tool to achieve these ends. The next chapter which introduces the thought of Marx, George, Bellamy, and Kropotkin – four thinkers influential on Howard, Wright, and Le Corbusier – is intended to set the tone for their understanding of this level of optimism about what people can achieve through cooperation, through genuine politics.

## Landscapes as Political Media

With this conception of politics in hand, what does it mean to claim that landscapes are, among other things, political media? There are two definitions of media that I would like to foreground. The first of these is that a medium is "a method or way of expressing something."[3] Landscapes express politics in at least two different ways. First, one can read in them the relations between people in a place or a society – one of the main premises of cultural geography and cultural landscape studies. Not only is equity and inequity between people who live in different neighborhoods regularly visible in the distribution of those neighborhoods throughout a metropolitan region relative to cultural and economic resources but also, in part, as the quality and arrangement of their landscapes including such things as access to public parks and their levels of maintenance, the character of streets and schoolyards, access to public amenities like transportation networks, and the prevalence and size of private landscapes associated with private residences. Similarly, one can read the relations between people in landscapes as they privilege one group's values in relation to another's through iconography, reference to cultural practices and expectations, and rules which define allowable use. The City Beautiful movement is a prime example of landscapes acting as political media to express differential social value in this way, as are landscapes organized around public art and statuary which reference particular and at times contentious and tendentious tellings of history. The second definition of media which I wish to bring to mind when I write that landscapes are political media is "a substance that something grows in, lives in, or moves through."[4] The access to and distribution of resources that is at the heart of politics happens spatially through the medium of landscape. When the members of a society make a determination, directly or indirectly, that a resource should be distributed amongst themselves in a particular way, this decision is instantiated and tangibly impacts the lives of its members through landscapes. Not only

20  *Landscapes as Political Media*

are landscapes media in which politics as relationships between people live, but they also have the power to encourage, support, reinforce, and construct as well as deny, deteriorate, destruct, and obstruct specific types of relationships. In many cases, the physicality of a place and the relationships they frame – taken together as landscape – develop into a self-reinforcing system: landscapes become media for iterative politics in the way that soil is a medium for plants. Different types of soil are beneficial to different kinds of plants. Different plants have different impacts on the soil they grow in, some fixing nitrogen and some depleting it, for example. Landscapes and politics are related to each other in the same way as are soil and plants. The location of agency within this relationship between landscape and politics is key to the main aim of this book – the consideration of how to initiate positive change in the world will be taken up directly in the conclusion.

This leads us to the question, what are landscapes? In the most prosaic but also in the most profound way, landscapes are tools for manipulating relationships between people and things in the world. These can be relationships between individuals and/or groups of people and they can be inclined toward a range of ends from providing for bodily and psychological pleasure to organizing the means and modes of production and the geographic distribution of the activities of life. To the degree that it is useful to think of a landscape as a thing, it should be thought of as an instantiated and inhabited web of relationships between people and between people and things in space. However, in an attempt to forestall the hubris of designers, it should be qualified that this embodied web of relationships is not deterministic. While landscapes install biases of various strength for or against particular forms of relationship, people can, and often do, work to overcome or step around these biases through policy and/or behavior. Landscapes, understood in this way, are not composed of only the material parts of the world which give them firmness and extent. Relationships between people and between people and things are as much a part of a landscape as its hardscape, its flora, and its fauna. In this way, the design of the physicality of a space is only part of designing a landscape. Rules for its use – by design giving preference to certain kinds of relationships – are also part of the landscape design. Olmsted's roles for social behavior were as much a part of his design of New York City's Central Park as were the locations of rocks, trees, and paths. It must be noted that a landscape with no rules for use only gives the power of making de facto rules for the use of public space to those who have or choose to take upon themselves the power to do so.

I find it useful to think of landscapes as political media in three different ways as prefigured above. While these three overlap and entangle, they yet collect specific kinds of relationships in productive groupings for use as tools of thought in the areas of history, policy, design, and critique. First, landscapes structure of the distribution of resources and access to them throughout space. In this way, landscapes can give body to such categorical complexes as capital/labor/land, live/work/play, and production/consumption and as well as solidity to social equity and inequity. Landscapes can reinforce existing conditions and

*Landscapes as Political Media*   21

categorical distributions, ameliorate their impacts, or reform them in foundational ways. Each of the three proposals considered in this text use landscapes to radically reform at least the capital/labor/land complex. Second, landscapes can, and almost always do, provide for specific political imaginations. How people imagine themselves politically has much to do with the spaces they imagine themselves allowed into or excluded from and, as importantly, how they understand their relations to others who share that space or don't. Histories of spatial segregation and exclusion across many societies, continents, and epochs provide the clearest example of this way in which landscapes are political media. Because both the act of reading and writing a landscape is based in part on what individuals or groups bring of themselves and their experiences to bear, one implication of this way in which landscapes operate as political media is that any given constructed space may make available a wide range of political imaginations – including some which are potentially contradictory. Third, landscapes provide for some of the characteristics of life that Giorgio Agamben refers to as form-of-life and describes as the ultimate goal of political life. He distinguishes between bare life – that which is merely the continuation of biological processes – and form-of-life – that in which the forms of living are inseparable from life itself. For him, a degree of self-determination and pleasure are key to the value of these forms-of-life which he claims are qualified by the intention toward happiness and individual power. In concrete terms, it is a life in which we can choose rewarding and uplifting daily rituals and processes which bring us value as we define it. While Agamben does not explicitly hinge happiness and power on such things as delight, wonder, surprise, comfort, pleasure, belonging, and security, I for one find it hard to conceptualize a life in which one has true power manifested in "the materiality of corporeal processes" and directed toward happiness that is not grounded in these concepts.[5] Landscapes are the political media in which these joyful aspects of a life of power are cultivated. In this way, beauty and pleasure in the landscape are political values. While this may seem overly abstract and theoretical, I suspect that few who observe the society around them would argue with the fact that there is a political dimension to who does and who does not have regular access to experiences of beauty, delight, and joy in their daily surroundings.

### Landscapes as Political Media Role #1: Structure of Resource Distribution and Access

Two texts exemplify the argument for understanding the organization of landscapes as giving structure to the distribution of and access to resources, one of the dimensions of landscapes operating as political media. The first is *Landscape Architecture as Applied to the Wants of the West* written by Horace Cleveland in 1873 with the intention of describing a broad scope for the profession, at least one that was broader than was popularly perceived at the time. He directly ties the expansion of the field of landscape architecture to the increased accessibility of suburban land following the growth of steam

## 22 *Landscapes as Political Media*

powered transportation. While he saw that books on landscape gardening by A.J. Downing and others had provided a valuable service to people with newfound realms within which to shape outdoor spaces, he felt that they provided "an inadequate conception of the scope of the art" because while they had explained "lucidly, and often in charming style, the esthetic principles of the art, and the management of the almost endless variety of combinations of natural and artificial decorations," the authors of such books had "confined themselves so exclusively to such details that the idea has became almost universal that landscape gardening is solely a decorative art."[6] He surmised that perhaps the authors restricted their scope to the decorative improvement of land because they imagined themselves writing for people who inhabit cities and suburbs already framed by the division of land into individual plots. He argued that it was obvious that "the new regions of the West require a vast amount of preliminary preparation before much attention can be paid to mere extraneous ornament."[7] His consideration of the role of landscape architecture in the West brought him to a formulation of the field's scope which leads clearly into understanding the arrangement and design of landscapes as an exercise of structuring the distribution of resources and access to them. "Landscape architecture," he wrote "is the art of arranging land so as to adapt it most conveniently, economically and gracefully, to any of the varied wants of civilization."[8] He claimed that when laying out towns, "the first question in the mind of a landscape architect should be: How can the area be divided so as to secure the best disposition of the different departments whose necessities can be foreseen and provided for?"[9] He also notes that the answer to this question must be grounded in "sanitary, economic, and esthetic sense."[10] It is noteworthy that he does not propose that the landscape architect can guide or influence the varied wants of civilization. Rather, landscape architecture is responsive to those wants – which it should be noted are based on perception by those who, typically, have the financial or political power to benefit financially and/or politically from the outcome of the arrangement of land. Indeed, he noted that the planning of towns had "reached the point when vast regions may be controlled by companies or individuals, and the sites and plans of towns can be selected and pre-ordained."[11]

The second text to bring forward in this context of understanding the role that landscapes play in the distribution of resources and access to them is *The New Exploration: A Philosophy of Regional Planning*, written by Benton MacKaye, a member of the Regional Planning Association of America, in 1928. MacKaye began this work with a description of the flows of people and goods, as seen from high above New York City's Times Square, as rivers which connect many landscapes and the people who live across the region. MacKaye followed, though did not reference, Adam Smith's notion of the invisible hand when he noted the incredible intricacy and detail of the organizational structure that underlay the seeming chaos, nor did he draw the same philosophical conclusion. He proposed that this stream could be "readily visualized as a flow of people from

*Landscapes as Political Media*    23

suburb to skyscraper and back again."[12] He describes the flow of goods into the metropolis as coming from an "industrial watershed" in which

> traffic streams take rise, first in small trickles and runnels, in farms, ranches, mines, forests, and then broadening into the vast streams of raw materials which go, as food or as basic products, into the homes and workshops of the world.[13]

He also wrote about the flow of development out of large cities in terms of water, specifically calling it a flood. In response, he proposed to shape the spread of development across whole regions of the country by using various mechanisms of land-use control which would direct the flow of people and goods in the same way that basins and levees direct the flow of water, beginning with natural features of the countryside that lend themselves to these control functions. He describes his proposal as an ordered civilization rather than a wilderness of civilization. Contrasting the two, he claimed that the elements of each – "factories and stores and residences and a host of other buildings and plants" – were the same just as "are the ingredients of a salad and a garbage pile the same."[14] Regional planning and the functional organization of landscapes, for MacKaye, is what makes the difference between the between the salad and the garbage pile.

Howard, Le Corbusier, and Wright proposed radical structural changes to the distribution of resources and access to them relative to what they saw around them – a hallmark of utopian thinking directed toward sweeping changes in society. Many people who have written about landscapes also proposed changes to structures of resources based on an idea of increased social good. In some cases, these proposed changes supported existing structures, in others they attempted to ameliorate the negative impacts of larger social and political patterns, and in yet others they sought to challenge and perhaps overturn or disrupt those patterns.[15] One such writer, Frederick Law Olmsted, argued repeatedly that the value of parks for health is a way to mitigate the impacts of urbanization driven by industrialization. "We may admit," he wrote, "that commerce requires that in some parts of a town there shall be an arrangement of buildings, and a character of streets and of traffic in them which will establish conditions of corruption and of irritation, physical and mental." Accepting that outcome of industrialization as given, he presented parks as ameliorative to these commercial corridors with "air that is disinfected by sunlight and foliage."[16] In a similar vein, he proposed that the "lives of women and children too poor to be sent to the country can now be saved in the thousands of instances by making them go to the Park."[17] In arguing for extensive parks and park systems on this basis, he was also effectively arguing for a change to the way that urban land was developed and for the construction of a public realm for public good with public monies. At the time, this was a significant challenge to the social imagination of what democratic governments could and should do with regard to land-ownership.

24    *Landscapes as Political Media*

However, it is also clear that he was not seeking a deep reorganization of the relationship between labor and capital – or the living and working conditions of laborers generally – with his emphasis on the benefits of parks. It is easily argued that this amelioration of the lives of the laboring class merely made them more fit to stay at work and generate more profit for industrialists – with the added benefit of making them less likely to riot through the neighborhoods of the owners of the means of production. This is not to say that the parks he proposed did not and have not improved the lives of many thousands of people in many places, it is merely to point out that his proposal propped up existing structures of inequity in society by ameliorating some of its impacts. It is telling that Olmsted felt that parks would help classes overcome their antagonism as well as reduce resentments that grew from the difference in wealth and its display through sharing space, but did not comment on the differential distribution of wealth itself or see landscapes as a tool to challenge or overcome inequity.[18] One can also contrast his statements about the inhabitants of the land that was to become Central Park with what we know about at least some of the actual residents of the land that would become the park, in particular those who lived in Seneca Village.[19]

Similarly, John Nolen, trained as a landscape architect and the first person to take 'city planner' as a professional title, supported some of the existing social and political structures while proposing ameliorations of others. He was involved in a wide range of activities including new towns, company towns, park plans, urban renovation proposals, and attempts to start farm-cities based on Howard's Garden City proposal in which the concept was to redirect small manufacturing interests to rural areas so that people could work part time in agriculture and part time in factories – changing both economic and settlement dynamics for those people but not proposing a significant shift in the dynamics of power in which rural and industrial labor was situated. He described his plans for cities in sometimes bombastic terms, indicating his intentions for the landscapes he designed. The subtitle to his plan for Mariemont, OH, stated that it was an "Interpretation of Modern City Planning Principles Applied to a Small Community to Produce Local Happiness: A National Exemplar."[20] However it should be noted that his proposed model for local happiness had a clearly segregated residential area for newly immigrated families who worked as industrial laborers. Nolen also proposed that existing cities could be reworked, especially small to mid-size cities. He proposed that these cities could change everything, with the power of what he called a great civic awakening, from the location of rail-lines, the use of waterfronts, the location of thoroughfares "by cutting new streets if necessary, and regrouping public buildings," the creation of park networks, and residential districts "helped to be attractive and delightful" through housing and lot-size standards, zoning, and standardization of street widths.[21] It must be recognized that though he argued for a reconfiguration of towns and industrial zones as well as agricultural patterns as a technical and practical solution to some of the problems of the distribution of resources and means of production relative to labor and to land cost, the organizational strategies he proposed were clearly grounded in the social and spatial separation of people by race and class and supported the continuation of those divisions within society.[22]

Both New Urbanism and Landscape Urbanism set out to ameliorate the impacts of industrial urbanization on the city, though in very different ways. Neither actively supports existing structures of resource distribution and access but neither actively attempts to challenge them either. In the introduction to the *Charter of the New Urbanism*, Jonathan Barnett writes that "decentralized metropolitan regions are the new reality, and we have to learn how to make them work."[23] The charter consistently describes the work proposed as restoration, reconfiguration, conservation, and preservation. By and large, the proposals found in the charter – as evidenced also in many if not most of the projects that have earned the moniker 'New Urbanist' – very consciously work within existing frameworks of profit-driven speculative development and the dictates of capital with relatively minor adjustments in investment. While there may be disagreement regarding how much effort should be spent trying to overcome these philosophical orientations of our society, New Urbanism does present a coherent strategy for change limited by the confines which the ideology accepts for itself. In the afterword to the charter, Peter Calthorpe dismisses – and rightly so – the misunderstanding of New Urbanism as nothing more than an aesthetically nostalgic enterprise. However, even the interworkings of policy and proposal across multiple scales which he described as the true core of the ideology still only mediate but do not challenge the political, economic, and social status quo in significant ways.[24]

While Charles Waldheim quickly dismisses New Urbanism as accommodating to "reactionary cultural politics and nostalgic sentiment" on one hand and dismisses mainstream urban design as being primarily concerned with "environments for destination consumption by the wealthy" on the other, his formulation of Landscape Urbanism explicitly situates itself as not more than a response to existing economic forces.[25] In his introduction to *Landscape as Urbanism*, Waldheim stated that "landscape has also been found useful as a way of thinking through the urban form in the wake of macroeconomic transformations" and that it "is invoked as a performative medium associated with the remediation of formerly industrial sites left in the wake of the Fordist economy's collapse." While he goes on to claim that landscape urbanism is focused on new forms of urban living, he states that these new ways are situated within "the spatial and social order of the contemporary city," not challenging it.[26] Alex Wall, in his essay from *Center 14: On Landscape Urbanism*, wrote about reprogramming the urban surface in response to changes in modern cities and proposed that we ought to rethink the ways in which we use urban surfaces to engage not only the city but each other. He gave a brief overview of several proposals that engage urban landscapes in this performative way and concludes that "the surface is not merely the venue for formal experiments but the agent for evolving new forms of social life."[27] Similarly, Chris Reed in his essay for the same volume points to the work of Stan Allen (while noting that he in turn

## 26  Landscapes as Political Media

relies on the work of Richard Forman) among others who look to find ways to encode open-endedness into the urban landscape which allows for appropriation and therefore, presumably, gives agency to the people using the landscape. His intention for the project he presents for illustration, The Papago Trail, is to "define a new public realm and to make available a new set of contingencies and provisional occupations for reiteration, application and adaptation."[28] While these writings by Wall and Reed go beyond Waldheim's prescription for staying within the bounds of neoliberal structures, it is not clear that they go beyond ameliorating the conditions of the contemporary city by affording space and structure to allow positive developments in public and social life to come forward from within the existing structures.

Some current works on urban food production seek to ameliorate the separation of food production from the structure of urban life by inserting spaces for food production within the existing fabric of urban landscapes. The relation between food production, industrialized work, and urban life is a concern common in varying degrees not only to Howard, Le Corbusier, and Wright but also to the four thinkers we are going to consider in the next chapter – Marx, George, Bellamy, and Kropotkin. *Public Produce* by Darrin Nordahl looks to public and underutilized land within the city to host a wide variety of possible food producing capabilities. *Urban Farms* by Sarah Rich and *Carrot City* by Gorgolewski, Komisar, and Nasr both offer illustrations for ways in which food production can be inserted within the city. However, neither aspire to propose a systematic overturning of the current social and spatial structure of food production relative to urban life broadly speaking. Other works, however, do. While not writing about landscapes directly, Thomas Lyson made an argument for dramatically restructuring our food system in *Civic Agriculture: Reconnecting Farm, Food, and Community* that would necessarily change much about how we distribute landscapes of food, agricultural production, and urban life. Similarly, *Second Nature Urban Agriculture*, edited by Viljoen and Bohn, frames a way to use the kinds of agricultural spaces described in the previously mentioned works to accrete large-scale systematic changes to the structures of food producing capacity relative to urban inhabitation which would have far-reaching economic and social implications.

Other writers have gone a step further and proposed significant changes to the distribution of resources through landscape design. While not fully utopian in his scope, Clarence Stein – known for his book *Toward New Towns for America* as well as his involvement in the Regional Planning Association of America and Sunnyside Gardens, Radburn, and the Greenbelt towns – did propose challenging at least two structural issues related to the distribution of urban space and the benefits of life in cities. He proposed to radically reorganize the landscape for people in a couple ways. First, he proposed – and exemplified in Radburn – separated pedestrian and vehicular traffic surfaces. This not only had the effect of giving people, and especially children, more freedom to move without concern about cars but it also had the effect of creating much more open space in the neighborhoods he proposed. Second and even more critically, he proposed shifting space from individualized, private control in typical neighborhood block plans to shared use and common ownership. He noted that new plans and new physical arrangements such as green belts, inner block parks, neighborhood superblocks, community centers, and the separation of pedestrian and automobile routes are needed, but not sufficient. "A new technique is required," he wrote, "another kind of legislative background and different ownership or control – at least control of land if not of building." Most directly bringing out the fundamental change he proposed, he wrote that "the objective of new towns is fundamentally social rather than commercial. Bluntly, the distinction is that between building for people or building for profit."[29] This attention to the legal control of land for the common good is a consistent theme in the proposals of Howard, Le Corbusier, and Wright as will be discussed further.

Lastly, Diane Balmori put forward in *A Landscape Manifesto* a clear call to use landscapes as tools to generate structural change – explicitly tying her proposal to industrialization. She wrote that, "to design a livable city that coexists with nature as a whole will require establishing different relationships among the parts. The harmful relations created by the nineteenth-century industrialization will have to be revised in some cases, reversed in others."[30] She develops this idea over the course of 25 theses illustrated by her own work and concludes that

> landscape must create a new kind of city, and it must broker a new type of relationship between humans and the rest of nature. For the first, we need to put the city into nature. For the second, we must undo the harmful model of industrialization.[31]

This statement of imperative for landscape design and arrangement offers significantly more direct challenge to the structures of resource distribution and access than, for instance, that proposed under the aegis of landscape urbanism.

The reader may at this point be considering the very broad scope that comes under the nominative umbrella of 'landscape' at this point given all that has been discussed above. Is there much if anything in the built environment which is not a landscape per this understanding of landscapes as political media which distribute resources and access to them? Perhaps not, but even if it is nearly all-encompassing, the term 'landscape' is still of value because it describes the *type* of relationships between people and between people and things that are embodied through landscapes in the world. It is also worth bringing it back to our attention that this book is about landscapes, not landscape architecture, and the consideration that landscapes are designed and arranged through many roles beyond landscape architecture and planning – including finance, law, engineering, and policy to name a few.

### Landscapes as Political Media Role #2: Political Imagination

The second way in which I propose landscapes operate as political media is through making specific political imaginations, how people imagine themselves

## 28  *Landscapes as Political Media*

in relationship to others, available to the people who use them – sometimes with and sometimes without the intention of the person or body that is responsible for the landscape's existence.[32] If politics is what happens between people, then one's political imagination is how one imagines oneself in relation to other people. Since people jointly partake of the world around them, their imagination of themselves in relation to the world necessarily carries with it how they imagine themselves relating to the world alongside other people. Political imagination can be carried in things and acts as overt as the megaliths of Stonehenge, the jar in Wallace Stevens' poem, the prominent and axial placement of statues of military figures and state leaders and their subsequent removal, and gold-domed statehouse set within viewsheds that attempt to ensure they are a prominent feature of the daily life of citizens. However, landscapes can also carry political imaginations in things as subtle as a rolling green sward or manicured and regimented plantings framing a fountain beyond which the sun rises and as seemingly unintentional as the sweeping view of a mountain range from a well-placed curve of a highway over a hill. These political imaginations are only made available however, not enforced, by landscapes, and are often not consciously emplaced. Often the political imagination of a place can be carried forward into the world based on an unconscious assumption on the part of the designer, policy maker, or financier who uncritically presumes a rightness and universality to their own political imagination – failing to recognize that it is in fact an imagination at all. These political imaginations made available through landscapes can also be contested, as is most viscerally available in the imagery of people pulling down prominent statues set up to embody a political vision which they do not or no longer share.

Some of the more amusing prose illustrating this proposal that landscapes make political imaginations available comes from Hirschfeld's *Theory of Garden Art*. Channeling Walpole, he disparages French gardens with the statement that "the French national taste, which grasps at trifles and glitter, has nearly eradicated any inclination toward country life" and exalts the British gardens with the statement that "the healthy taste of the English people makes country life valuable to them, and they devote as much to refining it as other nations commit to the support of their capitals."[33] He is clearly referencing not only the stereotypes of French gardens as formal geometricized environments and English gardens as large swaths of green picturesquely framed by masses of unmanicured trees but also their forms of government. While Hirschfeld's statements, with their attendant generalization and pomposity may seem trite and humorous to our contemporary ears, it is worth taking them seriously when considering the power of landscapes as political media. Not only was Hirschfeld, as Walpole before him, making a statement about the superiority of the British over the French in their national character and structure of governance as evidenced by their taste in gardening, he was also leading into a political statement directed at his native Germany when he commends three princes

> for the charitable spirit that they have lavished on their people [which] they have also turned to the improvement of nature, shaping with their

own hands, as they work the venerable, shady arbors where they pause just long enough to refresh their energy for further efforts that will benefit humanity.[34]

It is worth considering who was most properly British, or German, in Hirschfeld's thought if the national character was best exhibited in estates that were either held out of spatial and financial reach of the majority of people or designed and administered by the elite who could decide what political imagination should dominate social and public space.

Perhaps the most self-conscious use of landscapes as a tool for the management of political imagination is the City Beautiful movement exemplified in the United States by the many state and city capital projects in the United States – in particular the mall in Washington, D.C. While there were many components to the City Beautiful movement and disagreements, then and now, about the real motivations and the intent of the movement, it is undeniable that the consistent result was an organization of the visible representations of power within cities, and that these representations almost universally referenced a particular political heritage that – while perhaps not historically tied to the actual forms of government of antiquity – visually emphasized the continuity of power and political tradition. It is no accident that these constructions of centralized power – which their axes strongly emphasized in most cases – came at a time when native-born citizens of the United States were feeling the crush of immigration from Europe, and particularly of Germans and others who held distinctly different political views. This is perhaps most eloquently represented in John Nolen's design for the site of the Wisconsin state capitol building in Madison such that the capital building was ensured maximum visibility.[35]

Another proposal for using landscapes to support a particular political imagination can be found in *Making a Middle Landscape,* written by Peter Rowe. Bringing forward the social values behind arguments for the suburbs, in spite of their inadequacies and negative impacts, he described the debate between two positions on the suburbs in a section titled "Wasteful Fragmentation or Pure Democracy?" and concluded that, ultimately, "it is the darker underside of democracy, when people forget that it involves the common good as well as individualism."[36] He argued for a mythopoetics of modern pastoralism that would mediate between the machine and the garden, between the tradition of pastoralism and modern technical orientations and wrote that "a basic aspect of modern pastoralism's potential appeal as a legitimate, deeply seated cultural theme remains its incipient presence in the suburban landscape."[37] Rowe consistently sees the mediation between modern suburban growth depending on technology and shifting patterns of work and home life and the romanticist pastoral ideal as at least as much a mediation between imagination in the political sphere as a mediation in legal and financial frameworks.

In their book *Rethinking Urban Parks: Public Space and Cultural Diversity*, Low, Taplin, and Scheld take on the issue of diversity within a polity and how public spaces can support a political imagination that respects and honors diversity

## 30  Landscapes as Political Media

instead of marginalizing and excluding those typically set outside the dominant narrative of society. They study a number of parks regarding this issue of diversity and come up with six lessons for inclusive public spaces. Four of the six lessons speak directly to ways to encourage diverse populations to see a given park as a space for them – to seeing themselves as included in the political imagination of the place itself. These are: ensuring that their histories are represented in the public park; providing spaces for multiple and diverse populations in the same park; designing for different kinds of uses that may be particular to social classes and ethnic groups; and symbolically communicating the value of diverse cultural meanings in the park.

Landscapes can also bring forward a critique of a political imagination as well, a political counter-imagination if you will. For instance, Marth Schwartz's installation of a grid of golden frogs in a shopping mall surely brings to at least some readers of that landscape an instigation to critically consider commercialism, the role of mass-produced commodities in a society which claims to value unique identities, the role of wealth and accumulation in society, and capitalism – among other things. The fact that some may be simply intrigued by a phalanx of golden frogs worshiping a large sphere and think on it no further does not change the conceptual political imagination made available to the reader of that particular landscape. I would also argue that this political imagination is just as validly a part of the landscape whether or not the designer intended it to be read that way. *Wheatfield, Battery Park City – A Confrontation* by Agnes Denes is another example of a political counter-imagination. The artist temporarily planted two acres of wheat near the World Trade Center in New York City in 1982 as an explicit confrontation to the dominant political vision of land as a commodity and money as the ultimate measure of value. Denes made these intentions clear with the imagery of the project she promoted as well as her statements. She wrote that

> Planting and harvesting a field of wheat on land worth $4.5 billion created a powerful paradox. Wheatfield was a symbol, a universal concept; it represented food, energy, commerce, world trade, and economics. It referred to mismanagement, waste, world hunger and ecological concerns. It called attention to our misplaced priorities.[38]

As mentioned earlier, our imaginations of ourselves in the world at large also carry political connotations in that we can't help but imagine ourselves in relation to other people in the world when we imagine ourselves in relation to the world itself. A prime example of this, though not a landscape, is Wallace Stevens' poem "Anecdote of the Jar."[39] If we imagine for a moment that Stevens had the intent of bringing the wilderness to rise and meet the jar and make it no longer wild, the reader is led to ask how the hill was made to rise and meet the jar, and how did that make the wilderness no longer wild? Even more importantly, one must ask for whom was the wilderness no longer wild and what intellectual and epistemological equipment (baggage, perhaps) they were carrying that allowed

Stevens to alter the wilderness for them by situating the jar in a certain way? What did he know about his projected users of the landscape that allowed him to suspect this would work? What is it about the epistemological and sensual engagement of the site by the reader with whom Wallace is communicating with that allow the placement of a manmade object in the wilderness to have such power – to not only tame the wild, but demand that the wilderness rise to meet it? Wallace's situating of the jar on the hill isn't about the jar or the hill of course, it is about situating the reader as they imagine themselves in the landscape relative to their understanding of wilderness and – even more consequentially – their relationship to civilization as a device which gives order to wilderness. It is, ultimately, the reader of the poem as they imagine themselves as a reader of the landscape who is most consequentially situated.[40] Real landscapes can situate real readers of landscape in the same way.

While working at different scales, the installations by Christo and Andy Goldsworthy bring forward considerations of the fragility of the non-human world as well as an awareness of how we impact it. Christo's project *Surrounded Islands* couldn't help but situate anyone in the early 1980's in a consideration of human impacts on the environment. Goldsworthy's many pieces made with leaves, moss, sticks, and other ephemeral materials bring the viewer into a consideration of human intention, time, and the world around us. Works such as Spiral Jetty by Robert Smithson and Sun Tunnels by Nancy Holt situate the reader of the site in ruminations about temporality, mortality, geometry, the relationship between human reason and patterns of nature, and probably many other courses of thought that are more idiosyncratic to each reader.

The world at large within which landscapes situate us is not restricted to the more-than-human world as it is referred to by David Abrams in *The Spell of the Sensuous* and can situate us in human cultures as well. As fittingly described by John Dixon Hunt, Ian Hamilton Finlay's alluring use of thickets and other landscape devices to organize experience surely bring forward pure emotional delight.[41] Finlay's landscapes are also, however, richly invested with many references to human cultures and histories. Each person who experiences one of Finlay's landscapes will certainly bring layers of meaning to the experience from within their own history of experiences. However, while his references to such things as Greek mythology, battleships, and the French Revolution are by no means the sum total of Finlay's work, they are unavoidably a central part of it. His work is exemplary of landscape as a tool for manipulating relationships between people and things in order to produce meaning which is only available with particular cultural knowledge – following of course traditions that have been well established in picturesque gardens, even directly referencing some of them. In many instances, Finlay set down very particular meanings in stone and wood which can only be accessed with particular and occasionally obscure cultural knowledge. While some may claim that setting up landscapes that offer an intellectual relationship to historical events and ideas which are not widely accessible is elitist and condemn it as such, I would strenuously disagree. This capacity of landscapes to relate people to history and the history of ideas ought

## 32  Landscapes as Political Media

to be celebrated as one of the many ways landscapes can be used to enrich human life.

A critical volume with which the reader should explore this idea of landscapes as political media in the way that they carry political imagination is *Values in Landscape Architecture and Environmental Design: Finding Center in Theory and Practice*. The essays are invaluable throughout, but so is the way Deming frames the project. In the introduction to the book the author claims that "landscape is both a material and a conceptual medium that expresses social beliefs of ownership, control, status, power, virtue, spectacle, beauty, and faith, among many other things" and in the conclusion that "the most important thing that all of us can do is to help make personal landscape values publicly visible, especially in the context of shared decision-making about the world's resources."[42]

### Landscapes as Political Media Role #3: Form-of-Life

The ultimate goal of engaging in politics – that which happens between people to reiterate Arendt's formulation – is to live well. However, positioning living well as a static conclusion to politics is a dangerous concept that readily lends itself to abuses of power ranging from the 'mere' reinforcement of reductive ideologies to full blown authoritarianism. As discussed in the introduction, uniformity in defining the good life and especially in defining it for others is not the kind of utopianism that this book is putting forward for consideration. It is also, for creatures that seem to value open-endedness as much as do people, a dystopian concept well illustrated by movies such as *The Truman Show* and much of Phillip K. Dick's fiction. For these reasons, living well, which I would argue necessarily includes the experiences of beauty, delight, and joy in one's surroundings, cannot be an end of politics but must be one of its means. Arendt wrote that the end of politics is the continuation of politics. In a similar vein, Agamben argued in *Form-of-Life*, the first essay of his volume titled *Means without End*, that lives worth living are those that cannot separated from the forms of life – those daily practices and rituals which contribute to lives of happiness and power. Landscapes, as political media through which the relationships between people are expressed and in which they grow, provide not only the rudimentary frame of resources and important components of our political imagination as discussed in the last two sections of this chapter, but also significant components of the pleasure and satisfaction that is integral to the act of politically living well.

Sitwell's florid appreciation for the gardens of Italy exemplifies the kind of experience of pleasure in landscape to which I am referring. Sitwell rejected both what he defines as the unbending systems and formalism of the French as exemplified by Versailles as well as the mock-naturalism of the English garden with its "dead trees, and broken bridges" and "dreadful eruption of Gothic temples and Anglo-Saxon keeps…all with inscriptions in Greek or black-letter appealing to the eye of taste and to the tear of sensibility."[43] In contrast, he extolled the Italian garden and offered the most delightfully ekphrastic tours through several gardens to make his case for why "the Italian feeling for sensation has often been spoken of."[44] However, rather than discuss axiality, geometry, scale, perspective (in mathematical terms), or any of the other ways in which these gardens had been discussed, he focused on the sensorial and psychological experiences that avail themselves to the visitor. He wrote that the Duke of Lante's garden was a place of "enchanting loveliness, a paradise of gleaming water, gay flowers, and golden light" that is best approached by "striking upward by green lawns and ilex groves to follow from its source the tiny streamlet upon which pool, cascade, and water-temple are threaded like pearls on a string."[45] "Much there is," he wrote, "of mystery in the garden, of subtle magic, of strange elusive charm which must be felt but cannot wholly be understood" such that "the soul of the garden is in the blue pools which, by some strange wizardry of the artist, to stair and terrace and window throw back the undimmed azure of the Italian sky."[46] Clarifying what he thinks gardens are for, he wrote, that "gardens are for refreshment; not for pleasure alone, nor even for happiness, but for the renewing rest that makes labour more fruitful, the unbending of a bow that it may shoot the stronger" and that "in the ancient world it was ever the greatest of emperors and the wisest of philosophers that sought peace and rest in a garden."[47] The parks movement of the early 20th century also called to this idea and Olmsted and others also referred to the value of pleasure in the landscape in the terms of unbending the bows made taught by life in the industrializing city.

One finds similar claims in the direction which Laugier gave for the embellishment of gardens, the object of which, he claimed, "is to provide new attractions for an inclination that makes us all seek the relaxing atmosphere of the countryside."[48] He wrote that "in gardens, one should pay particular attention to places of a delightful and simple beauty," and that

> one must make use of all the fairness nature offers and embellish its creations by arranging them in a graceful and tender manner without ever taking away from them that simple and pastoral air which makes their charm so sweet.[49]

For him, the task of arranging elements in the landscape is to keep all of the favorable features of nature, doing so in such a way that allows us to "sense more keenly the contrasts and harmony yet does not efface the natural and the graceful."[50] Likewise, Walpole wrote that the landscape should be "chastened or polished, not transformed."[51] Even though both Laugier and Walpole expressed significant stylistic differences regarding the design of gardens, it is interesting and insightful they called to similar sensorial and psychological impacts on people to justify their less than open-minded descriptions of what should be considered the right style of gardening.

Books such as Gayle Souter-Brown's *Landscape and Urban Design for Health and Well-Being: Using Healing, Sensory and Therapeutic Gardens* propose a similar value to experiences organized through landscapes and present them as useful for supporting both physical and mental health.[52] While the focus of the work

34  *Landscapes as Political Media*

is on healing, it comes from a salutogenic stance – one that approaches healing with a focus on health, not on disease. Souter-Brown's description of what counts as a good garden design for healing, one which she claims is the same as the basis for any residential garden design, is "a range of plants to give height, texture, color, and fragrance, attract wildlife such as native birds and butterflies, and perhaps provide a fresh local food supply," surely speaks of landscapes that bring joy and delight. She continues that these gardens should "have comfortable seating from which to absorb and admire nature in all her glory."[53] Louv's *Last Child in the Woods* is conceptually grounded in a similar way of understanding the value of pleasure, joy, and wonder in the landscape though focused on wild landscapes rather than gardens.[54] Whether or not the reader accepts the romanticism that underpins Louv's thinking, accepts that the historical arc presented is fully accurate, or agrees with the author's conclusions about direct and necessary causal links between experiences of nature and healthy physical and emotional development, the narratives of childhood delights and wonders found in engagements with nature as Louv recounts and characterizes them are alluring and certainly describe experiences that enrich lives, both young and old.

There is also much to the pleasure and joy in gardens to be had in engagement with plants. On this front, Gertrude Jekyll comes foremost to mind. She spoke not only to the value of experiencing a garden but also the value in working in one when she wrote that the lesson she had learned and wished "to pass on to others is to know the enduring happiness that the love of a garden gives" and that she rejoiced when she saw

> anyone, and especially children, inquiring about flowers, and wanting gardens of their own, and carefully working in them. For the love of gardening is a seed that once sown never dies, but always grows and grows to an enduring and ever-increasing source of happiness.[55]

This fascination with plant material and the delight to be found in gardening is also evident in the plantings of Piet Oudolf, such as those along the High Line in New York.[56] While the re-inhabitation of an unused remnant of industry in the city as a significant outdoor urban space is significant and valuable, it would bring far less emotional value to its users without his planting designs which bring such pleasure to the experience. Among other works worth attention by those who are thinking of producing landscapes of wonder and pleasure through plant material are *Sowing Beauty: Designing Flowering Meadows from Seed* by James Hitchmough and *Rambunctious Garden: Saving Nature in a Post-Wild World* by Emma Marris. While much of Hitchmough's book has a technical focus on seed mixes, germination, soils, and such, he makes clear that beauty has been the driver for his work. In his attempt to find design methodologies that would include plant communities good for wildlife in urban areas but also be loved and therefore maintained by people, he describes his study of why people respond positively or negatively to landscapes. In the end he claims that, "of

*Landscapes as Political Media*   35

course, it doesn't matter how or why you find something beautiful, only that you do is quite sufficient. It isn't a competition about the nature of truth."[57] While Hitchmough is focused on what he refers to as naturalistic planting as a way of mediating the experiential needs and desires of people and the diversity needed by wildlife, Marris lucidly argues that this experience of beauty and wonder should not be thought of as something which is solely available in what we perceive to be natural areas. In opposition to finding beauty only in what we perceive to be pristine and taking up an ideologue's mantle with regard to native and non-native species, she claims that a "conscious and responsible and joyful cohabitation is the future of our planet, our vibrant, thriving, rambunctious garden."[58] One finds similar sentiments in John Dixon Hunt's description of the poetry to be found in drosscapes themselves as well as in designs which find and accentuate beauty and delight in the remnants of industrial sites and contemporary infrastructure. His description of Duisburg-Nord brings forward this aspect of the site with a readily discernible sense of joy. Duisburg Nord, Hunt writes,

> is a wonderful infusion of trees and planting into what was a toxic terrain: scents of blossoms mingle with the still palpable aroma of rust and coal, fragments of machinery become sculptural moments, water irises bloom in the River Emscher (previously hidden in a culvert), plants crowd into ruins and under the overhead walkways. What were abandoned, dark satanic mills renew our modern sense of sublimity.[59]

While considering joy, delight, beauty, pleasure, wonder, and other enrichments of life which can be offered through the media of landscape may be perhaps the most amorphous and least rationally definable one of the three ways in which landscapes operate as political media, it is nonetheless perhaps the most critical. If one imagines landscapes, or politics (that which arises between people, to remind the reader how that phrase is being used), which provide only for the first two – the structure of resource distribution and political imagination, it leaves one with a distinct impression of a life lived in places dry and colorless, devoid of the wit, whimsy, and delight that makes life what Agamben describes as one intended toward happiness in the visceral nature of daily living.

## Conclusion

Before heading into the work of Howard, Wright, and Le Corbusier, it is essential to understand works that were deeply influential on the political imaginations of their times and on ultimately on their proposals. These will be covered in the next chapter and are *Looking Backward* by Edward Bellamy, *Progress and Poverty* by Henry George, the works of Peter Kropotkin – especially *Fields, Factories, and Workshops,* and – of course – the first volume of *Capital* by Karl Marx. None of these works were by theorists or historians of landscape, yet

## 36   Landscapes as Political Media

they were all directly or indirectly foundational to the political imaginations of Howard, Le Corbusier, and Wright.

Among the vast array of individuals who wrote critically about changes within human society after the industrial revolution, these four thinkers who made connections between social form and landscapes stand out for both their attempts to propose changes across the whole system of human society and the reach of their work. Edward Bellamy wrote *Looking Backward* as a direct critique of the city and society in which he lived. The urban and rural landscapes in his book are framing devices central to his work. Henry George, as so many others, identified the private accrual of the socially produced speculative value of land, which he called the 'unearned increment,' as a foundational problem in modern society. As rents continue to outstrip wages in our day, *Progress and Poverty* continues to provide a timely critique of the way in which we have organized control over the unavoidable grounding of all human interactions – the land itself. The Russian anarchist Peter Kropotkin provided one of the most widely distributed challenges to the industrial organization of society in which agricultural modes of production were separated from other forms of production. His proposal has found echoes in the work of the Resettlement Authority in the United States and continues today, perhaps unwittingly, in the growing number of proposals for rural food hubs. All three of these writers presented direct critiques of capitalism as an organizational force in society if not directly of capital itself. Interestingly for anyone immersed in contemporary political discourse, none of these three – Bellamy, George, and Kropotkin – were fringe writings or theorists. Their work had vast popular audiences, so it should not be surprising that their works were referred to in one way or another by the authors of the proposals for the Garden City, the Radiant City, and Broadacre City. Lastly, one cannot discuss critiques of capitalism without considering Capital by Karl Marx. Though Howard, Le Corbusier, and Wright did not refer to his work directly, their work cannot but sit in the context of his analysis.

## Notes

1   Arendt and Kohn, *The Promise of Politics*, p. 95. I would ask the contemporary reader to overlook her use of the masculine pronoun as was dictated by the conventions of writing in her time and read for the deeper and more conceptual meaning she intended.
2   Gorz, *Strategy for Labor*, p. vii.
3   Medium. *Cambridge Dictionary.*
4   Medium. *Cambridge Dictionary.*
5   Agamben, *Means without End*, p. 12.
6   Cleveland, *Landscape Architecture as Applied to the Wants of the West*, pp. 13–14,
7   Cleveland, *Landscape Architecture as Applied to the Wants of the West*, p. 16.
8   Cleveland, *Landscape Architecture as Applied to the Wants of the West*, p. 17.
9   Cleveland, *Landscape Architecture as Applied to the Wants of the West*, p. 34.
10   Cleveland, *Landscape Architecture as Applied to the Wants of the West*, p. 34.
11   Cleveland, *Landscape Architecture as Applied to the Wants of the West*, p. 33.

12 MacKaye, *The New Exploration: A Philosophy of Regional Planning*, pp. 9–10.

13 MacKaye, *The New Exploration: A Philosophy of Regional Planning*, p. 14.

14 MacKaye, *The New Exploration: A Philosophy of Regional Planning*, p. 187.

15 While I did not use the language of reformist and non-reformist reforms from André Gorz book *Strategy for Labor: A Radical Proposal*, this argument was productive in arriving at this distinction.

16 Olmsted and Twombly, *Frederick Law Olmsted: Essential Texts*, p. 220.

17 Taylor, *Central Park as a Model for Social Control: Urban Parks, Social Class and Leisure Behavior in Nineteenth-Century America*, p. 448.

18 Taylor, *Central Park as a Model for Social Control: Urban Parks, Social Class and Leisure Behavior in Nineteenth-Century America*, p. 427.

19 The Central Park Conservancy, *Before Central Park: The Story of Seneca Village*.

20 Beck, *John Nolen and the Metropolitan Landscape*, pp. 83–116.

21 Nolen, *New Towns for Old*, p. 10.

22 See *John Nolen and the Metropolitan Landscape* for a discussion of his career at length.

23 *Charter of the New Urbanism*, p. 6.

24 *Charter of the New Urbanism*, pp. 15–21.

25 Waldheim, *Landscape as Urbanism*, pp. 178–179.

26 Waldheim, *Landscape as Urbanism*, pp. 4–5.

27 Center 14, *On Landscape Urbanism*, pp. 182–193.

28 Center 14, *On Landscape Urbanism*, pp. 224–237

29 Stein, *New Towns for America*, p. 219.

30 Balmori and Conan, *A Landscape Manifesto*, p. 1.

31 Balmori and Conan, *A Landscape Manifesto*, p. 221.

32 The reader will quickly be aware of the debt that this work owes to John Dixon Hunt's writings including specifically *Reading and Writing the Site* found in *Theory in Landscape Architecture; A reader* edited by Simon Swaffield.

33 Hirschfeld and Parshall, *Theory of Garden Art*, pp. 79, 96.

34 Hirschfeld and Parshall, *Theory of Garden Art*, p. 99

35 Beck, *John Nolen and the Metropolitan Landscape*, pp. 67–68.

36 Rowe, *Making a Middle Landscape*, p. 44.

37 Rowe, *Making a Middle Landscape*, p. 251.

38 Denes, *Wheatfield—A Confrontation: Battery Park Landfill, Downtown Manhattan*.

39 Stevens et al., *Anecdote of the Jar*.

40 I must at this point make it clear to the reader that these observations about not only Stevens' poem but also about the mental and emotional capacity of landscape that its consideration brings forward are grounded not only on John Dixon Hunt's writings but also on his insightful lectures which I enjoyed attending some many years ago.

41 Hunt, *Nature Over Again: The Garden Art of Ian Hamilton Finlay*, p. 18.

42 Deming, *Values in Landscape Architecture*, pp. 2, 233.

43 Sitwell, *On the Making of Gardens*, p. 7.

44 Sitwell, *On the Making of Gardens*, p. 41.

45 Sitwell, *On the Making of Gardens*, p. 16.

46 Sitwell, *On the Making of Gardens*, p. 19.

47 Sitwell, *On the Making of Gardens*, p. 11.

48 Laugier et al., *An Essay on Architecture*, p. 135.

49 Laugier et al., *An Essay on Architecture*, p. 135.

50 Laugier et al., *An Essay on Architecture*, p. 135.

## 38  *Landscapes as Political Media*

51  Walpole, *The History of the Modern Taste in Gardening*, p. 45.
52  Souter-Brown, *Landscape and Urban Design for Health and Well-Being: Using Healing, Sensory and Therapeutic Gardens.*
53  Souter-Brown, *Landscape and Urban Design for Health and Well-Being: Using Healing, Sensory and Therapeutic Gardens*, p. 36.
54  Louv, *Last Child in the Woods.*
55  Jekyll, *Wood and Garden Notes and Thoughts, Practical and Critical, of a Working Amateur*, pp. 1–2.
56  Oudolf et al., *Gardens of the High Line: Elevating the Nature of Modern Landscapes.*
57  Hitchmough, *Sowing Beauty: Designing Flowering Meadows from Seed*, p. 24.
58  Marris, *Rambunctious Garden: Saving Nature in a Post-Wild World*, pp. 169–170.
59  Hunt, *The Making of Place: Modern and Contemporary Gardens*, pp. 217–219.

## Bibliography

Agamben, G., 2000. Means without End: Notes on Politics, Theory Out of Bounds. University of Minnesota Press, Minneapolis.

Almy, D., University of Texas at Austin (Eds.), 2007. Center 14: On Landscape Urbanism, Center for American Architecture and Design, University of Texas at Austin School of Architecture, Austin. https://soa.utexas.edu/publications/center-14-landscape-urbanism

Arendt, H., Kohn, J., 2005. The Promise of Politics. Schoken Books, New York.

Balmori, D., Conan, M., 2010. A Landscape Manifesto. Yale University Press, New Haven.

Beck, J., 2013. John Nolen and the Metropolitan Landscape. Routledge, London; New York.

Cleveland, H.W.S., 2002. Landscape Architecture as Applied to the Wants of the West: With an Essay on Forest Planting on the Great Plains, American Society of Landscape Architects Centennial Reprint Series. University of Massachusetts Press in association with Library of American Landscape History, Amherst.

Deming, M.E. (Ed.), 2015. Values in Landscape Architecture and Environmental Design: Finding Center in Theory and Practice, Reading the American landscape. Louisiana State University Press, Baton Rouge.

Denes, A., 1982. Wheatfield – A Confrontation: Battery Park Landfill, Downtown Manhattan.

Gorz, A., 1971. Strategy for Labor: A Radical Proposal. Beacon, Boston.

Hirschfeld, C.C.L., Parshall, L.B., 2001. Theory of Garden Art, Penn Studies in Landscape Architecture. University of Pennsylvania Press, Philadelphia.

Hitchmough, J., 2017. Sowing Beauty: Designing Flowering Meadows from Seed. Timber Press, Portland.

Hunt, J.D., 2008. Nature Over Again: The Garden Art of Ian Hamilton Finlay. Reaktion Books, Londres.

Hunt, J.D., 2015. The Making of Place: Modern and Contemporary Gardens. Reaktion Books, London.

Jekyll, G., 1995. Wood and Garden Notes and Thoughts, Practical and Critical, of a Working Amateur, Repr. ed. Antique Collectors' Club, Woodbridge.

Laugier, M.A., Herrmann, W., Herrmann, A., 1977. An Essay on Architecture, Documents and Sources in Architecture. Hennessey & Ingalls, Los Angeles.

Leccese, M., McCormick, K., Congress for the New Urbanism (Eds.), 2000. Charter of the New Urbanism. McGraw Hill, New York.

Louv, R., 2008. Last Child in the Woods: Saving Our Children from Nature-Deficit Disorder, Updated and Expanded ed. Algonquin Books of Chapel Hill, Chapel Hill.

MacKaye, B., 1990. The New Exploration: A Philosophy of Regional Planning. Appalachian Trail Conference, Harpers Ferry.

Marris, E., 2013. Rambunctious Garden: Saving Nature in a Post-Wild World, Paperback ed. Bloomsbury, New York.

Medium. Cambridge Dictionary., 2022. Cambridge University Press, Cambridge, London.

Nolen, J., 2005. New Towns for Old. University of Massachusetts Press, Amherst, Boston in association with Library of American Landscape History, Amherst.

Olmsted, F.L., Twombly, R.C., 2010. Frederick Law Olmsted: Essential Texts, 1st ed. W.W. Norton, New York.

Oudolf, P., Darke, R., Hammond, R., 2017. Gardens of the High Line: Elevating the Nature of Modern Landscapes. Timber Press, Portland.

Rowe, P.G., 1991. Making a Middle Landscape. MIT Press, Cambridge.

Sitwell, G.R., 2003. On the Making of Gardens, 1st Softcover ed. David R. Godine, Boston.

Souter-Brown, G., 2015. Landscape and Urban Design for Health and Well-Being: Using Healing, Sensory and Therapeutic Gardens. Routledge, Abingdon, Oxon.

Stein, C.S., 1973. Toward New Towns for America, 5th Print. ed. MIT Press, Cambridge.

Stevens, W., Serio, J.N., Beyers, C., 2015. Anecdote of the Jar, in: The Collected Poems of Wallace Stevens. Vintage Books, New York.

Swaffield, S.R. (Ed.), 2002. Theory in Landscape Architecture: A Reader, Penn Studies in Landscape Architecture. University of Pennsylvania Press, Philadelphia.

Taylor, D.E., 1999. Central Park as a Model for Social Control: Urban Parks, Social Class and Leisure Behavior in Nineteenth-Century America. Journal of Leisure Research 31, 420–477. https://doi.org/10.1080/00222216.1999.11949875

The Central Park Conservancy, 2018. Before Central Park: The Story of Seneca Village. Central Park Conservancy Magazine. https://www.centralparknyc.org/articles/seneca-village

Waldheim, C., 2022. Landscape as Urbanism: A General Theory. Princeton University Press, Princeton and Oxford.

Walpole, H., 1995. The History of the Modern Taste in Gardening. Ursus Press, New York.


## Suggested Readings

Bohn, K., Viljoen, A. (Eds.), 2014. Second Nature Urban Agriculture: Designing Productive Cities. Routledge, Taylor & Francis Group, Abingdon; Oxon; New York.

Church, T.D., Hall, G., Laurie, M., 1995. Gardens Are for People, 3rd ed. University of California Press, Berkeley.

Ciucci, G. (Ed.), 1983. The American City: from the Civil War to the New Deal, 1st Paperback ed. The MIT Press, Cambridge.

Dorrian, M., Rose, G. (Eds.), 2003. Deterritorialisations: Revisioning Landscapes and Politics. Black Dog Publishing, London, New York.

40  *Landscapes as Political Media*

Forester, J. (Ed.), 2021. How Spaces Become Places: Place Makers Tell Their Stories, 1st ed. New Village Press, New York.

Francis, M., Hester, R.T. (Eds.), 1990. The Meaning of Gardens: Idea, Place, and Action. MIT Press, Cambridge.

Giesecke, A., Jacobs, N. (Eds.), 2012. Earth Perfect? Nature, Utopia and the Garden. Black Dog Pub, London.

Gorgolewski, M., Komisar, J., Nasr, J., 2011. Carrot City: Creating Places for Urban Agriculture, 1st ed. Monacelli Press, New York.

Hunt, J.D., 2000. Greater Perfections: The Practice of Garden Theory, Penn Studies in Landscape Architecture. University of Pennsylvania Press, Philadelphia.

Jackson, J.B., 1984. Discovering the Vernacular Landscape. Yale University Press, New Haven.

Jackson, J.B., 2000. Landscape in Sight: Looking at America. Yale University Press, New Haven, London.

Jacobs, J., 1992. The Death and Life of Great American Cities, Vintage Books ed. Vintage Books, New York.

Low, S.M., Smith, N. (Eds.), 2006. The Politics of Public Space. Routledge, New York.

Lyson, T.A., 2004. Civic Agriculture: Reconnecting Farm, Food, and Community, Civil society. Tufts University Press; University Press of New England, Medford; Lebanon.

Nordahl, D., 2009. Public Produce: The New Urban Agriculture. Island Press, Washington.

Olwig, K., 2002. Landscape, Nature, and the Body Politic: From Britain's Renaissance to America's New World. University of Wisconsin Press, Madison.

Olwig, K.R., Mitchell, D., 2009. Justice, Power and the Political Landscape. Routledge, London.

Rich, S., 2012. Urban Farms. Abrams, New York.

Shiffman, R., 2019. Beyond Zuccotti Park: Freedom of Assembly and the Occupation of Public Space. Project Muse, Baltimore.

Solnit, R., 2008. Storming the Gates of Paradise: Landscapes for Politics, 1st Paperback Printing ed. University of California Press, Berkeley; London.

Weilacher, U. (Ed.), 1999. Between Landscape Architecture and Land Art. Birkhäuser, Basel.

# 3 When the Social Order Was a Public Question

There was a time when discussions regarding the best and most equitable organization of society were not only philosophically available but also popular and publicly prominent. This is in distinct contrast to our own time, in the early 21st century, when public discourse seems to – at best – quibble around the marginal details of how to mitigate the worst of the inequities of a neoliberal world order as it blindly accepts the questionable proposal that there is no legitimate alternative to free-market capitalism which, it should be noted, offers freedom only to a select and privileged few. In order to read the utopian proposals of Howard, Le Corbusier, and Wright effectively – in a way that allows us today to think through what we might glean of value from them – it is helpful to set a contemporary reading of their texts in the time they wrote, when the best and most equitable social order was still very much treated as a public question. This chapter is an attempt to provide this context through a very brief overview of four influential and widely read books. Some influenced these three utopian writers more directly than others, but all influenced the mindset from which they wrote. All four works presented in this chapter challenged capitalism and other structures of power which have allowed the few to have power over the many and the wealthy to subjugate the poor. More importantly for our purposes, all four enjoyed a significant level of popular readership and influenced public debate regarding the organization of society. The contemporary reader will profit most from this chapter not by attempting to argue for or against the analyses and proposals within these works, especially based on the necessary extreme brevity of their presentation herein. Nor will the reader benefit by dismissing these proposals because they are well outside what is available for public political discussion in our time. Rather, it is suggested that the reader use this chapter to open questions in their own mind regarding the best and most equitable social order at the fundamental categorical level of land, capital, and labor as a precursor to evaluating the works of Howard, Le Corbusier, and Wright for the value they offer us today. In particular, it is suggested that the reader focus on opening questions regarding the balance between private benefit and collective action. Anyone tempted to dismiss these works given their priority on collective action, particularly in the area of control over land, is encouraged to challenge

DOI: 10.4324/9781351053730-3

42    *When the Social Order Was a Public Question*

the bases for their intuitions by bringing them up against the problems we face in the contemporary world as given as a motivation for utopian thought today in Chapter 1 and their ties to capitalist ideologies. These four works are *Capital: A Critique of Political Economy* (1867) written by Karl Marx, *Progress and Poverty* written by Henry George (1879), *Looking Backward: 2000–1887* (1887) by Edward Bellamy, and three works by Peter Kropotkin, *The Conquest of Bread* (1892), *Fields, Factories, and Workshops* (1898), and *Mutual Aid: A Factor of Evolution* (1902).

## Capital

Writing from exile in England, Karl Marx published the first volume of his intended three-volume work titled *Capital: A Critique of Political Economy* in German in 1867. *A Critique of Political Economy* is commonly referred to as simply *Capital* or *Das Kapital*. It was translated into French by 1875, republished three more times in German by 1890, and first published in full in English in 1887. While it is now a text most typically read within only a small subset of academic settings, this was not the case in the first decades after its publication. As early as 1883, sections of *Capital* were translated into English and published in serialized form in a British magazine titled *Today: A Monthly Gathering of Bold Thoughts*. Between 1885 and 1889, the magazine, retitled as *To-Day: Monthly Magazine of Scientific Socialism*, published the first ten chapters of *Capital* in English. The first popular distribution of the work in the United States was in German language periodicals from 1868 to 1871 that catered to German socialists who had emigrated to the country. The first English excerpts in the United States were distributed as "The Workingmen's Voice on the Normal Working Day" in 1872 by the American section of the International Workingmen's Association. English summaries by chapter were later published in 13 installments in a weekly journal *The Socialist* beginning in 1876. The volume was also extracted into a series of ten installments in another publication, *Labor Standard*, in 1878.

It is important to begin with the reasons that Marx wrote this work. While he was clearly responding to treatises on political economy by writers such as David Ricardo, John Stuart Mill, and Adam Smith, his years of engagement with working class organizations in England and the publication of *The Communist Manifesto* with Friedrich Engels in 1848 make clear that this was not a dispassionate intellectual pursuit. In the preface to the first publication of *Das Kapital*, Marx explained to his German language readers why the examples in the book were from England. He claimed that at the time of his writing, England was the purest and most completely documented example available of "the capitalist mode of production, and the conditions of production and exchange corresponding to that mode." He continued with the warning to Germans reading his work that "where capitalist production is fully naturalized among the Germans (for instance, in the factories proper) the condition of things is much worse than in England."[1]

*When the Social Order Was a Public Question*   43

Marx argued that capitalists exploit laborers through expropriating the value they create surplus to what is necessary to merely sustain themselves and then use this expropriated surplus value as capital to further increase their economic and social power. According to Marx, if the total value of labor was paid to laborers, capitalists would see no profit.[2] The foundational part of this work, for our purposes, is Marx's analysis of why the laborer has no choice but to sell their labor to the capitalist on the capitalist's terms. "Labour," wrote Marx, "is, in the first place, a process in which both man and Nature participate, and in which man of his own accord starts, regulates, and controls the material re-actions between himself and Nature."[3] The earth itself is a universal instrument of this labor and the soil and the water of the earth are the universal subject of human labor. A subject of labor in Marx's terms is that to which human labor makes changes for the purpose of increasing its value. An instrument of labor is that which is used by labor to make these value-increasing changes. Marx writes that the earth is a universal instrument of labor for the basic fact that one must stand on the earth to labor – simply put, people must labor somewhere. Other instruments of labor are the result of previous labor and Marx notes that these include things such as canals, roads and workshops.[4] The subjects of labor and the instruments of labor, taken together, constitute the means of production.[5] The greater the percentage of control that capitalists have over the means of production at the expense of laborers, the greater the potential for exploitation of laborers by capitalists because without access to the means of production, laborers have nothing to work on and nowhere to work from.

Marx questioned how, presuming that people are truly equal, it came to be that some people had the power to control the means of production (including the very earth itself) and others did not, such that the latter had to accept the conditions for life offered by those who held power over production – no matter the associated impoverishment. Marx noted that the typically told story, one that continues to echo in contemporary discussions of poverty, is that the separation of society into those with control of the means of production and those with control of only their own labor was the result of a history in which one group of people was "diligent, intelligent, and above all frugal" while the other was comprised of "lazy rascals, spending their subsistence, and more, in riotous living."[6] Contrasting what Marx described as this "insipid childishness … preached to us in the defense of property," he claimed that the true history of separating people from the means of production which was a necessary precondition to the development of capitalism was a history in which "conquest, enslavement, robbery, murder, briefly force, plays the great part" and that the expropriation of the means of production began primarily with the denial of agricultural producers the right to use land.[7] While the particulars may vary from country to country, this is always the first step, according to Marx, in producing a class of laborers who have no alternative but to labor under the conditions set forward by those who control the means of production. As is the case throughout *Capital*, Marx uses the history of England – which includes their domination of other countries – as the classic form of

## 44 *When the Social Order Was a Public Question*

the violent expropriation of the means of production by an elite class. Capital tells a story worth reading about the many confiscatory laws, wars, violent disregard for law and humanity, and other abuses of power the result of which was that England shifted from being a nation in which most people had some form of ownership of the means of production including access to land and therefore the ability to subsist as free people in the late 14th century to a nation in which the vast majority of people had no choice but to sell their labor and that of their children to capitalists in the middle of the 19th century. It is a history of bloody and violent cruelty that included brandings, whippings, mutilations, and executions by the church as well as the nobility – one which, he wrote, can be found "in the annals of mankind in letters of blood and fire."[8] While he focused on England, he also noted parallel developments across many countries.

The enclosures of the commons played a central role in this denial of people the rights to the means of production and the ability to be self-sufficient. It is worth noting that Marx recounts and references the same history told by Sir Thomas Moore regarding the destruction of villages and removal of peasants from their land in order to pasture sheep for the production of wool. This was one of the first significant steps, after the Norman conquest of England, in the chain of the separation of people from the means of production. It led, in turn, to the pre-conditions for the development of capitalist modes of production and the inherent inequalities between those who generate capital through the control of the means of production and those who have only their labor to sell.

Hand in hand with the destruction of rural villages and the removal of people from the right to support themselves came the destruction of rural domestic industry. Not only did the enclosures of the commons remove the possibility of self-subsistence, it also removed access to raw materials for artisanal production and disrupted the traditions of communal inter-reliance. Now that people were separated from the land and its raw materials such that they could not manufacture goods for household use or sale in local economies, they necessarily became consumers of domestic products produced for profit by those who controlled the means of production. Once labor was beholden to the owners of the means of production for both income and daily needs, it was a short and accelerating path to large factories where capitalists made use of laborers as inputs to machine processes while reducing the skill level required to keep the machines running. This reduction in required skill made individual laborers as interchangeable as any other part of the machine and undercut the potential for laborers to resist capital by withholding skill. This led, as Marx quoted from another source, to children as young as seven being

> consigned to the charge of the master-manufacturers; they were harassed to the brink of death by excess of labour…were flogged, fettered and tortured in the most exquisite refinement of cruelty; … they were in many cases starved to the bone while flogged to their work and … even in some instances … were driven to suicide.[9]

*When the Social Order Was a Public Question*   45

Larger and larger cities are another logical outcome of the capitalist means of production founded on the separation of people from the means of production in combination with the increasing scale of production required to compete for profit. Concurrent to capitalists drive to reduce wages relative to the volume of production, laborers were also squeezed by this accelerating growth of cities in another way. Since land became a means of financial production through the collection of rent and the land in cities was held by a small number of landlords for whom renters were as interchangeable as laborers were for factory owners, the poverty of the working class was driven to the point of bare subsistence from both directions – income and expense. It should be noted that what needed to subsist, from the point of view of the capitalist and the landlord, was a class of laborers and renters. Individual laborers and individual renters were irrelevant to their balance sheets and therefore to their interests.

The solution, for Marx, was to expropriate control of means of production back to the people in common so that laborers have the right to the benefit from all their labor, not just the bare minimum which the owners of the means of production share with them in order to keep the machines running and support their further accumulation of capital. It is critical to note that the means of production did not only mean the factories and other instruments of labor but also meant the subjects of labor including the very earth itself. This inclusion of land and the proposal for re-organizing its control, use, and benefit for the common good as an alternative form of social organization was not distant from public discourse during the formative years of Howard, Le Corbusier, and Wright – as will be even more clearly seen in the next book to be discussed which had an even wider popular reception, *Progress and Poverty* by Henry George.

## Progress and Poverty

While many people have at least a passing familiarity with the works and thought of Karl Marx, few have heard of Henry George even though George's work was quite popularly known and debated through the early years of the 20th century. Unlike Marx who had extensive formal education, Henry George left school at a young age and worked in a variety of roles with newspapers and ran for local office in California and in New York on several occasions. Observing the growing disparity between the increase in production and wealth on one hand and the increase in poverty and despair on the other, he felt he had found the key to this dilemma in the way land value was held within society. *Progress and Poverty* was published in 1879 and, while that was several years after the first serialized English translations of *Capital* became available in the United States, there is no evidence that George was significantly influenced by Marx's work. He had formed the core thesis of his analysis and published it in a work titled "Our Land and Land Policy" in 1871. In 1905, his son wrote in the preface to the 25th anniversary addition that by conservative estimate, more than two million copies had been sold in several languages – with at least

## 46  *When the Social Order Was a Public Question*

three translations into German.[10] It is claimed that in the 1890's *Progress and Poverty* sold more books than any book other than the Bible in the United States. Whether or not this is an accurate claim, the fact that one could credibly make such a claim speaks to the popularity of his work which remained high for many years. The *Single Tax Year Book* published in 1917 listed five national organizations and 56 state organizations dedicated to his ideas in the United States alone.[11]

While the even broader readership and public discussion of George's work compared to Marx's may have well been that the book was approximately half the length and required far less historical knowledge and specialized philosophical background to access the material, it is also true that George offered – at least to the growing middle class – a far more palatable solution to the problem of poverty in the face of great abundance that he, Marx, and so many others identified. He stated that "it is true that wealth has been greatly increased, and that the average of comfort, leisure, and refinement has been raised; but these gains are not general. In them the lowest class do not share."[12] However, his solution for reducing disparities in wealth did not pit class against class, nor does it require deep structural changes to the foundations of society. In fact, he stated in his introduction that one of his primary goals was to find a solution to offset the power of "charlatans and demagogues" who offered all sorts of what he saw as dangerous proposals.[13] His interest in resolving this enigma, while genuinely concerned with the poverty and deprivations lived by laborers, was also specifically intended to forestall proposals for radical, violent solutions.

George stated that throughout the field of political economy it was commonly but mistakenly claimed that the source of this inverse relationship between progress and poverty was an inverse relationship between capital and wages – that wages were equivalent to the capital available for productive use divided by the number of workers available to engage in productive activity. He offered both observational and theoretical arguments for why this was inaccurate. In order to discover the real reason for the enigma of increased poverty that attended increased progress and a solution to resolving both poverty and social conflict, George began by defining the relationships between land, labor, and capital that support production and the generation of wealth. He too, like Marx, turned to the control of land as a critical component in this equation.

There are three factors of production in George's scheme – land, labor, and capital. Of these, only land and labor are essential to the production of wealth. He has an expansive definition of land which

> includes, not merely the surface of the earth…but the whole material universe outside of man himself, for it is only by having access to land, from which his very body is drawn, that man can come in contact with or use nature.[14]

The significant implication here is that things such as rich agricultural fields, veins of ore, access to steady flows of water for generating power, and other relative or locational advantages which facilitate the output of labor are not capital but are rather included in the category 'land.' Further, he claimed that all people have equal right to land and that private ownership of land (though not improvements made upon it) is an unjust institution, a 'maladjustment of man.' He wrote that

> the equal right of all men to the use of land is as clear as their right to breathe air — it is a right proclaimed by the fact of their existence. For we cannot suppose that some men have a right to be in this world and others no right. ... This is a right which is natural and inalienable; it is a right which vests in every human being as he enters the world ... There is on earth no power which can rightfully make a grant of exclusive ownership of land.[15]

The second necessary factor of production, labor, has a much simpler definition. Labor, for George, "includes all human exertion."[16]

Capital, as George framed it, is more complicated. Capital is a form of wealth and wealth is comprised of such things that "consist of natural substances or products which have been adapted by human labor to human use or gratification."[17] He explained this with an analogy between the way that wealth stores labor for later use and the way that coal stores the heat of the sun. However, labor which provides directly for the satisfaction of desire does not produce wealth. "Only labor which gives value to material things," also called productive labor by George, produces wealth. Similarly, "nothing which nature supplies to man without his labor is wealth."[18] George also excludes such items as bonds, mortgages, promissory notes, bank bills, and other devices for transferring wealth from being wealth themselves.

Capital, George argued, is wealth put to use in aid of the production of more wealth. He made the distinction between money set aside for use in business or speculation as capital and money set aside for household use. Similarly, grain that a farmer sets aside as seed for the next year is capital, grain set aside for household consumption through the next harvest is not. A sewing machine for home use is not capital, but a sewing machine for commercial use is. Since wealth is characterized by use or gratification, the goods produced must be delivered to the location at which they will be used or provide gratification. Therefore, all the things from railroad engines to telegraph lines which facilitate the transfer and delivery of goods to be enjoyed as wealth are capital. Since the three factors of production are land, labor, and capital but capital is a subcategory of wealth which is ultimately generated by storing labor in land, both wealth and capital are derivatives of the application of labor to land and therefore only labor and land are primary categories. George's own observation was that therefore capital is put to use by labor, not the other way around.[19] This is critical to his argument that capital does not have the power to control labor ascribed to it by some and therefore that it cannot, categorically, be the source of inequity. This understanding also negates the possibility that class antagonism between labor and capital will resolve the issues of poverty and disparity of wealth.

48 *When the Social Order Was a Public Question*

Another way in which his scheme of production minimized the role of capital in the creation of gross inequity is to point out that capital cannot be put to use without labor. While labor can produce wealth by engaging with land if it has access to it, capital can do nothing without labor because in and of itself, unlike labor, capital has no motive power. "Stop labor in any community," wrote George, "and wealth would vanish almost as the jet of a fountain vanishes when the flow of water is shut off."[20] Capital is merely an aid which makes the process of applying labor to land in order to generate wealth more productive. The classic example of capital in George's sense is a tool. One can carry grain to market on one's back if one chooses. But one can carry more grain to market with the same amount labor if one has a wagon. The wagon is a tool for producing wealth, and therefore it is capital. However, it took many tools – implemented as capital – to produce the wagon. This chain of capital formation is a long and continuous history of human labor being mixed with land from the first rudimentary tools up to modern mechanisms of transportation such as railroad cars and large ships. All along the process, matter has been transformed into wealth through the storage of labor in land, the latter to which everyone also has equal right. Since the right to land is equally held and all wealth and therefore all capital is land imbued with labor, then both wealth and capital have a partial basis in what George claims is the common and inalienable right to land.

The question is, how then – if all wealth production is based in part on the contribution of commonly shared land – did access to wealth become so unequally distributed. George's understanding of the source of modern inequality starts in much the same place as do the understandings of More and of Marx. He quoted from More's introduction to *Utopia* to illustrate the history of violent appropriation of the control of land and poverty.[21] He ties all land ownership to the use of force without right – whether in the New World or in the Old – and claims that none have had the right to give "the exclusive possession of that which nature provides for all men."[22] He goes further to claim that "the ownership of land will always give the ownership of men... [and] ...when starvation is the alternative to the use of land, then does the ownership of men involved in the ownership of land become absolute."[23] He noted, by way of calling out the absurdity of private land ownership, that

> thirty thousand men have the legal power to expel the whole population from five-sixths of the British Islands, and the vast majority of the British people have no right whatever to their native land save to walk the streets or trudge the roads.[24]

George concluded his narrative about the source of inequality with a focus on the rent for the use of land. Once all land is privately held, he claimed, those who control land have monopoly control over the production of wealth, having control of all land to which labor can be applied. They also, therefore, have effectively total control over labor since labor has nothing to apply itself to in order to generate wealth which includes not just capital and luxuries, but the basics of life such as food and shelter. This monopoly control of land gives the class of landowners control over those who don't own land that for George is equivalent to the control that slaveowners have over enslaved people. Illustrating his understanding of the relationship between land, labor, and wealth, George connected the free availability of land in the New World — without in any way acknowledging indigenous rights in the New World it must be noted — and the motivation for importing enslaved people from Africa. Since land was freely available to settlers from Europe who could generate wealth by washing gold out of streams or taking up agricultural production for themselves, the large landowners of the South had no way to compel labor from people through monopoly control of land as is foundational to capitalism and was typical at the time in Europe. Therefore, their only option to increase their wealth through exploitation was to import people whose labor could be appropriated by force. While enslaved people were obviously controlled in many more violent ways, George's accurately observed that restricting them from travel and from owning land of their own achieved the same wealth-generating benefit for slaveholders that capitalist landowners saw due to the monopoly control over land. He went so far as to propose that the 14th Amendment to the Constitution in the United States did not, ultimately, abolish slavery and that only the abolishing of private property will fully accomplish that end.

His solution is rather simple, conceptually speaking. He claimed that, based on the natural right to land which all people share based simply on their humanity, any person using land to generate wealth should pay rent for the use of land to the public since the public as a body was the rightful owner of land as a common resource. It is important to note that he distinguishes between land and improvements to land, using the example of a house. The house is wealth and can be privately owned, and he acknowledges that in order for progress to be made and for people to invest in the production of durable wealth — particularly durable wealth that is used as capital — there must be security in holding that wealth. This does not, however, mean that the land itself becomes privately owned because a private house is bult on it and he proposes that the homeowner should pay rent to the society for the use of the land that is integral to their enjoyment of the benefits of their labor as wealth. He argues against the re-appropriation of land back to common ownership as a needless shock to the systems of production that were generating historically unprecedented accumulations of total wealth. All that was needed to resolve the enigma of extreme poverty in the context of extreme wealth, he proposed, was a confiscation of the rent that is being wrongfully and privately accumulated. He further claimed that this is the only tax that would be needed and the only tax that could be justified, hence his proposal is commonly known as the Single Tax Movement.

50  *When the Social Order Was a Public Question*

## Looking Backward: 2000–1887

Rather than putting forward a theory of the right social relations that would alleviate poverty and inequality if instituted, Edward Bellamy's 1887 book *Looking Backward: 2000–1887* uses the framework of a romantic fiction to describe a society in which the gross inequities of industrialized society of the late 19th century had been overcome. It sold over 400,000 copies in the United States before the turn of the century and was similarly widely read in Britain after its publication there in 1890. Over 150 Bellamy clubs formed to promote the vision Bellamy offered of a society characterized by equality, material comfort, and security for all. While the ideas were not unprecedented, the book was widely influential and spawned a small library worth of literature by people both critiquing and supporting the ideas it contained. One likely reason for its popularity was that it portrayed a society which overcame disparities in wealth without the need for widespread social violence, coming out only one year after the Haymarket Riot – only the most notorious of many politically motivated riots of the time. If the reader is interested in a deeper understanding of concerns about violence at the time, *Urban Masses and Moral Order in America* by Boyer, *Urban Disorder and the Shape of Belief* by Smith, and *The Great Riots of New York* by Headley are good places to start.

While Bellamy does not explicitly impugn capital or take on directly economic language in this text, he does define the basis of inequity in society as the fact that some live in idleness on the return on inherited investments while the rest of society toils to live meagerly as they support the idle rich. He describes the society of his day with an analogy to a carriage in which a select few enjoy inherited seats on the top of the carriage with pleasant views and breezes, but the largest mass of humanity is consigned to drag the carriage along with ropes. The situation of those pulling the carriage is a spectacle which distresses those who sit on top of the carriage, especially when the carriage comes to a bad spot in the road and the riders observe "the desperate straining of the team, their agonized leaping and plunging under the pitiless lashing of hunger" while many "fainted at the rope and were trampled in the mire."[25] He wrote that they would, at the sight of such suffering, "call down encouragingly to the toilers of the rope, exhorting them to patience, and holding out for hopes of possible compensation in another world for the hardness of their lot" or contribute "to buy salves and liniments for the crippled and injured" yet in practical effect only cling to their own seats the more tightly so not to fall off and have to pull the ropes themselves.[26] He chalks the persistence of this situation to two things: first the belief that there was no other way to organize society, and second, what he calls the "singular hallucination" that the people on top of the coach were somehow not like those who pulled the coach – that they were made of "finer clay, in some way belonging to a higher order of beings."[27] This delusion of a natural and innate difference between the people pulling the carriage of society and the people

*When the Social Order Was a Public Question* 51

riding in ease was, in his view, explained the indifference that the privileged members of society felt toward the working class. When, toward the end of the book, the main character Julian West who held a seat on top of the metaphorical carriage, tried to challenge both of these beliefs at a dinner party – that the wealthy are naturally superior and that there is no better, more just, and more productive to organize society, he was met with aversion, dread, reprobation, contempt, and cries of "Madman! Pestilent fellow! Fanatic! Enemy of Society!" and thrown to the street by his fellow elite.[28]

However, at the beginning of the narrative, Julian West's main concern, other than insomnia, was the delay that labor strikes of 1887 are causing to the completion of his house which is, in turn, was delaying the timing of his wedding. He tries to overcome the insomnia and get away from the stress of the strikes by retreating to a specially made underground vault. While he remains asleep for 113 years, all of society is reorganized and the city of Boston is vastly improved. He wakes in the year 2000 in the house of his host, Dr. Leete, who found the underground chamber during an excavation. Dr. Leete explains to Julian West the changes to society and to the city that occurred in the intervening time. He recounts that the change was bloodless and without violence because public opinion had become ripe for a new understanding of the most equitable, and efficient, means of controlling and organizing production. Dr. Leete makes the argument that the expansive increase in production under capitalism was undeniable, even to its foes, but that the parallel contrast between extreme poverty on one hand and extreme wealth on the other was just as undeniable, even to capitalism's supporters. While one proposal could have been to return to a pre-consolidation era of small producers to achieve greater equity between people, the efficiency and therefore the scale of production would have been lost. Instead, Dr. Leete explains that,

> early in the last century the evolution was completed by the final consolidation of the entire capital of the nation. The industry and commerce of the country, ceasing to be conducted by a set of irresponsible corporations and syndicates of private persons at their caprice and for their profit, were intrusted to a single syndicate representing the people, to be conducted in the common interest for the common profit. ... In a word, the people of the United States concluded to assume the conduct of their own business, just as one hundred odd years before they assumed the conduct of their own government, organizing now for industrial purposes on precisely the same grounds they had then organized for political purposes. ... the obvious fact was perceived that no business is so essentially the public business as the industry and commerce on which the people's livelihood depends, and that to entrust it to private persons to be managed for private profit is a folly similar in kind, though vastly greater in magnitude, to that of surrendering the functions of political government to kings and nobles to be conducted for their personal glorification.[29]

## 52   *When the Social Order Was a Public Question*

There are several aspects of Bellamy's vision that are particularly salient for the writing of utopian urban proposals. West at first thinks that someone is playing an elaborate joke on him by telling him he had been asleep for so long but is finally convinced when Dr. Leete takes him to the roof of his house to see what had become of Boston while he slept. While he recognizes the shape of the Charles River and the Boston harbor with its islets, he is astonished by the change to the city. At his feet lay a great city with "miles of broad streets, shaded by trees and lined with fine buildings" which "stretched in every direction" while "every quarter contained large open squares filled with trees" such as was not comparable to any city he had ever seen.[30] Dr. Leete explains to Julian West that in 1887

> the excessive individualism which then prevailed was inconsistent with much public spirit. What little wealth you had seems almost wholly to have been lavished in private luxury. Nowadays, on the contrary, there is no destination of surplus wealth so popular as the adornment of the city, which all enjoy in equal degree.[31]

Three changes to the city in particular are evidence of this shift from the city of the 19th century characterized by competition and the city of the year 2000 which is characterized by cooperation and public spirit. First, there is no smoke and there are no chimneys. The society of the future had come to the realization that they could more efficiently produce heat and power as a public utility rather as an effort undertaken at the scale of the individual residence and the private factory. The second is that sidewalks are not only consistent and passable in the rain, but that there are covers over the sidewalks for everyone. His host comments that

> the difference between the age of individualism and that of concert was well characterized by the fact that, in the nineteenth century, when it rained the people of Boston put up three hundred thousand umbrellas over as many heads, and in the twentieth century they put up one umbrella over all the heads.[32]

Furthermore, Dr. Leete points out the drips off the edge of all 300,000 umbrellas fell on someone else in the crowded streets of 19th-century Boston.

The commercial life of the city had also been entirely remade. There were no banks or lenders, which were seen as being anti-social, and there were no advertisements for goods. Each ward of the city had its own store which was within five to ten minutes of every residence, closely echoing More's description of Utopia. Everybody in society had equally distributed credits to use at these stores, and were able to shop for what they needed at will. Cooking, laundry, repairs and such household activities were all done at public operations. Each ward also had communal dining halls which were social centers of life in the city. This organization around communal utilities and equal distribution of

*When the Social Order Was a Public Question* 53

credits to all people in society was made possible by the organization of production into a centralized affair in which all people were expected to work in what Bellamy described as an industrial army. People, for the most part, had a large say in what work they did based on their preferences. Anyone refusing to work and contribute to the wealth of society and the benefits they enjoyed from it, was imprisoned on bread and water until they agreed to do so.[33] Different jobs were not paid in different numbers of credits, but the hours and conditions were adjusted as necessary to make the contributions to production fairly distributed. If there were a job that was harder or more dangerous or in some other way less desirable, the hours expected to fulfill that job were reduced until it was attractive enough that there were a sufficient number of people voluntarily selecting it.

Commercial and other aspects of relations between nations were also wholly remade while West had been asleep. Not only had the United States made this conversion to organized production for common good, but so had the whole world in Bellamy's projected world of the year 2000. Trade between nations happened much as the way it happened between individuals – everything was balanced out to the benefit of all between nations as well as within them. In addition to the increase in productive capacity of society as a whole and the efficiency of enjoying luxuries in common rather than hoarding them privately, there were also no military expenditures since all nations had realized that the real enemies were not other nations but rather poverty and poor health. This lack of military spending allowed an even higher percentage of total production to be put to the good of society.

As was the case in George's proposal, one of Bellamy's main points was that society could be reorganized to resolve massive poverty and inequality through reasoned argument and cooperation. While he did not go as far as George to say that there is no reason for class antagonism, he did propose that with a cooperative spirit, class antagonism can be overcome for the good of all. Whereas the other writings we look at in this chapter bring in land and to a degree urban form as a philosophical category that needs to be understood and used to achieve a solution, one of Bellamy's greatest contributions to the popular discourse around poverty and the city at his time was an imagination of what a resolution would look like in the flesh.

## Fields, Factories, and Workshops

Peter Kropotkin wrote several volumes, all centered around the idea that cooperation was the historical norm prior to industrialization and the state, was the natural condition of human interaction, and remained a moral imperative for organizing society in an equitable way. These are *The Conquest of Bread* (1892), *Fields, Factories, and Workshops* (1898), and *Mutual Aid: A Factor of Evolution* (1902). In particular, he argued for a re-integration of agriculture and industrial production under the control of small cooperative units. Like the other writers considered in this chapter, and the three utopians whose major works

54    *When the Social Order Was a Public Question*

will be examined in depth in the following chapters, Kropotkin concerned himself with finding a resolution to the grinding poverty and exploitation that accompanied the spectacular growth of wealth in the modern world. He proclaimed that

> the day when the labourer may till the ground without paying away half of what he produces, ... the day when the worker in the factory produces for the community and not the monopolist – that day will see the workers clothed and fed and there will be no more Rothschilds or other exploiters.[34]

Kropotkin also tied the poverty and inequality of his day to centuries past and the violent, or at least unscrupulous, expropriation of land. In one descriptive narrative he offered, a feudal baron takes claim to a valley but "might as well possess property on the moon" if there are no people to work it and pay him tribute.[35] The baron then offers free land, which was never really his except by claim, to those laid destitute by wars, droughts, and pestilence in exchange for a certain number of years free of tax and payment. Once, however, they have built the roads and improved the soil as well as settled into cottages and villages which they hold only at the pleasure of the baron, he or his heirs gradually build their fortunes through increased rent and "little by little, with the aid of laws made by the barons, the poverty of the peasant becomes the source of the landlord's wealth."[36]

Kropotkin was born into a Russian aristocratic family and later denounced the structure of privilege and advocated for an anarchist communism, subsequently living much of his life in exile. While anarchism is often portrayed as a violent ideology, this is not the case and not at all what Kropotkin was arguing for. Anarchy simply means the organization of society without government. Those who espouse anarchy as an ideal form of society, like Kropotkin, present it as a political form in which cooperation and equity replace control and privilege. "Every society, on abolishing private property will be forced," Kropotkin wrote at the beginning of his chapter "Anarchist Communism" in *The Conquest of Bread*, "to organize itself on the lines of Communistic Anarchy. Anarchy leads to Communism, and Communism leads to Anarchy, both alike being expressions of the predominant tendency in modern societies, the pursuit of equality."[37] Even those societies grounded in individualism, according to Kropotkin, necessarily tend toward anarchist communism because while individualism can be "explained by the efforts of the individual to protect himself from the tyranny of Capital and of the State" the limitations of being able to operate as free individuals using money as a medium of relations was becoming clear.[38] His argument that people would see the value in cooperation and ultimately choose it over competition is similar to the history that Dr. Leete recounted to Julian West. Kropotkin continued with a description of how principles of communal labor and consumption have been maintained in rural townships and continue to succeed "except when the State throws its heavy sword into the balance" and

*When the Social Order Was a Public Question* 55

points out that communist principles are expressed as a matter of practicality in several form of infrastructure.[39]

Like Marx, George, and Bellamy, Kropotkin argued that wealth is socially produced and should not be appropriated to the enjoyment of a few individuals either through current violence or on the foundation of a history of violence. However, he was the only one who specifically claims that the drive toward equity between people, as people become aware of what it implies, must lead ultimately to anarchist communism. He claimed that the perception of a need for a State is a superstition promulgated by whole systems of philosophy, the press, and of course politicians themselves who proclaim that if they are given power, they will free people from misery.[40] He proposed that the history of the last half of the 19th century shows that, as an alternative to the state, society can be more effectively and more justly organized when people "satisfy their need for organization by the free contacts between individuals and groups pursuing the same aim."[41] To the modern ear, this ideal taken in isolation reads as if from a neoliberal playbook. However, one must remember that the foundation for this free contact he proposed between people was his claim that wealth was socially constructed and all property was rightly owned in common. "A society," he wrote,

> founded on serfdom is in keeping with absolute monarchy; a society based on the wage system and the exploitation of the masses by capitalists finds its political expression in parliamentarianism. But a free society, regaining possession of the common inheritance, must seek in free groups and free federations of groups, a new organization, in harmony with the new economic phase of history. Every economic phase has a political phase corresponding to it, and it would be impossible to touch private property unless a new mode of political life be found at the same time.[42]

Central to the new economic phase which he saw as inevitable and the mode of political life that accompanied it was an integration of industrial and agricultural production directly at odds with the principle of the division of labor. It is this critique of the division of labor that gives the most solid footing to the spatial solutions Kropotkin offered.

Kropotkin argues against the division of labor, most famously proposed by Adam Smith, which guided specialization not only of people but of regions and nations. Kropotkin claimed that the division of labor was "organized so as to permit the owners of the land and capital to appropriate for themselves, under the protection of the State and historical rights, the yearly surplus of human production."[43] His argument for change is twofold. First, as long as land and capital are held by the few under the protection of the State, then a just and equitable distribution of the benefits of society will be out of reach because people do not have the ability to feed themselves unless they accept wages and conditions offered by the owners of land and capital. The division

## 56   *When the Social Order Was a Public Question*

of labor, organized and controlled by the owners of factories and those who control trade for both raw materials and finished goods, ensures that no consensual group of people can provide for their needs independently. He noted that German, French, Russian, and Austrian governments had all actively denied syndicalization (unionization in current terms) that villages and artisan groups sought in order to have bargaining power to balance negotiations with the owners of capital.[44] Writing in 1898, he noted that in Germany, "even now a mere co-operative association for the sale of artisans' work is soon reported as a 'political association' and submitted as such to the usual limitations."[45] He was as critical of socialists who want to perpetuate the division of production within society as he was of capitalists and the State when it comes to the role which specialization of industry plays in keeping people powerless as members of free communities. He argued instead for an integration of industry, and particularly an integration of industry and agriculture. He claimed that

> it is to the advantage of every region, every nation, to grow their own wheat, their own vegetables, and to manufacture at home most of the produce they consume. This diversity is the surest pledge of the complete development of production by mutual co-operation, and the moving cause of progress, while specialization is now a hindrance to progress.[46]

It is important to note that when he wrote about regions and nations, he was not writing about the collected benefits of individuals who live in those regions and maintain their wealth individually but rather the nation and region as a collective whole that is organized so that all people in it can achieve well-being.

The second component of Kropotkin's argument against specialization is that along with reclaiming wealth and land back to the common good, the only way that people will hold power – rather than a governing elite – is the integration of factory production and agriculture. He presented this idea most completely in *Fields, Factories, and Workshops* though it is supported by his other works. While he proposed many reasons for this integration, the first and foundational reason is that this integration of fields and factories would blunt the impact that hunger and poverty have on political power. He noted in *The Conquest of Bread* that revolutions must first solve the question of bread rather than being occupied with "endless discussions on the forms of government" as the middle class were. He also claimed that middle class were, ultimately, displeased with the proposal of equality in the form of food, shelter, and clothing for all because "they are quite alive to the fact that it is not easy to keep the upper hand of a people whose hunger is satisfied."[47]

This was partly about the productive capacity expected of agriculture during his day which relied on machinery for working the fields, transportation, irrigation, and other aspects of agricultural production. Similar to the idea that under the specialization of labor, laborers were beholden to some industrialists for their ability to work and others for the production of their basic needs, the specialization of manufacturing agricultural implements beyond the control of people working the land left them vulnerable to exploitation by those who provided, and could withhold, the necessary agricultural technology. Not only did this particular component of Kropotkin's proposal directly influence Howard's proposal more than the others – it also had long reach into proposals for new towns and direct impact on the Greenbelt proposals of United States housing policy through Howard's ideas, though they were only partially carried forward.

Kropotkin felt that this integration of agricultural work with industrial society was as inevitable as was communist anarchy. Once the workers seized hold of the factories and subsequently the trade for raw goods and finished products was stalled, people would have no choice but to turn to agricultural production in order to feed themselves. However, rather than producing food "in the same manner as the present peasants who wear themselves out, ploughing for a wage that barely provides them with sufficient food for the year," because "a Paris jeweler would object to that," people would turn to a better form of agriculture. This better form of agriculture would be carried out by joyous groups of people as they follow "the principles of the intensive agriculture, of the market gardeners, applied on a large scale by means of the best machinery that man has invented or can invent."[48] He argued for an agriculture that is more cognizant of the maintenance of soil at this smaller scale. While he noted the great success in volumes of harvest obtained by extensive agriculture such as was found in the Midwest of the American prairies, "which takes the soil from nature without seeking to improve it" and "when the earth has yielded all it can" it is abandoned in the search for "virgin soil, to be exhausted in its own turn," he was also clearly critical of these practices.[49] He proposed that instead, the new kind of agriculture would naturally develop once the factories were taken by the workers and economic life becomes locally organized as one which cares for soil and in which the "object is to cultivate a limited space well, to manure, to improve, to concentrate work, and to obtain the largest crop possible."

## Conclusion

While Marx, George, Bellamy, and Kropotkin held differing positions in some aspects of their proposals for a better society, they all saw cooperation as the underlying principle of a just and equitable society. However, it was not that they felt that if only people would cooperate then society would be improved. Rather, they saw that society was already cooperating but that there were political, legal, and social mechanisms by which the benefits of that cooperation were not equally distributed to the people who were doing the work. Not only was the appropriation of the value of cooperation benefitting some members of society more than others, it was depressing the quality of life for those who provided the basic labor for production

# 58 *When the Social Order Was a Public Question*

to the level of bare material subsistence if not below – and certainly not leaving them with security, joy, and rest as an expectation of life. While these four disagreed about the role of capital as a social force and capitalists as a class, they agreed about the role of land and in particular about the role of land ownership. All four proposed that land could not legitimately be privately owned and that the benefits which grew from the use of land should accrue to all – though the details of that accrual vary somewhat across the four. In the next chapter, we will examine these categories – land, capital, and labor – in the proposal for the Garden City, the Radiant City, and Broadacre City. Though these three utopian proposals approach the details of labor and capital in different ways, they all take the same position relative to land as that of Marx, George, Bellamy, and Kropotkin. Howard, Le Corbusier, and Wright all propose that the benefits of owning land should be based on a social good – though Wright's proposal comes at the topic from a very different angle than the others. Furthermore, all three proposals are organized around the same conceptual value of cooperation as a replacement for competition.

## Notes

1  Marx et al., *Capital*, p. 8.
2  Marx et al., *Capital*, p. 465.
3  Marx et al., *Capital*, p. 151.
4  Marx et al., *Capital*, p. 153.
5  Marx et al., *Capital*, p. 154.
6  Marx et al., *Capital*, p. 617.
7  Marx et al., *Capital*, p. 617.
8  Marx et al., *Capital*, p. 618.
9  Marx et al., *Capital*, p. 654.
10  George, *Progress and Poverty*, p. 7.
11  Miller, *Single Tax Year Book*, pp. 444–448.
12  George, *Progress and Poverty*, p. 16.
13  George, *Progress and Poverty*, p. 18.
14  George, *Progress and Poverty*, p. 32.
15  George, *Progress and Poverty*, p. 207.
16  George, *Progress and Poverty*, p. 32.
17  George, *Progress and Poverty*, p. 34.
18  George, *Progress and Poverty*, p. 34.
19  George, *Progress and Poverty*, p. 124.
20  George, *Progress and Poverty*, p. 97.
21  George, *Progress and Poverty*, p. 180.
22  George, *Progress and Poverty*, p. 209.
23  George, *Progress and Poverty*, p. 212.
24  George, *Progress and Poverty*, p. 233.
25  Bellamy, *Looking Backward: 2000–1887*, p. 12.

When the Social Order Was a Public Question    59

26  Bellamy, *Looking Backward: 2000–1887*, p. 12.
27  Bellamy, *Looking Backward: 2000–1887*, pp. 12–13.
28  Bellamy, *Looking Backward: 2000–1887*, p. 159.
29  Bellamy, *Looking Backward: 2000–1887*, p. 33.
30  Bellamy, *Looking Backward: 2000–1887*, p. 24.
31  Bellamy, *Looking Backward: 2000–1887*, p. 26.
32  Bellamy, *Looking Backward: 2000–1887*, p. 77.
33  Bellamy, *Looking Backward: 2000–1887*, p. 65.
34  Kropotkin, *The Peter Kropotkin Anthology (Annotated)*, p. 48.
35  Kropotkin, *The Peter Kropotkin Anthology (Annotated)*, p. 49.
36  Kropotkin, *The Peter Kropotkin Anthology (Annotated)*, p. 49.
37  Kropotkin, *The Peter Kropotkin Anthology (Annotated)*, p. 36.
38  Kropotkin, *The Peter Kropotkin Anthology (Annotated)*, p. 38.
39  Kropotkin, *The Peter Kropotkin Anthology (Annotated)*, p. 39.
40  Kropotkin, *The Peter Kropotkin Anthology (Annotated)*, pp. 42–43.
41  Kropotkin, *The Peter Kropotkin Anthology (Annotated)*, p. 42.
42  Kropotkin, *The Peter Kropotkin Anthology (Annotated)*, p. 46.
43  Kropotkin, *The Peter Kropotkin Anthology (Annotated)*, p. 472.
44  Kropotkin, *The Peter Kropotkin Anthology (Annotated)*, p. 641.
45  Kropotkin, *The Peter Kropotkin Anthology (Annotated)*, p. 641.
46  Kropotkin, *The Peter Kropotkin Anthology (Annotated)*, p. 204.
47  Kropotkin, *The Peter Kropotkin Anthology (Annotated)*, p. 63.
48  Kropotkin, *The Peter Kropotkin Anthology (Annotated)*, pp. 206–207.
49  Kropotkin, *The Peter Kropotkin Anthology (Annotated)*, p. 214.

## Bibliography

Bellamy, E., 2018. Looking Backward: 2000–1887. DIGIREADS COM, Place of publication not identified.

George, H., 2016. Progress & Poverty. Aziloth Books, Great Britain.

Howard, E., Osborn, F.J., 2001. Garden Cities of To-morrow, 11th Print ed. MIT Press, Cambridge.

Kropotkin, P., 2020. The Peter Kropotkin Anthology (Annotated): The Conquest of Bread, Mutual Aid: A Factor of Evolution, Fields, Factories and Workshops, An Appeal to the Young and The Life of Kropotkin. CSA Publishing, Coppell.

Le Corbusier, 1964. The Radiant City: Elements of a Doctrine of Urbanism to be Used as the Basis of Our Machine-Age Civilization. The Orion Press, New York.

Marx, K., Engels, F., Moore, S., Aveling, E.B., Untermann, E., 2017. Capital. Volume 1, Digireads, USA.

### Suggested Readings

Bender, T., 1975. Toward an Urban Vision: Ideas and Institutions in Nineteenth-Century America. University Press of Kentucky, Lexington.

Boyer, P.S., 1978. Urban Masses and Moral Order in America, 1820–1920. Harvard University Press, Cambridge.

60　*When the Social Order Was a Public Question*

Eagleton, T., 2018. Why Marx Was Right, 2nd ed. Yale University Press, New Haven.

Fishman, R., 1982. Urban Utopias in the Twentieth Century: Ebenezer Howard, Frank Lloyd Wright, and Le Corbusier, 1st MIT Press pbk. ed. MIT Press, Cambridge.

Giunta, E., Trasciatti, M.A. (Eds.), 2022. Talking to the Girls: Intimate and Political Essays on the Triangle Shirtwaist Factory Fire, 1st ed. New Village Press, New York.

Hall, P., 2014. Cities of Tomorrow: An Intellectual History of Urban Planning and Design Since 1880, 4th ed. Wiley-Blackwell, Hoboken.

Harvey, D., 2018. The Limits to Capital. Verso, London.

Harvey, D., 2012. Rebel Cities: From the Right to the City to the Urban Revolution. Verso, New York. Headley, J., 2004. The Great Riots of New York 1723–1873. Thunders Mouth Press, New York.

Howe, F., 1912. The City, the Hope of Democracy. Charles Scribner's Sons, New York.

Jameson, F., 2005. Postmodernism, or, The Cultural Logic of Late Capitalism, 11th Printing in Paperback ed, Post-contemporary Interventions. Duke University Press, Durham.

Lang, G., 2021. Jane Jacobs's First City: Learning from Scranton, Pennsylvania, 1st ed. New Village Press, New York.

Lefebvre, H., 1991. The Production of Space. Blackwell, Oxford, Cambridge.

Lefebvre, H., 2003. The Urban Revolution. University of Minnesota Press, Minneapolis.

Mill, J.S., 2002. On Liberty, Dover Thrift Editions. Dover Publications, Mineola.

Miller, Joseph Dana, (ed.). 1917. Single Tax Year Book: The History, Principles and Application of the Single Tax Philosophy. Single Tax Review Publishing Company, Sun Building, New York City.

Mohl, R.A., 1985. The New City: Urban America in the Industrial Age, 1860–1920, The American History Series. H. Davidson, Arlington Heights.

Patten, S., 1968. The New Basis of Civilization. The Belknap Press of Harvard University Press, Cambridge, Massachusetts.

Ricardo, D., 1971. On the Principles of Political Economy and Taxation. Penguin, Harmondsworth.

Schuyler, D., 1993. The New Urban Landscape: The Redefinition of City Form in Nineteenth-Century America, New studies in American Intellectual and Cultural History. Johns Hopkins University Press, Baltimore.

Scott, J.C., 2008. Seeing like a State: How Certain Schemes to Improve the Human Condition Have Failed, Nachdr. ed, Yale Agrarian Studies. Yale University Press, New Haven.

Smith, A., 1981. An Inquiry Into the Nature and Causes of the Wealth of Nations. Liberty Fund, Indianapolis.

Smith, C.S., 2007. Urban Disorder and the Shape of Belief: The Great Chicago Fire, the Haymarket Bomb, and the Model Town of Pullman, 2nd ed. The University of Chicago Press, Chicago.

Smith, N., Mitchell, D., Siodmak, E., Roybal, J., Brady, M., O'Malley, B.P. (Eds.), 2018. Revolting New York: How 400 Years of Riot, Rebellion, Uprising, and Revolution Shaped a City, Geographies of Justice and Social Transformation. The University of Georgia Press, Athens.

Soule, G., 1932. A Planned Society. The Macmillan Company, New York.

Steffens, L., 2004. The Shame of the Cities. Dover Publications, Inc., Mineola, New York.

Thompson, E.P., 1966. The Making of the English Working Class, 1st Vintage ed. Vintage Books History. Vintage Books, New York.

Wiebe, R.H., 2007. The Search for Order, 1877–1920, 47th Print ed. American History. Hill and Wang, New York.

# 4 Land, Capital, and Labor

As introduced in Chapter 1, Ruth Levitas proposed in *Utopia as Method* that productive utopian thought would provide a holistic imagination of the reconstruction of society with an eye toward the equitable and participatory flourishing of the world. With this as our jumping off point, it is clear that the intertwining categories of land, capital, and labor are central to any utopian proposal. They and their relationships are all central components to the reimaginations of society put forward in the influential works by Marx, George, Bellamy, and Kropotkin covered in the previous chapter. There are echoes of these in the proposals for the Garden City, the Radiant City, and Broadacre City for which land, labor, and capital are also central. Understanding the relationships between the conceptual categories of land, capital, and labor around which the three utopian proposals under discussion are organized is critical to understanding their full intent and their distinct imaginations of what human flourishing entails.

For Karl Marx, the ability of capital to expropriate the value created by labor was tied to its expropriation of the control of land from common ownership. He noted that the history of this expropriation was a narrative of the violent establishment of power "written in the annals of mankind in letters of fire and blood."[1] An argument about the return of land to common ownership is logically embedded in the argument that the means of production should be returned to common ownership so all people benefit equitably. The means of production, for Marx, is composed of the subjects of labor and the instruments of labor. Subjects of labor are those things which are altered by labor to generate value. Instruments of labor are those things which are used in the process of laboring. While it may be a truism that all things come from the Earth, Marx points out that both the subjects and instruments of labor come from the earth to emphasize the point that as long as the earth can be privately owned, labor will always be at the mercy of capital and inevitably exploited by it.

Henry George also tied the vast inequalities he saw in society around him to the private ownership of land. Whereas Marx proposed that capital controlled land as a means by which to exploit labor, George proposed that the private ownership of land was opposed to both capital and labor which cooperated to generate wealth. George centered his analysis around the production of

DOI: 10.4324/9781351053730-4

Land, Capital, and Labor    63

wealth – the manipulation of the natural world for human use or gratification. He understood wealth as labor stored in natural materials. Capital, for George, is only a subset of wealth – that wealth which is set aside to generate more wealth, meaning that capital cannot be necessary to the production of wealth. Interestingly, George retells a similar history of the bloody and violent taking of land from common ownership by power. And even more noteworthy, both George and Marx recount a parallel history to that told by More about the role of the enclosure of the commons in the production of poverty in England. George proposed that the most common-sense and least disruptive solution to the enigma of poverty in the face of progress would be for society to recover through taxation the increase in value derived from land to which all people have a right, rather than letting the increase in value accrue to private accounts.

While George and Marx analyzed of the structure of inequality and argued for changes to the relationships between land, capital, and labor, Edward Bellamy used as critique a romantic fiction in which these relationships had already been reconstructed so that all people could flourish. The essential plot is that a privileged individual, Julian West, falls asleep in 1887 and wakes in the year 2000 to find a completely remade society and city. In Bellamy's fictional Boston of 2000, all production is centrally managed. His host, Dr. Leete, explains that as the benefits of consolidation became clear, eventually all agreed to the consolidation and the nationalization of all industry – and therefore nationalization of all land as a means to turn production to the benefit of all people without sacrificing the progress achieved through industrial efficiency. Most notably, the expression of this arrangement of society was the beautification of the city since, as the main character of the book points out, people have joined in common to embellish and enrich the public spaces used by all rather than hoarding wealth to beautify their own private enclosures. This results in cities which are adorned by parks and public institutions that extend conviviality throughout society while eliminating the prevalence of advertising and smoke of manufacturing. Furthermore, woven into the life and fabric of the city was a deep respect between people across professions and the pervading imperative of equality.

While all three of these individuals included agricultural concerns in their proposals, Peter Kropotkin prioritized the integration of agriculture into the social production of wealth and gave it the most complete treatment. Kropotkin, arguing for an anarchist communism, wrote that the quest for equality was a quest against the cooperating tyrannies of capital and the state. To achieve his political ideal of freely chosen association, he, like Marx, George, and Bellamy, proposed that the foundational step toward achieving genuine equality is the abolishing of private property in land and a return to cooperation rather than competition as the basic form of human relationship. Among his several reasons for the integration of factory and agricultural work, two reasons are here most pertinent. First, the production of food within freely associating political organizations was critical to their independence and the ability of their members, acting cooperatively, to resist being exploited. Secondly, in his view

## 64   Land, Capital, and Labor

it was explicitly the division of labor, particularly at a regional or national level, that allowed certain individuals to maintain control of others through controlling the basics needed for survival.

## The Garden City

In his 1945 introduction to a reprint of *Garden Cities of To-Morrow*, Lewis Mumford stated that Ebenezer Howard was deeply influenced by both Henry George and Peter Kropotkin. Howard himself noted the influence that George's work had on him in a footnote to a critique of George's ideas in which he wrote that he hoped it was not "ungrateful in one who has derived much inspiration from *Progress and Poverty* to write thus."[2] Howard was also influenced by *Looking Backward*. F.J. Osborne, introducing the 1965 reprint of *Garden Cities of To-Morrow*, claimed that it was Bellamy's book which initially inspired Howard and that Howard was instrumental to having Bellamy's book republished in England.[3]

### *Capital in the Garden City*

Howard did not rail against capital or capitalism the way that Le Corbusier and Wright would after him, but he was by all accounts a more humble and less dogmatic individual. He did, however, view the world of his day as being organized around the conflict between vested interests of labor on one hand and of capital on the other. In fact, when he argued for the use of eminent domain to support the extension of his proposed garden city into a national system of garden cities, he imagined that the vested interests of capitalists and landlords would at first resist the idea but that their resistance would be overcome (nonviolently, of course) by time and by the "vested interest of those who work for their living, whether by brain or hand."[4] Like Wright after him, he made a distinction between capitalism that is supportive of community interests and capitalism that is not. After arguing that the housing in his garden city proposal should be built primarily through cooperative building societies and not financed by profit-taking banks, he wrote that "the true remedy for capitalist oppression where it exists, is not the strike of *no work*, but the strike of *true work*, and against this last blow the oppressor has no weapon."[5] By true work, Howard meant work that is cooperative, organized, and pro-municipal.

Howard saw a place for capitalism as the investing of money in order to better one's financial position as long as it was subservient to community interests and kept under collective control. This is seen most clearly in the system of commerce he proposed for the Garden City. Since the Garden City operated as a municipality in that it served the residents of the town but was also legally a private landowner and therefore could make different rules for its occupants than could a truly publicly incorporated town, Howard argued that it actually had greater powers with which it could to serve the interests of the community.[6] One of the ways this power was to be expressed was in the limitation of competition between commercial interests in the Crystal Palace – the Garden City's large indoor commercial and recreation facility. Howard described how the typical competition between rival business owners led to lower quality and service as business owners lowered prices to remain competitive and profitable. Competition of this sort was, ultimately, good for neither the consumer nor the shop owner. On the other hand, Howard clearly saw the negative potential of monopoly control of any one good or service. His solution was to let the corporation decide on the number of shops of each type that could serve the community, and in most cases limiting providers to one per type.[7] As long as that one provider was offering high quality at reasonable prices, the people in the community would be well served and the shop owner would make a decent living. But if the people in the community felt that prices were too high or quality too low, they could offer a lease in the arcade to a competitor – and just the threat of this, Howard proposed, would keep the interests of capital in check. Each of these business owners would, he noted, "be in a sense a municipal servant."[8] He had similar proposals to balance the interests of the community with those of agricultural and industrial proprietors who paid rent for land to the town the same way that commercial owners did.

At a more fundamental level, Howard relied deeply on capital to make his Garden City proposal work. The enterprise turns on the ability to buy agricultural land at agricultural prices as the initial investment and he went to great lengths to calculate that the financial returns on the land would be beneficial to the investors while still benefiting future residents of the Garden City. This initial land purchase rested on the willingness of "four gentlemen of responsible position and of undoubted probity and honour, who hold it in trust, first, as a security for the debenture-holders, and, secondly, in trust for the people of Garden City."[9] In other words, Howard's entire vision relied on finding enough individuals with capital to invest in the initial land purchase and the initial utility and road construction who were also willing to realize less than the full potential profit of the enterprise in two ways. First, these individuals were imagined by Howard to be willing to invest their capital for a return of only 4 percent – well below what they could get for the investing in other enterprises. Second, he imagined that they would be willing to turn over the landownership of what would be a highly profitable enterprise to the residents themselves once the original capital was repaid along with 4 percent interest. Howard was not alone in this wishful proposal. Charity at 4 percent was a common progressive proposal of the time.[10] The Achilles heel of Howard's proposal, which may also indicate why history did not bear out his belief that Garden Cities were nearly inevitable, is his assumption that "in every man there is some measure of the reforming instinct; in every man there is some regard for his fellows."[11]

### Labor in the Garden City

A central motivation for Howard's proposal is his perceived need to balance the distribution of labor across England– though he clearly imagined his

66   *Land, Capital, and Labor*

proposal to be an example of the solution of a more universal problem of the human condition of his contemporary world. He gave the impetus for the book as being that "it is deeply to be deplored that the people should continue to stream into the already over-crowded cities, and should thus further deplete the country districts."[12] In order to demonstrate widespread support for his concept, he noted that his observation about this imbalance between cities and the countryside was agreed upon across many groups in society who were morally opposed to each other across other issues as divisive as temperance, politics, and religion. He quoted Tom Mann, an organizer in the British labor movement as observing that "the congestion of labour in the metropolis is caused mainly by the influx from the country districts of those who were needed there to cultivate the land."[13] While it is often a contemporary presumption that people left agricultural areas for the cities because mechanized agricultural processes decreased the need for rural labor, this is not the case. Advances in agricultural technology – particularly the development of cheap and easily installed drainage tile in England – actually expanded the need for agricultural labor. Rural labor shortages were not uncommon. Of course, periods of extreme destitution due to crop failure, international market competition, and capital shortages were also common in the countryside. The reason that laborers moved to cities was that, as bad as the conditions were for laborers in cities, they were still worse in rural areas. There were also no real chances of advancing out of a laborer position into more desirable work given that there was only one industry in the countryside. There was also little chance to stay in the countryside and earn even a meagre living during years of agricultural economic downturn. This doesn't mean, of course, that there were not periods of significant unemployment in the city – only that there were more possibilities for finding alternative work.

Howard used magnets as a rhetorical device to describe the attractions of the town, the country, and his proposal – the town–country. Howard illustrated the benefits he was seeking to build into the garden city by contrasting the attractions of his new proposal with the attractions and drawbacks of existing towns and the existing countryside. While he noted that in the town there were high money wages (for excessive hours), there were also high rents and prices. There were chances of employment, but also an army of unemployed. There were slums as well as palatial edifices. There were places of amusement, but also the isolation of crowds. In the country, by contrast, there are none of the social attractors. There were still hands out of work, long hours and low wages, crowded dwellings, and deserted villages. The only real advantages that Howard listed for the country have to do with the proximity to the beauty of nature, water, sunshine, and forests whereas in the city one deals with foul air and murky skies. In his proposed town–country magnet which he sought to construct with the garden city, there would be high wages but low rents and prices, social opportunities within reach of the beauty of nature, and bright homes and gardens without the smoke or slums.[14] This new industrial system had much to do with the distribution of labor and work.

Howard took issue with both sides of the debate between those who proposed that poverty could be solved by increasing production without addressing unequal distribution of the wealth on one hand and those who proposed that there was no need to increase production but only to redistribute existing wealth on the other. Rejecting that the options for addressing poverty were restricted to this dichotomy, he claimed that his proposal opened a broad path that,

> through a creation of new wealth forms, to a new industrial system in which the productive forces of society and of nature may be used with far greater effectiveness than at present, and in which the distribution of the wealth forms so created will take place on a far juster and more equitable basis. Society may have more to divide among its members, and at the same time the greater dividend may be divided in a juster manner.[15]

While Howard described the agricultural estate in detail and first in the sequence of his economic argument, less time is spent on the nature of industrial work. Because of the proximity of agricultural production to a ready market in the Garden City, Howard's imagination for agricultural work consisted primarily of local farms growing for local markets. While this may seem to be a pipedream to the contemporary reader, in the 1890's the prime characteristic noted in advertisements for agricultural land listed for sale in England was the distance to a rail-line and the nearest large city which that rail-line served. The most profitable agriculture in England at that time was market gardening to supply fresh produce to large cites. Since land in the Garden City was rented from the city, presumably by owner-operators rather than being owned by large landholders who hire labor without concern for their living conditions, and because the agricultural production consists of more high-value vegetable crops rather than simple commodities open to competition across vast distances, the labor of agricultural production was more highly remunerated in the Garden City than in the areas represented by Howard as the magnet of the countryside. Howard had similar arguments for the position of labor throughout the Garden City. Since the land on which labor worked was rented from the community as a whole, the wages paid for labor and the working conditions of their labor were both part of the negotiation for access to land between the community and the potential proprietor. Of course, this was only a functional way to improve the lot of laborers given the assumption that most people working in the Garden City also lived there and vice versa.

### Land in the Garden City

Much hay has been made of the fact that the center of Howard's Garden City was in fact a large garden and that the entire town was bounded by a greenbelt. However, it is often elided in histories and in most applications of his ideas that the productive, primarily agricultural, character of the greenbelt was critical to

## 68  *Land, Capital, and Labor*

Howard's theory. It was not intended to be simply a buffer of open space. Just as important to the functioning of garden cities as this expanse of agricultural land outside the town is the outer band of industrial land situated close to the intermunicipal rail-line which connects industrial firms more readily to natural resource inputs as well as markets for their outputs. This situation also greatly reduces traffic through the residential and civic areas as well as keeps the smoke from industrial production dispersed and away from the central areas of the city. Howard's detailed diagram lists a range of industrial activities from boot factories and cycle works to jam factories and stone yards. This distribution of land uses benefits laborers as well. All of those who work in both agriculture and industry have not only ready access to the social advantages of the city within a short distance but also to homes with gardens rather than the slums and deteriorating shacks which industrial and agricultural laborers respectively lived in at the time. These improvements to the quality of life for laborers across the spectrum of work are made possible by Howard's proposed restructuring of the ownership of land. The community has control over land use and tenancy decisions and can therefore make decisions that benefit the community as a whole in broad terms.

Restructuring of the use of capital and the application of labor as previously discussed is made possible by the recovery of the pecuniary benefits of land ownership from private accounts to communal good. Howard proposed that this recovery of benefits to the common good had far-reaching benefits for society well beyond a more just relationship between capital and labor. Howard, in one of his few florid passages, proposed that holding land in common was

> the key to the problem how to restore the people to the land – that beautiful land of ours, with its canopy of sky, the air that blows upon it, the sun that warms it, the rain and the dew that moisten it – the very embodiment of Divine love for man – is indeed a Master Key which will solve problems of intemperance, overwork, anxiety, poverty, government interference, and the relations between man and God.[16]

Howard explicitly refers to four conceptual proposals for addressing the distribution and inhabitation of land: *Art of Colonization* by Wakefield, proposals for restructuring land tenure by Thomas Spence and by Herbert Spencer, and a model city proposal by Buckingham.[17] While Wakefield was not writing about 'home colonies,' Howard thought his description of the right way to set colonies up for success as whole communities was constructive. He noted that Wakefield accurately foresaw that the real financial benefits of a colony would accrue to landholders and owners of the railroads serving the colony at a greater rate than to the colonists themselves, and followed to question why the community should not reap those benefits that existed only because the community made use of them. The contemporary critique of colonies and colonization was not a significant part of the discourse at this time, as the contemporary reader is most likely aware. Howard follows this question with the proposals by Spence and Spencer which suggested just this – that the benefits of land ownership should be retained for the residents in common. Howard saw two problems with these the positions of Spence and Spencer however; the use of the force by the state to acquire and/or own land on one hand and the difficulty of finding a price at which existing landowners could be justly recompensed while allowing the settlement to pay for itself on the other. His solution was the middle strategy to buy land in rural areas at agricultural prices and then settle the land in a way that would build the value to be held in common by the new population as a whole.

This explains why Howard spends so much of his book on calculations of rent, taxes, and the financial plausibility of his proposal. It is particularly telling that he begins the title of all three chapters after his introductory chapter with "The Revenue of the Garden City."[18] These three chapters, plus the fourth on "Further Details on Expenditure" take up over 25 percent of the entire volume. Howard's basic proposal for land being held in common was that with the capital put forward as described above, agricultural land would be purchased at agricultural prices and basic infrastructure put in place. Subsequently, the land would be turned over to the garden city corporation once the initial debt was paid off at a modest rate of interest. Howard calculated that once the land and initial infrastructural investments were paid for, the income from the rental of residential, commercial, agricultural, and industrial land will well exceeds the costs of maintaining the community. This surplus income will then be turned to social benefits such as pensions for retirees and support of charitable institutions. Because the land cost would not be ratcheted upward by speculation and competition for space as it is in cities, the amount paid as rate-rent (what Howard argues replaces both rent and taxes) in the garden city would remain significantly lower than what is commonly paid for taxes and rent in the city.

Residential rents in the garden city would be held at reasonable levels in part because of the greater profitability of agricultural, industrial, and commercial land that he expected would come from the planned efficiencies and benefits of garden cities. Howard surmised that these agricultural leaseholders will be willing to pay more than they currently did for land because their profits would increase at an even greater rate than the increased land costs due to the ready markets for their crops without the cost or burden of long-distance transportation and similarly due to the increased income from higher value perishable crops which this proximity allowed. He made similar arguments to support his calculations of income from rent to industrial and commercial interests. He also proposed that sewage from the garden city would be freely available as fertilizer to farmers, reducing their operating costs. While this may seem strange to modern sensibilities, sewage farms were a common way to manage effluent from cities well into the 20th century.

Howard proposed that speculation in land would be effectively undercut in two ways. First, because the population was to be held at or below a given maximum and the possibility for employment was presumed to be balanced with that population, there would be no incentive for people to move into the

## 70    Land, Capital, and Labor

garden city once it was full and thereby compete for residential space. Second, all property in the garden city was held in common so rate-rent would be set to the benefit of all and it is hard to imagine that any given community would price themselves out of their own community. This, of course, presumes a unity of purpose and an equal care for all members of the community. Howard proposed that this rate-rent be set in perpetuity at 4 percent per annum of the original cost of the land since he calculated that the income from the agricultural, commercial, and industrial estates would more than cover all other costs and benefits of the garden city.[19] It is also worth note that long-term leases up to 99 years were common in England, far more so than individual sole ownership of residential property. The concept of private sole ownership of residential property was far from universal in Howard's time and therefore this proposal which may seem so radical to modern ears was actually quite uncontroversial–except for the quite radical proposal regarding the common ownership of land as opposed to ownership by landlords.

## The Radiant City

When Le Corbusier looked at the city around him, he also saw poverty in the face of privilege which he likewise tied to land tenure – though in a very different way than Howard. Immediately following his title page, he asserted in large bold font "MOBILIZATION OF THE LAND FOR THE COMMON GOOD."[20] Under a heading of the same title later in the book, he expanded on his observation. "The machine age," he claimed, had "gnawed away at our cities, rotted them, destroyed them" and "destroyed the joys of life."[21] The contemporary city allowed the privileged classes to avoid the negative impacts on life that came with the industrial revolution and the growth of cities, but "as a result, millions of human beings are henceforth being deprived of the *basic pleasures*" and would be for their whole lives.[22] Like Howard, Le Corbusier proposed that private land ownership was a foundation to the problems of poverty so readily apparent at the time. Unlike Howard though, Le Corbusier did not propose that holding land privately directly generated unequal wealth in society. His main issue with the private holding of land was that it stood in the way of the ability to generate and implement a plan which would make the city efficient and distribute the benefits of what he proposed would be the second machine age to all people. These included the basic pleasures for all – sun, greenery, space, and active, participatory citizenship.[23] In answer to his own rhetorical question as to whether there was an obstacle to the life he imagined in his proposed new city, one that was productive, recuperative, joyful, and healthy, he wrote "Yes. The present form of land tenure, which is invested with private rights antagonistic to the public right."[24] For Le Corbusier, nature is the model, and problems in society – all of which he wraps up in the denial of basic human pleasures – can be solved by looking to the mechanism by which nature functions. "Although the entire phenomenon of nature is one of uninterrupted movement, circulation, development, cycles, regularity and harmony," he wrote, "contemporary activity is hidebound by the esteemed and enduring institution of unproductive property."[25] What he means by unproductive property in this instance is property that is not being used to support the provision of the basic human pleasures for all.

### Land in the Radiant City

Le Corbusier's proposal for land in the city, made possible by technology as will be discussed in the Chapter 5, was that 110 percent of the city's land area would become available to the pedestrian. All buildings and most commercial transportation would be lifted off the ground to provide covered recreation areas, thereby making the full surface of the city freely available to people walking. Roof gardens which could also be used for walking, sports, and sunbathing – all amidst flowers, trees, shrubs, and grass – provided the additional 10 percent of open space. He proposed swimming pools, tennis courts, sports fields of several types including soccer and basketball, sand beaches for sunbathing, and wide paths for walking throughout the new urban landscape. "Paths and walks are everywhere," in his proposed city where it would be "possible to cross the entire residential area from end to end, in any direction, either entirely in the open air or entirely sheltered from sun and rain."[26] In addition to sports fields and all manner of spaces for passive and active recreation to be found directly outside of all residences, he also proposed nurseries, kindergartens, and primary schools for children through the age of 14 placed in parks attached directly to residential buildings. The modern reader who may be accustomed to looking, perhaps in distaste, at the massive and monolithic buildings in Le Corbusier's grand urban proposals is asked to return to all of his renderings and plans of open spaces and mentally populate them with these outdoor activities for a different imagination of what life in his proposed city would have been like and then ask if, maybe, with such amenities immediately at hand living in such large and impersonal edifices might not be worth the bargain.

Le Corbusier did not only concern himself with urban land and urban uses. Reorganization of rural land and the "revision of the peasant family's status with regard to the land" were just as important to him.[27] Like Howard, he proposed that the problems of cities could not be addressed until issues in rural life, and therefore rural land, were addressed. "We shall not be able to empty the cities of their superfluous population," he wrote, "until the land has been materially and spiritually redeveloped."[28] Unlike Howard who expected people to move back to the land as if drawn by a magnet, Le Corbusier expected that people would be sent back to the country by the authorities.[29] On a short page of commentary that Le Corbusier inserted before the table of comments in the 1964 reprinting of the book, he wrote that the book as originally printed offered "at one go, an organism (The Radiant City) capable of housing the works of man in what is from now on a machine-age society. This description serves as a key to a social and economic revolution."[30] The first of the three events which he stated that the book announced are "those which will bring about agricultural

## 72    Land, Capital, and Labor

exploitation" by which he meant a better form of agricultural production relative to both the lives of the people who worked the land and the produce generated.[31] Whereas the urban dweller in the Radiant City was largely free to use the landscape for recreation, the rural peasant's working life was deeply embedded in the landscape. Agricultural land was to be redistributed into larger farms than what existed after a long history of the division of estates through inheritance. The result would be family-unit farms surrounding co-operative villages which would act as hubs of rural commerce and culture. He argues that the land in France,

> to be properly tended, ... must benefit from the attentive activity of a family group attached to a particular locality and whose combined wisdom is applied to all the diverse circumstances determined by so complex a topography and so varied a climate.[32]

He included many plans, models, and perspectives of these radiant farms showing what we would today call diversified agriculture with dedicated spaces for poultry, pigs, and sheep as well as kitchen gardens, orchards, and field crops.

### Capital in the Radiant City

While Le Corbusier wrote that "we must concern ourselves with man, not capitalism or with communism," he continued his train of thought by distinguishing between happiness and company dividends and between satisfaction of people's instincts and the corporate race for success.[33] He excoriated money and the interests of money throughout the book, calling the dominance of money and its pursuit – among other things – wretched, shady, a disease, violent, savage, cruel, ruthless, insatiable, and voracious.[34] He had numerous ideological problems with the concept and use of money and with capitalism, whether or not he consistently admitted to such ideological leanings. The core to his distaste for money was that it was both the driver of and medium for competitive interests between private actors which opposed the possibility of cooperative, coordinated efforts aimed at satisfying what he described as the basic pleasures. He described society based on competition for money thus:

> We have finally allowed ourselves to be taken over entirely by what we call free competition, which is to say a form of slavery, which means that any effort is immediately countered by an opposing effort…we have become merely a flock of rams, horns locked together, all trying to push one another backwards…we can make no progress![35]

Money stands in the way of his proposal for a city that meets human needs and desires in the machine age in three ways. Most importantly, the private ownership of land and the resulting speculative building forestalls the coordinated efforts that would be needed to realize his proposed reorganization of the

Land, Capital, and Labor 73

landscape to equally benefit all. Secondly, competition around money leads to what he sees as gross inefficiencies in the provision of the goods of society. Lastly, a significant volume of resources is taken up by the production of what are – in his view – useless consumer goods when production is driven by supply rather than by demand – claiming that "modern industry, organized according to the laws of supply has inundated us with useless consumer goods."[36]

Le Corbusier wrote that a fundamental postulate of the city is that it is "part of an economic complex."[37] Much of the form of the city he proposed is based on the arrangement of the most economical way to provide goods and services to people – from the communal provision of services such as laundry to the transportation system designed to deliver food and other goods efficiently to residential units. As opposed to the "insane chaos of carts and trucks thundering daily into the central markets of today" and the need to "trudge out shopping in the rain, then trudge back again," he proposed centralized, coordinated refrigeration and transportation. This would not only do away with the unpleasantries of traffic and shopping but would also increase the efficiency of the whole operation. Would it "also mean doing away with thousands of little private businesses?" Le Corbusier answered his own hypothetical question, "Of course! That is clearly one way to exorcise waste in the city, and therefore to bring down the cost of living."[38] While the reader may immediately consider the fate of all the small business owners and their employees in such a proposal, one must remember that Le Corbusier proposed that the benefits of social action needed to be distributed such that everyone had not only the right to eat but also the "right to expect a serene end to life that had been filled with fruitful labors" and the right to know the value of and need for the work they performed.[39] He was not proposing that shopkeepers be put out of work and livelihood, but rather that all of society should be reorganized so that daily work was drastically reduced through economic and spatial efficiency. As will be discussed shortly, he also imagined that five to six hours of work a day per person would be sufficient for maintaining all people with these benefits of modern production.

A significant component of his plan, motivated not merely by his indignation at the continued production of bric-a-brac and other things not suitable to the machine age, is the establishment of "a plan for producing permissible goods; to forbid with stoic firmness all useless products" and to "employ the forces liberated by this means in the rebuilding of the city and the whole country."[40] He proposed an economy based on demand which would do away with salesmen and advertising agents. Of course, for Le Corbusier, this demand must be defined by some person or some agency with the authority to determine which demands were allowable and which were not. This reorganization of the economy to produce only useful things would, according to Le Corbusier, redirect industry toward its true aims; "providing work for all and guaranteeing every man his daily hours of freedom."[41] He saw this shift to a demand-driven economy as the just and inevitable outcome of industrial development which would lead to the greatly expanded leisure time around which

74   *Land, Capital, and Labor*

the landscapes in the Radiant City would be organized. Replacing a voracious and ruthless kind of money – by which he means not money as a thing but money as a motivation – with a new and honest money is part of a program to produce for consumption of essential products. What are essential products for Le Corbusier? "Bread, clothing, housing, and the spiritual fruits of life."[42] Le Corbusier did not have a problem with capitalism because it was based on one group exploiting another but because the individual decisions made under its aegis thwarted an overall coordinated approach that would benefit everyone. This included not only land use decisions as discussed earlier, but also decisions about consumer goods as noted here. Both required significant and potentially disturbing roles for authority and the issues of agency and authority will figure heavily later in this book.

### Labor in the Radiant City

Le Corbusier did not write at length about labor. However, he claimed that "in order to distribute the fruits of human labor differently, we must first organize that labor, set precise and fertile goals for it."[43] Furthermore, he wrote that "waste," which he equated with slavery, "that snickering and drunken tyrant, at present claims all our labor, all our sweat."[44] This waste included the inefficiencies of everything from transportation of people and goods through the antiquated city form to housework in unhygienic houses to the inefficiency of useless products. He equated all of these with slavery because of the number of unpaid hours that people were forced to work to support them. He proposed that a reorganization of labor would, in part, recover the hours and effort lost to waste which he estimates takes up six months of work out of every 12. While he does not give a specific outline for how he proposes that the fruits of human labor would be distributed differently, it is clear that he expected that the increased capacity of machines, alongside his proposals for better organization of the city, should result in a reduction of the need for work (quota of collective labor) to five or six hours a day and a great expansion of time for leisure and productive work "*on a human level:* body and mind."[45] "Consider," he asked his readers regarding families, workers, and managers, "what the difference will mean to them between our present dislocated organization of labor, the products of which are all intended for one caste … and this new, organized form of activity."[46] Agricultural work, of course, was driven more by seasons of planting and harvesting than by the repetition of the machine, so rather than having consistently shorter daily work hours, he proposed that the average hours of work in agriculture would also decrease in parallel with those who performed their quota of collective labor in industry, but the hours worked per day would continue to vary with the seasons.[47]

Leisure, which he described as a threat that he was proposing to solve, ultimately, with the Radiant City, was only one of the ways in which Le Corbusier assumed that people would use their newly freed time. True work was at least as important to his imagination of life in the Radiant City. Le Corbusier defined

Land, Capital, and Labor 75

true work in the machine age as something distinct from industrial labor using machines to generate the essential products and allowable goods. The true work of people during this new age was not labor for basic production but rather time spent in the freely chosen work during non-laboring hours. As examples of this kind of freely chosen work, he offered Pasteur's scientific body of work, the Radiant City proposal he was putting forward, and "playing about with some piece of cabinetmaking" by "even the humblest member of society."[48] This freely chosen work which advances the arts, literature, and science echoes Bellamy's imagination of a future society in which one's worklife ends by age 45, freeing one for such pursuits to the overall benefit society.

## Broadacre City

Like Le Corbusier, Wright imagined a society in which people would spend much less time laboring and in which they would have much greater choice over the labor they performed. He similarly connected problems of labor to machine production. He claimed that the poor man was usually a wage-slave at some machine and that the "unearned increment of the machine itself" was one of the three great economic artificialities, the profits of which are "funneled into pockets of fewer and more 'rugged' captains of industry" and "only in small measure…where they belong; that is to say, with the man whose life is actually modified, given, or sacrificed to this new common agency for doing the work of the world. This agency we call 'the machine.'"[49] While he stated that "common realty achieved by way of taxation on communal resources, as Henry George pointed out with complete logic, is entirely democratic," he also felt that the tax proposal was only an expedient and "never intended to be taken as a complete solution to our land problem."[50] While George claimed that the nationalization and redistribution of land would create an unnecessary upset to the social order, Wright felt that if this "economic liberation of land and money" were achieved, "none may say how far man's cultural liberation may go with greater aesthetic uses of his ground by way of the vast mechanical resources developed in the last century" and proposed just such a solution.[51]

### Land in Broadacre City

While Wright's foundational critique of his contemporary society was that it was organized around rent − primarily rent for land, but also rent for money and rent for ideas, he felt that the form of rent that contributed most significantly to social inequality was rent for land. "The first and most important form of rent contributing to overgrowth of cities, resulting in poverty and unhappiness," he claimed, "is rent for land."[52] The ability of some to claim rent for the use of land he described as nothing more than "some fortuitous fortune's accidental claim to some lucky piece of realty, private but protected by law."[53] It was this exclusive claim on land, and therefore the ability of some people to charge others rent for space to merely live, that Wright most aggressively targeted. His

76 *Land, Capital, and Labor*

proposal is logically simple – he proposed that every man, woman, and child in the United States would get no less their own acre of land. To account for population growth, he proposed that land be held in forests that could be distributed as population grew. He claimed that this amount of land was a minimum and could be expanded, since if the population of the world stood close together, they would "scarcely occupy the island of Bermuda."[54] If this seems implausible to the modern reader, it might come as a surprise that if land area of the United States were distributed equally to the country's population as of 2022, there would be nearly seven acres for every person, including all children. If only existing agricultural land in the United States were considered, there would be over two and a half acres of land per person.[55] Furthermore, if only the existing farmland in the United States were divided equally amongst the entire population of North America – including the United States, Mexico, and Canada – every person would get just shy of two acres. This is in stark contrast to the fact that the largest individual landowner of agricultural land in the United States at this moment owns 242,000 acres.[56] To put that number in land-use context, there are currently only 93 cities in the United States with populations over 242,000. Every other city in the nation could be accommodated, at an acre per person, within this one individual's land holdings.

It is noteworthy that Wright did not acknowledge that the land in question was occupied prior to colonization and settlement by Europeans or even acknowledge that this is an issue to consider. However, he was consistent and did not recognize the rights of any current landholders either. Wright's alignment with the economic theory of Henry George and his critique of the ownership of land means that Wright did not acknowledge the current ownership of land by anyone, anywhere. He repeatedly attacked the ownership of land as an accidental foundation of irrational privilege. He made his disregard for the institution of private property law which stands in the way of distributing the benefits of the earth for the benefit of all clear when he stated that in Broadacre City, "landlaws are established as subordinate to the rights of the human being."[57] Echoing Henry George and others, Wright claimed that good ground is the birthright of every person, that "co-operative sharing of increase in land values is past due to society," and that in the contemporary situation, the owners of land "hold all man-made improvements on the land *against* the man on his land."[58] In other words, people who own land – because of their right to control access to land – have the capacity to effectively use any person's improvements on land such as houses and factories as leverage to charge rent up to just shy of the point it is worth abandoning the investment. On the map in the front of the book Wright included two principles illustrating his views on the ownership of land: "No private ownership of public needs," and "No public ownership of private needs."[59] While Le Corbusier and Howard proposed that land itself is held in common, Wright's proposal was significantly different – that the right to distribute the benefits of land is held in common. While he did not propose that it would become illegal for large landholdings to be compiled for cooperative use, it seems clear that he imagined that the benefits of being

*Land, Capital, and Labor*  77

able to opt out of wage-based employment would be enough to maintain the granularity of the rights to land at an acre per person achieved after breaking up what he described as a hold-over from aristocratic privileges.

### Labor in Broadacre City

While this decentralizing distribution of land that Wright proposed would allow for a re-integration of life and the freedom which would make democracy possible because every individual would have the freedom to be employed or not given that they would not be beholden to others for food or a place to live, he did not propose that everyone will support themselves in agriculture. He was clear that his proposal did not "mean that every man must be a genius or farmer" even though "there will be no longer excuse for any man to the kind of parasite the machine power of centralization is now so busy making of him – only to ensure him 'employment' on the terms of a wage slave."[60] This freedom to choose employment, and the inversion of the current power structure of capital and land ownership is summarized in the conclusion to Wright's work where he claimed that "No man need be a kept or 'Yes' man; if he goes intelligently to his birthright in nature he is now independently a 'No' man, if he so chooses."[61]

Even though Wright valorized the small family farm and ended his volume with a single appendix, printed in red, which includes a selection of an essay on farming by Ralph Waldo' Emerson, it is important to pay attention to the fact that he still imagines a landscape heavily laden with an engaged communal life of the arts, sport, and the functions of county government. Large buildings, even skyscrapers, are distributed throughout his proposed landscape. The map of Broadacre City included in the original volume as a fold out sheet, shows widely distributed polo grounds, music gardens, factories, sectarian and non-sectarian temples, research facilities, a zoo, clinics, cinemas, educational centers, and other amenities – all made available by a system of roads. He described at some length the social functions of community centers, design centers, hospitals, universities, schools, and markets. These all clearly imply not only leisure but varied kinds of work.

The core idea of Wright's proposal is that for a true democracy to thrive, the people who participate in it must be free and able to live a daily life centered around an authentic aesthetic of daily life and appreciation of their relationship to each other and to the earth. Large cities, according to Wright, preclude this kind of life. Much of this has to do with the work people do in cities. What he described as the "properly citified citizen" neither "creates or operates more than mere machinery, nor is he going to be much more than a machine himself" until the city is replaced with a new kind of settlement pattern.[62] This person, psychologically fitted to the big city,

> becomes a broker of profit-system ideas, a vendor of gadgetry, a salesman dealing for profit in human exaggeration … a speculator in frailties, … [a] puller of levers, pusher of the buttons of vicarious power, … a parasite of the spirit.[63]

78    *Land, Capital, and Labor*

The city dweller was trapped in work by two things according to Wright – continual rent paid merely for space to live and the lack of the ability to opt out of employment and support themselves if they so choose. It is not just the poor who are impoverished in spirit by the city in his analysis. Wright claimed that "it is not true that the poor are poor because the rich are rich" and stated that the rich were as parasitic as the poor – both were equally trapped by the three forms of rent, even if not equally compensated for their entrapment.[64]

Wright described full employment as "a more subtle form of rent or conscription" and "the baited hook that keeps the worker dangling."[65] Similar to the others, he set some of the blame for this situation at the foot of machine production. He claimed that "big time production's flagrant greed" alongside "the abuse of surplus machine power and orthodox finance" make people poorer through making them useless.[66] While it was the use of machine production that led to a society in which all were beholden to the owners of the machines, Wright did propose that the use of machine power could also lead to a reduction of effort required to provide for the basic goods of life, as did Le Corbusier. While the machine was a central feature of what Wright saw as a system of wage-slavery that defined work in modern society, he also thought that machine power could set people "free from all conscription whatsoever – whether military, moral, economic, or artistic."[67] Given the productive capacity of machines, he also felt that only a few hours of paid labor a day would be necessary – especially if life were lived in such a way that income from employment would be combined with food and income from gardens and small farms.

Not only would the ownership of small farms impact the need to work for a living, but so would the decentralization of work throughout the landscape Wright described through offering more readily available options for employment. Given the low density of both residences and places of work, transportation to a chosen form of work would be easy. He claimed that the decentralization he proposed would allow that "every citizen may choose any form of production, distribution, self-improvement, enjoyment within the radius of, say, ten to forty minutes of his own home."[68] One component of life, if democracy were working, would be that everyone would have "freedom to work at what he believes in, what he likes to do."[69] However, Wright clearly felt that working the land and having a close association with it was the highest form of work. His proposals for schools for children included the maintenance of garden and flower beds as part of their education. "A callus on the palm would be a mark of honor" he projected, and "each young worker would learn of the potentialities of soil" as well as other skills of hand and mind through engaging in observing and working with the natural world.[70]

### Capital in Broadacre City

Wright projected that this decentralization of the power of landownership and the subsequent reintegration of life would overturn what he described as the "indiscriminate wealth by way of fortuitous survivals of despotisms: feudal

*Land, Capital, and Labor* 79

money-getting and property-holding. ... an economic order more suited to monarchy and despotism than freedom" in which "unnatural reservoirs of capital accumulation" stood in the way of a genuine culture and a true democracy.[71] Wright regularly distinguished between false capitalism and true capitalism – the former presented as an upside-down pyramid resting on its apex and propped up by laws protecting privilege, and the latter as a pyramid resting on its base as the result of decentralization offering freedom from rent. It must be noted that Wright's true capitalism shares nothing with capitalism as we understand that term today while what he defines as false capitalism is closely aligned with it. In contrast to the children of his proposed schools for whom callouses are badges of honor, he mocks the "rugged individualism" of the "rugged captains of our rugged industrial enterprises" which have led in the development of "a crude, vain power: plutocratic 'Capitalism.'"[72] This, he claimed, was not true capitalism but was contradictory to a genuine democracy. The false capitalism of his day, he claimed, was "individualism gone rank or riot, producing either isolationist, authoritarian or unconscientious objectors."[73]

Making it clear that he understood his proposal for the new city of freedom as a proposal about power, Wright states that those with vested interests in the current political and economic order would "never voluntarily agree to the loss of their immediate quarry which lies in some form of rent" short of the use of force or educational revolution.[74] He saw these vested interests as part of a system which "concentrates money-power in fewer and fewer hands" as the "inevitable centripetal action of capitalistic centralization proceeds by tactfully extended channels of control."[75] He saw that the spiritual needs of people were opposed by the profit system, asserting that "money power itself is only another vicarious power," and proposed that "money should have no power whatever in itself."[76] Similarly, he understood the development of a natural economic order and an organic law as an opposition to "avaricious money and land power."[77]

The commerce that grows out of the broad distribution of land and the resulting freedom of people to have genuine power in political and economic spheres is characterized by small businesses. "Instead of the big fixations of banking and insurance," he projected, "would rise multiplicity of fluid small individual charming human establishments. Freedom at last economic!"[78] Banks would become non-profit institutions of public good in Wright's new city, rather than institutions of power. While he did not propose the mechanics for how this would function, he claimed that in this new system "the credit of the People would therefore be in their own hands without unfair exploitation by broker or any system of interlocking insurance" and that the banker would be "an integrated, dedicated member of his society."[79]

His imagination of the public market as a civic institution was emblematic of the true capitalism which he proposed based on small land holdings and a genuine production of not only the basics needs for life but also cultural goods. The public market was an outlet for people who would use the production of their land as a way to generate economic freedom for themselves and their families. Not only would these markets, which developed from gasoline service

80 *Land, Capital, and Labor*

stations, provide the infrastructure of the transportation system which made all of Wright's proposals possible, but they would replace commercial centers and commercial traffic made up of "the congested crowds senselessly swarming in from the country to hard pavements and back again."[80] These diversified road-side markets, outlets for locally produced goods as well as standardized industrial products, would – in Wright's imagination – be "great spacious roadside pleasure places" that "might resemble our county fairs."[81] They would include spaces for open-air concerts as well as cafes, good restaurants, theaters, and luxury motels. While today we may look with skepticism at the inclusion of spaces for live community theatre, for instance, in commercial centers centered around gas stations, it is worth giving this seeming incongruity the benefit of the doubt and allowing it to generate a deeper understanding of Wright's imagination of an economic system based on the small-scale production of goods and local culture. If we can accept, at least for a moment, that the production of goods for purchase and the production of local amateur theatre which he imagined would replace the stars of stage and screen, were equivalent in their attachment to the local place and the creative energies of the people living there, we can access Wright's imagination for Broadacre City as a deeply democratic society of free people genuinely engaging with each other in economic activity as a cultural, not as a power-seeking, activity.

## Conclusion

These imagined and utopian restructurings of the relationships between land, capital, and labor were not put forward as theoretical texts focused on just those philosophical categories. Each of these utopian proposals relied on particular technological forms and had implications for their implementation. They each held a vision for a different form of agricultural production with implications for changes in not only the growing but also the distribution and consumption of food. Since all were responding to the demands of industrial life, it is not surprising that each proposed a vision of leisure and social life, often connected to specific visions of nature and how people interact with it. Lastly, there are significant and challenging ideas underlying all three of these utopian proposals regarding the relationship between freedom and authority, between the individual and the collective. It is to these considerations that the following chapters turn.

## Notes

1 Marx et al., *Capital,* p. 618.
2 Howard and Osborn, *Garden Cities of To-morrow,* p. 136.
3 Howard and Osborn, *Garden Cities of To-morrow,* p. 20.
4 Howard and Osborn, *Garden Cities of To-morrow,* p. 147.
5 Howard and Osborn, *Garden Cities of To-morrow,* p. 108.
6 Howard and Osborn, *Garden Cities of To-morrow,* p. 193.

Land, Capital, and Labor 81

7 Howard and Osborn, *Garden Cities of To-morrow*, pp. 98–99.
8 Howard and Osborn, *Garden Cities of To-morrow*, p. 100.
9 Howard and Osborn, *Garden Cities of To-morrow*, p. 51.
10 Adam, *Profit and Philanthropy: Stock Companies as Philanthropic Institution in Nineteenth Century Germany.*
11 Howard and Osborn, *Garden Cities of To-morrow*, p. 149.
12 Howard and Osborn, *Garden Cities of To-morrow*, p. 42.
13 Howard and Osborn, *Garden Cities of To-morrow*, p. 44.
14 Howard and Osborn, *Garden Cities of To-morrow*, p. 46.
15 Howard and Osborn, *Garden Cities of To-morrow*, p. 130.
16 Howard and Osborn, *Garden Cities of To-morrow*, p. 44.
17 Howard and Osborn, *Garden Cities of To-morrow*, p. 119.
18 Howard and Osborn, *Garden Cities of To-morrow*, p. 5.
19 Howard and Osborn, *Garden Cities of To-morrow*, p. 66.
20 Le Corbusier, *The Radiant City*, p. 1.
21 Le Corbusier, *The Radiant City*, p. 187.
22 Le Corbusier, *The Radiant City*, p. 187.
23 Le Corbusier, *The Radiant City*, p. 86.
24 Le Corbusier, *The Radiant City*, p. 139.
25 Le Corbusier, *The Radiant City*, p. 9.
26 Le Corbusier, *The Radiant City*, p. 115.
27 Le Corbusier, *The Radiant City*, p. 322.
28 Le Corbusier, *The Radiant City*, p. 197.
29 Le Corbusier, *The Radiant City*, p. 330.
30 Le Corbusier, *The Radiant City*, p. 3.
31 Le Corbusier, *The Radiant City*, p. 3.
32 Le Corbusier, *The Radiant City*, p. 325.
33 Le Corbusier, *The Radiant City*, p. 69.
34 Le Corbusier, *The Radiant City*, pp. 14, 69, 341 for some highlights.
35 Le Corbusier, *The Radiant City*, p. 68.
36 Le Corbusier, *The Radiant City*, p. 68.
37 Le Corbusier, *The Radiant City*, p. 188.
38 Le Corbusier, *The Radiant City*, p. 116.
39 Le Corbusier, *The Radiant City*, p. 176.
40 Le Corbusier, *The Radiant City*, p. 152.
41 Le Corbusier, *The Radiant City*, p. 69.
42 Le Corbusier, *The Radiant City*, p. 341.
43 Le Corbusier, *The Radiant City*, p. 176.
44 Le Corbusier, *The Radiant City*, pp. 73, 342.
45 Le Corbusier, *The Radiant City*, p. 190.
46 Le Corbusier, *The Radiant City*, p. 342.
47 Le Corbusier, *The Radiant City*, p. 191.
48 Le Corbusier, *The Radiant City*, p. 68.
49 Wright, *The Living City*, pp. 148, 33.
50 Wright, *The Living City*, p. 85.
51 Wright, *The Living City*, p. 85.
52 Wright, *The Living City*, p. 33.
53 Wright, *The Living City*, p. 33.
54 Wright, *The Living City*, p. 79.

## 82 Land, Capital, and Labor

55 National Agricultural Statistics Service, *Farms and Land in Farms 2019 Summary.*
56 Duffy and Kay, *Bill Gates Is America's Biggest Owner of Private Farmland, and His 242,000 Acres Could be Split in His Divorce.*
57 Wright, *The Living City,* p. 26.
58 Wright, *The Living City,* pp. 147–8.
59 Wright, *The Living City,* map, frontmatter.
60 Wright, *The Living City,* p. 78.
61 Wright, *The Living City,* p. 219.
62 Wright, *The Living City,* p. 17.
63 Wright, *The Living City,* p. 17.
64 Wright, *The Living City,* p. 147.
65 Wright, *The Living City,* p. 73.
66 Wright, *The Living City,* p. 147.
67 Wright, *The Living City,* p. 90.
68 Wright, *The Living City,* pp. 118–119.
69 Wright, *The Living City,* p. 164.
70 Wright, *The Living City,* p. 188.
71 Wright, *The Living City,* pp. 39–40.
72 Wright, *The Living City,* p. 46.
73 Wright, *The Living City,* p. 110.
74 Wright, *The Living City,* p. 81.
75 Wright, *The Living City,* p. 34.
76 Wright, *The Living City,* pp. 138, 201.
77 Wright, *The Living City,* p. 200.
78 Wright, *The Living City,* p. 121.
79 Wright, *The Living City,* p. 167.
80 Wright, *The Living City,* p. 168.
81 Wright, *The Living City,* p. 168.

## Bibliography

Adam, T., 2014. Profit and Philanthropy: Stock Companies as Philanthropic Institution in Nineteenth Century Germany. Voluntas: International Journal of Voluntary and Nonprofit Organizations 25, 337–351.

Duffy, K., Kay, G., 2021. Bill Gates Is America's Biggest Owner of Private Farmland, and His 242,000 Acres Could be Split in His Divorce. Business Insider. https://www.businessinsider.com/bill-gates-land-portfolio-biggest-private-farmland-owner-in-america-2021-1

George, H., 2016. Progress and Poverty. Aziloth Books. Great Britain.

Howard, E., Osborn, F.J., 2001. Garden Cities of To-morrow, 11th Print ed. MIT Press, Cambridge.

Le Corbusier, 1964. The Radiant City: Elements of a Doctrine of Urbanism to be Used as the Basis of Our Machine-Age Civilization. The Orion Press, New York.

Marx, K., Engels, F., Moore, S., Aveling, E.B., Untermann, E., 2017. Capital. Volume 1. Digireads, USA.

National Agricultural Statistics Service, 2020. Farms and Land in Farms 2019 Summary. https://www.nass.usda.gov/Publications/Todays_Reports/reports/fnlo0220.pdf

Wright, F.L., 1958. The Living City. Horizon Press, New York.

## Suggested Readings

Agnew, E., 2005. Back from the Land: How Young Americans Went to Nature in the 1970s, and Why They Came Back. Ivan R. Dee, Chicago.

Crawford, M., 1995. Building the Workingman's Paradise: The Design of American Company Towns, Haymarket series. Verso, London; New York.

Fishman, R., 1982. Urban Utopias in the Twentieth Century: Ebenezer Howard, Frank Lloyd Wright, and Le Corbusier, 1st MIT Press pbk. ed. MIT Press, Cambridge.

Ghirardo, D.Y., 1989. Building New Communities: New Deal America and Fascist Italy. Princeton University Press, Princeton.

Hartog, H., 1983. Public Property and Private Power: The Corporation of the City of New York in American Law, 1730–1870, Studies in Legal History. University of North Carolina Press, Chapel Hill.

Hayden, D., 2004. Building Suburbia: Green Fields and Urban Growth, 1820–2000. Vintage Books, New York.

Perin, C., 1979. Everything in Its Place: Social Order and Land Use in America, 1st Princeton Paperback ed. Princeton University Press, Princeton.

Wilentz, S., 2004. Chants Democratic: New York City and the Rise of the American Working Class, 1788–1850, 20th Anniversary ed. Oxford University Press, Oxford.

Wright, G., 1981. Building the Dream: A Social History of Housing in America, 1st ed. Pantheon Books, New York.

# 5 Technology

The degree of technological advancement that Howard, Le Corbusier, and Wright witnessed during lifetimes was staggering, but so was the acceleration of inequality facilitated by industrial production as well as the increase in other negative impacts such as the density of coal smoke that enveloped growing cities and the high rates of industrial accidents. All three were optimistic about the possibilities of technology while also being highly critical of how it was being implemented at the time. And to be fair, both their criticisms and their optimisms were warranted. Howard claimed that vast changes in everything from building technology, communications, instruments of war, and machinery had undergone extensive change in the 60 years prior to his writing and projected similar developments in the future as he contemplated the discovery of "new motive powers, new means of locomotion, perhaps, through the air, new methods of water supply, or a new distribution of population."[1] Le Corbusier wrote that the machine should descend from its current position to that of a servant and that if it did, it could "from the slavery to which it has subjected us ... lead us to emancipation."[2] Wright felt that if the machine could be forced to go to work for people, it would free them from conscription and give them freedom as citizens. He wrote that people had become mere pushers of buttons and pullers of levers and machine-age conscripts in the city of his day but that in Broadacre City there would be freedom for all as long as machines were put to work for them, by them.[3] In contrast, he claimed that in the city of his day "the unearned increment of the machine itself" – defining the machine as "this new common agency for doing the work of the world" – was merely funneling profits to ever fewer people instead of to the people "whose life is actually modified given, or sacrificed" to mechanized production.[4] On one hand, machines extend human capacity for production in a number of ways – hence the optimism about machines and what they could to do lighten the load of labor. On the other hand, machines also replace labor and reduce the human skill needed for production – hence their ability to be used to benefit only the few. The real concern that Howard, Le Corbusier, and Wright had regarding machine production at their time had to do with how the benefits of machine production were distributed, not for the most part the use of machines per se. Chapter 3 presented four works which grappled with that question as well, all

DOI: 10.4324/9781351053730-5

of which directly or indirectly influenced Howard, Le Corbusier, and Wright; *Capital* by Karl Marx, *Progress and Poverty* by Henry George, *Looking Backward* by Edward Bellamy, and three books by Peter Kropotkin including *Fields, Factories, and Workshops*. The previous chapter on land, labor, and capital brings forward how Howard, Le Corbusier, and Wright positioned their thinking in relation to this question of the just distribution of the benefits of industrial production in society. In each case, the proposals for urban life and urban form that make up their utopias are attempts to solve this problem of just distribution.

While Howard's tone was less aggressive than either Le Corbusier's or Wright's, he did imply a direct critique of how the benefits of industrial production were distributed. Predictably because of both witnessing the least technological development of the three and the nature of his proposal, Howard relied on technological change the least and made fewer grand claims about it. However, electrification of factory production and a highly developed transportation network are critical to his vision. He stated that the goal of his work was to generate "a new industrial system in which the productive forces of society and of nature may be used with far greater effectiveness than at present, and in which the distribution of the wealth forms so created will take place on a far juster and more equitable basis" and that his proposed garden cities would be a "stepping stone to a higher and better form of industrial life."[5] Le Corbusier wrote that the first century of the machine age had brought destruction, desolation, misery, and danger whereas what he called the "second era of the machine age," which would be heralded in by the changes he proposed for both urban and rural landscapes, would be "the age of harmony."[6] As much as Le Corbusier despised some of what they were producing, he wrote that factories were the single exception to the fact that society was crouched "in a pool of dead things … under the influence of antiquated junk."[7] He noted that his entire proposal for city planning to produce a machine-age environment which would "provide every individual with personal liberty and the basic pleasures" was based on an architectural revolution and modern techniques.[8] The plan, which was Le Corbusier's ultimate authority as will be discussed in Chapter 7, was for him "a product of technology."[9] Electrification and mechanical mobilization, on which Wright's proposal rests, are two of the three "miracles of technical invention" that he wrote must be reckoned with.[10] Looking to the future with optimism he wrote that "we now know that these new machine forces may be potential, great liberators" and that it was "within the power of these very mechanical forces to automatically destroy any system that continues to deprive humanity of all but a small fragment of its potential benefits."[11] However, Wright felt that because technology was directed by "the same landlord, machine-lords, and money-lords that operate rent and operate the city," technology could not fulfill its liberating potential until the stranglehold of capital and rent were broken as he proposed Broadacre City would do.

The main areas of technology that these three urban visions relied on were electrification, transportation, building materials and processes, and communications. All three relied on electrification as a source of energy to

86  *Technology*

power factories, primarily as a means to deal with the oppressive clouds of toxic smoke generated by coal-powered industrial production that hung over the cities of their age. All three also relied on changes in transportation technology and its organization, though with significant variations that fit their proposals for population density and open spaces. Modern, industrialized building technology and premanufactured building components were foundational to the Radiant city proposal but also significant to Broadacre City. Changes in communication technologies were critical to Broadacre City but played far less of a theoretically foundational role in either the Garden City or the Radiant City

A brief overview of the level of technological change they experienced up to the point they published their visions will be helpful to set the context in which these three utopian proposals were generated. Ebenezer Howard was born in 1850 and his work *Garden Cities of To-Morrow* was published in 1902. Some of the things invented during this period were the motorized sewing machine, the internal-combustion engine, the elevator with safety brakes, the escalator, dynamite, the telephone, the lightbulb, and the zipper. In addition to many important inventions, other things were not new but became commercially available due to large-scale manufacturing during this period. These include items as seemingly insignificant as fountain pens and toilet paper and items as revolutionary as the typewriter and the automobile. The first paper was mass manufactured from wood pulp in 1870 and by 1891 printing presses could print and fold 90,000 four-page papers a single hour. In the decade before Howard was born, the railway system in England expanded fourfold to approximately 6,000 miles. By 1875, it had more than doubled to over 14,000 miles. The first underground railway was completed in London in 1863 and by 1890 the underground trains in the city switched to electric engines.

Le Corbusier was born in 1887 and published *The Radiant City* in 1933. The Wright brothers flew the first airplane in 1903 and when World War I started in 1914, there were only a small number of airplanes in military service – used primarily for reconnaissance. By the end of the war in 1918, the combatant countries had manufactured more than 200,000 airplanes in a wide variety of specialized configurations from high-altitude reconnaissance planes to bombers to fighters. The first commercial international flight between London and Paris took place in 1919. Charles Lindbergh flew nonstop from New York to Paris in 1927. The first commercial refrigeration was developed shortly before Le Corbusier was born but by the 1930s when he published *The Radiant City,* refrigerators were common household appliances. Reinforced concrete was invented about 20 years before Le Corbusier was born, the technology for rolling steel rails for construction was developed shortly after that, and the Eiffel Tower was built in 1889, when he was two years old. Arc-welding became a building construction technology in 1920 and the 77 story Chrysler building was built in 1929. Global steel production nearly tripled from 10 metric tons per year in 1870 to 28.3 metric tons per year in 1900, and nearly tripled again by 1913 to 79 metric tons per year.

Frank Lloyd Wright was born in 1867 and exhibited the first large model of Broadacre City in 1935. Alexander Graham Bell received a patent on the telephone in 1876 and ATT had 5,800,000 customers by 1910. The first radio broadcast was produced in 1910 in New York City's Metropolitan Opera House. The first commercial radio station in the United States started broadcasting in 1920 and the first baseball game was broadcast in 1921. The Federal Radio Commission in the United States was created in 1927 and by 1930 – only 3 years later, 12 million American households had radios and there were 618 active stations with a combined advertising income of $40.5 million – the equivalent to slightly more than $650 million in 2022 currency. The model T was introduced in 1908 and by the mid-1920s one car was being produced every 10 seconds. By 1929 Americans alone owned over 23 million cars. The first modern television was invented in 1927 and the first television station started broadcasting in 1928.

## Electricity

The Garden City, the Radiant City, and Broadacre City all relied on the widespread use of electricity as a foundational technology in different ways. While this reliance may seem banal today, large cities such as London, Paris, and New York only installed their first electric lights in the mid to late 1880s. Rural areas in the United States and in France did not see significant electrification until the 1930s and in England not until the 1950s. It wasn't until after the turn into the twentieth century that utilities started producing power for clients in the United States, and as late as 1914, only half of all electricity in the country was generated by utility companies and distributed to clients.[12] Prior to large scale utility distribution of electricity, factories had to produce their own power on site. It is notable that developing what would essentially be a local electrical utility was one of the cost-saving strategies Howard proposed for the Garden City. While the primary reason for using electricity was abating the smoke that was generated by coal-fired factories, producing electricity in one facility for all the industrial activity in the town would also, Howard proposed, reduce the cost of electricity for streetlights and other uses.[13] He wrote that, in the cities of his day, "the sunlight is being more and more shut out, while the air is so vitiated that the fine public buildings, like the sparrows, rapidly become covered in soot, and the very statues are in despair."[14] One drawback to the town as represented in his diagram of the magnets that described the attractions of the town, the country, and his proposal – the town-country – was foul air and murky sky in the town which contrasted with the fresh air and open skies of the country. His proposed resolution, the Garden City, would have pure air and no smoke while retaining the social and economic advantages due to industrial activity found in the town. Expecting that this would be achieved through the growth of electricity as a power source for manufacturing, he wrote that "the smoke fiend will be kept well within bounds in the Garden City; for all machinery is driven by electric energy."[15]

88  *Technology*

Le Corbusier did not write this directly about the use of electrical power, but two critical technologies which the Radiant City would rely on are only functional with electrical power – air conditioning equipment and elevators at the scale of Le Corbusier's proposal. He was also concerned with pure air like Howard, but more directly with air inside of buildings. He proposed that we should be breathing "good, true God-given air" instead of the air in cities which he describes as "devil's air." Following a collection of information about lungs, the process of inhalation and exhalation, and a table of the number of bacteria in per 10 cubic meters of air in locations ranging from isolated mountaintops and the open sea (0) to the rue de Rivoli in Paris (55,000), he stated that "the normal temperature of air fit for breathing is 64.4 degrees Fahrenheit." He proposed the use of filters, driers, humidifiers, and disinfectors "to send exact air into men's lungs, at home, at the factory, at the office, at the club and the audi- torium."[16] Of course, since the outside environment in the Radiant City was not characterized by narrow streets and congested traffic, le Corbusier would have imagined that air in the Radiant City would have been close to that of the mountaintops or open sea. The elevator, also necessarily relying on electricity for buildings of the scale of the Radiant city, is central to the spatial planning of his utopian proposal and the open landscapes that he imagined would dom- inate the experience of living in the Radiant City. Along with concrete and steel construction which will be discussed later in this chapter, the elevator is a critical technology allowing the height of building and concentration of popu- lation over small building footprints that opened the land for free pedestrian use. "It is a crime," he wrote, "to make anyone walk up more than three flights of stairs."[17] These elevators, meant to be run by elevator operators both night and day, were imagined on a grand scale, serving up to 100 apartments per floor and connecting interior horizontal streets throughout his city. Without them, not only would the open sports fields and landscapes for passive recreation not be feasible, neither would the system of elevated interior streets that were inte- gral to his urban proposal.

Wright also saw the role of electrification as key to his proposal – noting it as the first miracle of technological invention that was driving changes in culture as well as the built environment. For him, it made communications and entertainment at a distance possible and provided a source of light which extended the day for human occupation. These two things, he claimed, led to "radical change in the entire basis of civilization."[18] Wright is the only one of the three to rely significantly on developments in communication technology. Various forms of electronic communication, in particular, are foundational to Wright's proposal since he based his proposed decentralization on its ability to overcome distance. Without this technology, he could not conceptually propose a solution to his observation "that ultimate human satisfactions no longer depend upon but are destroyed by density of population."[19] He listed the telegraph, the telephone, radio, and television as some of the technologies that would allow time to overtake distance as the critical factor in productive human interactions. With these technologies in hand, he claimed that "there is no advantage in a few blocks apart, over a mile or two or even ten."[20] The ancient city was appropriate to its time because "human intercommunication could only be had by direct personal contact" and therefore that "commercial or social communication was slow and difficult."[21] According to Wright, now that this was no longer the case, the ancient city no longer served as an appropriate model for human social life and should be replaced with his proposal for a decentralized city fit to the newfound ability for people to cooperate at a distance.

## Transportation

Common to all three utopian ideals was an emphasis on the separation of traffic by speed and type. Whereas Le Corbusier and Wright projected significant advances in transportation technologies – though not anything outside the realm of imaginable technological progress in their day based on the change they had seen in their lives – Howard stayed quite soberly with the transportation technologies that existed at his time, organizing them into logical and efficient patterns. This is not to say that transportation, particularly the railroad, was not a key component of Howard's utopian proposal. Each garden city would be encircled by a railroad that would connect the factories on the perimeter of the city to a main line which in turn connected them to a national network of railroads. This perimeter railway allowed goods to come and go from the manufacturing area at the perimeter of town while allowing for the restriction of traffic internal to the garden city to local deliveries. It is telling that Howard described the journey from the center of town to the perimeter as a walking tour; he imagined life in the Garden City to be largely a pedestrian affair. The efficiency of the transportation network he proposed played a significant role in the viability of the Garden City in another way. It is typical of Howard's approach that he calculated the reduction in cost of maintaining roads within the Garden City due to the minimization of commercial traffic through the town.[22] Another critical factor in the Garden City's financial viability related to transportation was the increased profitability of agriculture due to farms closer proximity to consumers willing and able to buy higher value products which led to farmers willingness to pay higher rental income for agricultural land to the town. He claimed that this proximity would not only help the local farmer compete with the wheat producers of America and Russia given their transportation costs to market, but help make local dairies more profitable – calculating that saving a penny of shipping costs per gallon of milk for a population of 30,000 would save producers over £1,900 a year in 1902, the equivalent of approximately £250,000 in 2022.[23] He also proposed that local farmers would be more likely to grow vegetables – which were not only healthier but offered a higher profit margin – because of the ready access to market and reduced rate of spoilage during shipping. The efficiency of the transportation system and technology of the Garden City and the higher profitability of agricultural production was critical to the maintenance of the green belt of productive

90   *Technology*

land around the town proper, and therefore to the political imagination of the Garden City as a cooperative whole.

Howard also imagined that after the first Garden City proved itself successful, the concept would grow as clusters of garden cities were developed and connected by inter-city rail, electric tramways, and other planned forms of efficient transportation networks. He criticized the fact that legislation which would have given Parliament planning control over the railway systems in London had been denied in order to maintain profits for individual rail companies and claimed that the English would not "suffer for ever for the want of foresight of those who little dreamed of the future development of railways."[24] Once the value of the garden city was established, he felt that "there would be no great difficult in acquiring the necessary Parliamentary powers to purchase the land and carry out the necessary works step by step."[25] This included, of course, the land for his proposed system of rail transit which tied the network together. Howard's proposal was not only that transportation technology would support changes to the landscapes of the city, but also support a rational change to how settlement happened across England.

The Radiant City also relied on several interconnected transportation networks and a variety of transportation technologies. These range from a freight network moving goods and building materials between the city and the countryside to trolleys for movement within the city to the elevators which Le Corbusier referred to as "a means of public transportation."[26] He gave five principles for his proposed organization of traffic. First, the classification of speeds so that "normal biological speeds" would not be "forced into contact with high speeds of modern vehicles." Second, the creation of one-way traffic to increase efficiency. Third, clearly designated uses for high-speed vehicles. Fourth, attention to the functions of heavy vehicles. Lastly, "The liberation of pedestrians."[27] He offered several landscape sections showing how these different modes of transportation would be separated where they cross or are adjacent to each other.[28] His integration of transportation systems to allow high-density cities with open landscapes was, in part, a response to his criticism of the organization of living into urban areas where one worked and suburbs or dormitory towns where one slept. He described the latter as garden cities and, while that may not have been an accurate representation of the theory of the garden city put forward by Howard, it was accurate to the way his ideas were being applied. This flow of people led Le Corbusier to claim that "the garden city is a pre-machine age utopia" based on "idealistic, ruinous and inoperative figures recommended by urban authorities still imbued with romantic ideology."[29]

His proposed network of large high-speed elevators would be professionally run and operate as vertical public transportation elements connecting the elevated streets that ran throughout his proposed buildings. He proposed that a bank of four such professionally run elevators could serve a population of 2,400 people.[30] Without the scale of these elevators, his urban proposal could not function. Thinking typologically, it was the elevator that allowed the front door

Technology    91

of each residence to be separated from the ground-level street, thereby allowing the stacking of floors and the shrinking of the footprint of buildings and the opening of the ground plane to pedestrian use for sport and passive recreation.

Transportation within the Radiant City was separated into types. Automobile circulation within the city was strictly separated from pedestrian circulation – typically with pedestrian routes going under routes for any motorized transportation. Le Corbusier claimed that in his plan no pedestrian would ever meet an automobile.[31] There would be no busses in the Radiant City either because while they were "the most marvelous and adaptable form of mass transport for *cities in chaos*," the streetcar was less costly, better suited to ordered cities, and so in the Radiant City would "regain its pre-eminence."[32] While the personal transportation needs of the city would be served by streetcars, freight and high-speed automobile traffic would be accommodated by elevated highways which allowed trucks to serve the communal food services that would save people time and expense through removing waste from the food provision and facilitating more efficient centralizing refrigeration, handling, and preparation. His diagram for a residential traffic networks shows an elevated parking deck for every building which not only provides parking for the residents but also connects the highways to service bays for each building's catering service. He also emphasized the rational separation of traffic. While he was a convert to the value of the automobile, he regularly villainized traffic and in particularly traffic congestion throughout his text. One of the many justifications he gave for the need to design new cities was the change in speeds of travel with the automobile as a tool with people travelling "at ten times, at twenty times, at forty times" the speed which was biologically available by foot and horse on which historic city form was based.[33] His solution was not to get rid of the vehicles, but to rationalize their use through large parking areas tied to his buildings as well as the separation of speeds. While tower buildings were the most visible urban elements in his perspectives, plans of the buildings themselves show how extensive the automobile infrastructure would be – all 5 meters above ground level.[34]

One of the first constructions that Le Corbusier lauds in his book is a road through the Spanish countryside, stating that "Spain now has a continuous road that is the most beautiful I have ever seen, sometimes miraculous, a magnificent invention of modern times. It cuts right across land that has been under the plow for centuries."[35] While the modern reader may likely cringe at this idea of a modern road cutting across prime agricultural land that had been in production for centuries, one must think of it from the position of living on that land with scant and frustratingly slow access to the benefits and markets of modern society. Whereas the railroad had created, in Le Corbusier's view, a civilization of great concentrations, the automobile would open up both the countryside and the opportunity for a new civilization.[36] This access – from door to door and working in opposition to the concentrating function of railroads – was, according to Le Corbusier, going to make the countryside accessible and led him to proclaim that "The *land* is being brought back to life! We only have to open our eyes and pave the way!"[37] However, new transportation equipment

92   *Technology*

in the forms of cars, trucks, and buses that he referred to as death-dealing missiles which cut villages in two "as though by a saber stroke" required new transportation infrastructure in the form of roads of the type he admired in Spain.[38] While he saw the automobile as a tool for making the countryside accessible and rural areas attractive enough that people would settle in them, he was derisive of the idea that automobiles would make "the mystic belief in deurbanization" possible.[39]

While Wright would not call it de-urbanization, the decentralization of cities that Le Corbusier was criticizing is, of course, exactly the point of Broadacre City – which also relied heavily on a range of transportation technologies. Wright's drawings of personal helicopters and futuristic cars are perhaps the most iconic representations of this reliance.[40] Mechanical mobilization was one of the three miracles of the modern age which would make new city forms possible according to Wright and the individual automobile and the freedom that it gave people was critical to his proposal and the life he imagined for the residents of Broadacre City. He proposed that "it is significant that not only have *space* values entirely changed to *time* values, now ready to form new standards of movement-measurement, but a new sense of spacing based upon speed is here."[41] He wrote that "the amorphous herds of humanity swarming in narrow erstwhile village lanes and caverns may now take wings as well as go on wheels" and that "the door of the urban cage is surely opening wide" due in large part to the "motorcar invasion and collateral inventions in the air and on the rails...leading up to the total mechanization of transit."[42] While the highways were to be returned to the individual in their own automobile, Wright does not propose the end of freight traffic or the abandoning of railroad rights-of-way. On the contrary, those rights-of-way – which he argues belong to the people, would become repurposed and expanded to accommodate not only local and long-distance heavy trucking but also bus traffic alongside the railroad lines.

Illuminating that Wright saw Broadacre City as a proposal for the just and equal distribution of the benefits of society, he proposed that transportation should be subsidized for the poor. Without subsidizing transportation, he argued, it would be meaningless to give them an acre of land. "If at first there must be a subsidy...why not subsidize transportation? ... Modern mobility can be so easily arranged for these citizens," such that "rescue and restitution are now ready for 'the poor man' in a new city. Especially by way of a bus or a motor car" he wrote.[43] Subsidizing transportation would allow the poor individual of the city, currently living as a wage-slave, to "go not backward but forward to his native birthright: the good ground."[44] Ultimately, Wright's social and political proposal of the potential for self-reliance to remake the economic framework of society and eliminate vast differentials of power, and therefore the nature of citizenship, rests on the ability of people to move freely to and from home, work, and cultural amenities. And access to this technology, he thought, should be made publicly available as a public good, at least until all people were in a position of economic stability.

## Building Technology

Howard made no significant reference to building technology. However, we can infer something of his aesthetic imagination of the city from his description of the street with relationship to housing and in this the pragmatic imagination for the use of technology becomes clear. While on his imagined walk from the center of the city to the agricultural estate at the perimeter, he noted that upon

> noticing the very varied architecture and design which the houses and groups of houses display – some having common gardens and co-operative kitchens – we learn that general observance of street line or harmonious departure from it are the chief points as to house building, for, though proper sanitary arrangements are strictly enforced, the fullest measure of individual taste and preference is encouraged.[45]

He also had no need for advanced building technology beyond what was readily available in his day because his proposal was modelled on villages of single family homes which would have not reached higher than two or at most three stories. Even the larger public buildings that were integral to his proposal such as libraries and civic buildings would not have required any construction materials or methodologies which were not common at the time.

Wright, on the other hand, grounded his proposal partly on advances in building technology – though not to the degree that Le Corbusier did. Wright suggested that the prefabrication of building materials and components made possible by new materials and processes would allow that "buildings may be so economized by intelligent standardizing that 'home' may now be open to environment and be designed to broaden the life of the individual family, making site and building a unit" and that, rather than being "bound to his employers' machine," the poor should be using the machine to build his own home.[46] He also specifically mentioned the use of steel and concrete in a tension/compression paring along with glass, plastics, plywood, sheet metal, and concrete as critical to organic architecture and therefore to its contribution to the realization of democracy. Wright also imagined that what he described as ill-smelling and inefficient groups of poorly adapted buildings on farms would be replaced with assembled and prefabricated buildings which "could well be delivered to the farmers at low cost by machine production intelligently expanded and standardized" and assembled on site.[47] It should be noted that while Wright did not wax poetical or philosophical about the use of concrete and steel in the larger buildings integral to his proposal as did Le Corbusier, his renderings clearly show buildings of those materials. In addition, a significant part of any given citizen's ability to customize a house and living arrangement to their desires was not only the use of these modern construction materials, but access to premanufactured privies, bedrooms, living-rooms, and other building elements. These, he proposed, would be "varied in general scheme of assembly to suit either flat land or hillside, in various materials so designed as to make not

94    *Technology*

only a dignified but well-planned appropriate whole."[48] He decried the available standardized building units of his time and their lack of good design as well as their inability to "add up to a practical gracious whole."[49] He proposed that this would change when the factories shifted from prioritizing production and profit to prioritizing consumption and good design. This would happen naturally, he proposed, when factory production was directed by and for the workers based on what would improve their lives rather than what could be most cheaply made to satisfy the imperatives of capital. While few people connect Wright's imagination of industrial production which would serve society to that of Marx, it is perhaps not quite the stretch that some might at first imagine. Wright's ultimate goal of an intimate and personal relationship with land as a basis for democracy relied significantly on the use of prefabricated building component technology to reduce the cost of that fitting of land to the desires of life, which he saw as the outcome of workers controlling the means of production.

Le Corbusier stated that his entire proposal rested on new materials and construction techniques. He wrote that "today, iron and reinforced concrete give us convenient means of carrying out the sort of city planning which responds to the profound social and economic revolution caused by the machine age" and that the basic materials of city planning are "sun, sky, trees, steel, cement, in that strict order of importance."[50] Without the latter materials, it would not be feasible to build at the scale and site density that Le Corbusier's proposal required. His proposal for a construction system of pilotis and horizontal surfaces raised above the ground – artificial sites as he called them – was not a proposal about building form per se, but a political proposal about the use of land. Whereas apartment buildings in cities had risen to six stories, Le Corbusier proposed that it was now possible to "perch 20 or 30 or 50 artificial sites on top of one another, a thing which until now was not feasible" with stone walls and wooden floors.[51] This building technology and the imagination of massive structures also allowed him to propose the linear buildings integrated with highways such as he proposed for Algiers.

In addition, Le Corbusier also relied heavily on prefabrication even more than did Wright. Rather than being built in exposure to the elements, he proposed that houses should be built in factories where they would be "subjected to the rhythm of modern methods of work, to the discipline of timetables, of machines and of our construction programs."[52] These prefabricated homes, which he suggested should be thought of as domestic equipment, would be bolted together to make buildings from 60 to 600 feet tall on site. Prefabrication in factories, he noted, had brought the cost of a single automobile from 200,000 francs when hand built, down to 30,000 francs and he expected the same scale of cost reduction for housing to follow a similar shift in production techniques. The prefabricated house equipped internally for modern life was also intended to be a source of happiness and liberty as it would save the occupant time and reduce unpleasant household tasks. The benefits to prefabrication, at least financially, were tied to the time-saving aspects of communal services that were

Technology 95

made available by the density and building typology Le Corbusier proposed. However, Le Corbusier noted that, "before building the prefabricated house we must plan the cities."[53]

For Le Corbusier, technological advances such as prefabrication and advancements in building materials should be in service of "the basic pleasures," by which he means, "sun, greenery and space" which "penetrate into the uttermost depths of our physiological and psychological being" and "bring us back into harmony with the profound and natural purpose of life."[54] It is in light of this primary goal that everything else, including the home itself, is reduced to its minimum. The aesthetic he proposed for homes is ultimately focused on the reduction of economic and material effort needed to live an aesthetic life outside in public and in serene privacy at home, hence his many studies for the minimum house. He described a friends' summer shack, by way of example, as a "modest and eloquent witness to the validity of 'the minimum house'" where they had "carved out a life at their ease; functions were given a precise statement and found an architectural response."[55] He based his proposal for housing on the concept of the cell which should be "biologically good in itself (in conformity with the individual's needs) and also susceptible of multiplication to infinity (by means of modern techniques)."[56] These cells, based on a standard of 14 square meters per person should, he noted, "be thought of in relation to the roof beaches, to the sports grounds in the parks all around, to the sea of trees visible for 200 to 300 meters through the 12 meters of plate-glass window, to the clouds floating by in the immensity of the sky" and would be characterized by "bright light, cleanliness everywhere" and "efficient equipment to meet every domestic need."[57]

## Technologies of War, Political Will, and Landscape

All three authors assumed that the political will that would be necessary to implement their visions was inevitable to different degrees. However, Le Corbusier and Wright had particular reasons to believe it could be accomplished which Howard did not. Le Corbusier published his proposal after World War I. Wright presented the model of his idea after World War I and published *The Living City* after the World War II. They both responded to this in similar ways. First, both Wright and Le Corbusier felt that their designs responded to the new technologies of war – particularly various forms of aerial warfare – in ways that further justified their proposals. Le Corbusier noted the proportion of roof area to total city area in his proposal would make armor plating the roof of every building more economical and that in the Radiant City, "the danger of fire is eliminated" and that "the scattered arrangement of the buildings considerably limits the effectiveness of bombs."[58] He also observed that the open landscape would limit the effectiveness of gas warfare because the breezes would keep it from stagnating and that the infrastructure for delivering exact air to all occupants would be "widely spaced, very well sheltered and almost invulnerable."[59] Wright was also concerned about airborne attack and proposed that

96   *Technology*

his proposed decentralization would provide an advantage in modern warfare as well. He wrote that "at proper points along or under railways or highways safe, spacious underground refuge should be constructed for the various kinds of storage uses in peacetime" which also "might afford protection under attack from the air; making such attack unprofitable."[60]

Secondly, and more importantly, Le Corbusier and Wright both witnessed clear examples of the feasibility of a vast scale of technological and financial mobilization necessary to realize their visions, if only the political will necessary could also be generated. Both directly called out the technological advances as well as the scale of technological production that had been mobilized for the destructive purposes of war and subsequently decried the difficulty in mobilizing the same technological capacities for peace. World War I saw significant improvements in tank, machine gun, airplane, field medicine, and naval technology as well as significant increases in manufacturing capacity. Between them, the combatant powers had produced over 220,000 tanks, nearly 9,000 naval vessels, and over 400,000 aircraft in a span of approximately five years to fight World War II.[61] In answer to those who objected to the scale of his vision, Le Corbusier wrote,

> Gentlemen, we were able to carry on a major war for five years, one that involved the mobilization of millions of men, the feeding of millions of men, the construction of cannons and dreadnoughts, the creation of an aviation industry, the fabrication with clockwork precision of the storms, the tempests, the hurricanes, the typhoons unleased by bombs and shells... We were able to perform miracles of transportation...there was no human energy we did not press into service... We even mobilized our churches! We conscripted Jesus Christ![62]

He concluded his work with a call to the mobilization of land, people, and production to make his vision a reality and achieve happiness in society, claiming that society should be using the same organization of technology for peace that was used for war but "first of all, the mobilization of enthusiasm, that electric power source of the human factory."[63] The final sentence of *The Radiant City* is, "Simply choosing CONSTRUCTION instead of accepting DESTRUCTION."[64]

Wright similarly argued that the political will that had organized such a massive technological expenditure of human effort for the ends of war should be put to the ends of peace. Concluding a short description of the damage done to society and the environment by the industrial revolution, he noted that it was a pity that all the billions of dollars had been wasted when they could have "been spent to create a more fruitful example of a truly liberal democratic life."[65] "What irony!" he continued that "peace has never been organized for the innate glory of America – only for or against war! Or the fear of war."[66] Wright went one logical step further and claimed that if these resources were put to the ends of peace, war itself would be defeated because nobody would be motivated to fight it. He claimed that "if with true aesthetic sensibility we should scientifically see in perspective the vast resources with which we continually go to war but with which we have certainly never learned how to go into creative work," society would be able to realize true freedom. He concluded by drawing a connection between industrialism and war. "By total industrialism war," he wrote, "more war is always in sight, paid for in advance – all but the bloodshed."[67] If, on the other hand, peace were to be as organized as war, "war could never defeat peace on any terms whatsoever."[68] Once true peace and freedom were established by a renewed and empowered citizenship in a decentralized and reintegrated city and society, he felt that "war would look as sinister to children and the citizen called upon to wage it as it really is" and that "the teenager and the citizen would soon compel 'the interests' to pay the price for peace in terms of peace and by their own contribution."[69]

## Conclusion

In all three of these utopian proposals, we must remember that even though they relied on technology for their realization, and at least the Radiant City and Broadacre City relied on significant technological advances, none of them looked to technology as an end unto itself. Rather, technology was a means to the end of putting in place a pattern of landscape use which met their social end of addressing the negative repercussions of industrialism and rapidly expanding cities. Furthermore, in each case the use of landscapes as political media as presented in Chapter 2 was reliant on particular technologies and technological systems.

## Notes

1  Howard and Osborn, *Garden Cities of To-morrow*, p. 135.
2  Le Corbusier, *The Radiant City*, p. 29
3  Wright, *The Living City*, pp. 27, 20–21, 82.
4  Wright, *The Living City*, p. 33.
5  Howard and Osborn, *Garden Cities of To-morrow*, pp. 130, 138.
6  Le Corbusier, *The Radiant City*, pp. 92, 340.
7  Le Corbusier, *The Radiant City*, p. 8.
8  Le Corbusier, *The Radiant City*, p. 182.
9  Le Corbusier, *The Radiant City*, p. 154.
10  Le Corbusier, *The Radiant City*, p. 64.
11  Le Corbusier, *The Radiant City*, p. 79.
12  Du Boff, *The Introduction of Electric Power in American Manufacturing*.
13  Howard and Osborn, *Garden Cities of To-morrow*, p. 55.
14  Howard and Osborn, *Garden Cities of To-morrow*, p. 47.
15  Howard and Osborn, *Garden Cities of To-morrow*, p. 55.
16  Le Corbusier, *The Radiant City*, pp. 40–42.
17  Le Corbusier, *The Radiant City*, p. 38.
18  Wright, *The Living City*, p. 64.

98   *Technology*

19   Wright, *The Living City*, p. 69.
20   Wright, *The Living City*, p. 68.
21   Wright, *The Living City*, p. 67.
22   Howard and Osborn, *Garden Cities of To-morrow*, p. 55.
23   Howard and Osborn, *Garden Cities of To-morrow*, p. 61.
24   Howard and Osborn, *Garden Cities of To-morrow*, p. 145.
25   Howard and Osborn, *Garden Cities of To-morrow*, p. 146.
26   Le Corbusier, *The Radiant City*, p. 38.
27   Le Corbusier, *The Radiant City*, pp. 121–122.
28   Le Corbusier, *The Radiant City*, p. 126.
29   Le Corbusier, *The Radiant City*, p. 94.
30   Le Corbusier, *The Radiant City*, p. 39.
31   Le Corbusier, *The Radiant City*, p. 108.
32   Le Corbusier, *The Radiant City*, p. 126.
33   Le Corbusier, *The Radiant City*, p. 121.
34   Le Corbusier, *The Radiant City*, p. 165.
35   Le Corbusier, *The Radiant City*, p. 10.
36   Le Corbusier, *The Radiant City*, p. 180.
37   Le Corbusier, *The Radiant City*, p. 197.
38   Le Corbusier, *The Radiant City*, p. 196.
39   Le Corbusier, *The Radiant City*, p. 74.
40   Wright, *The Living City*, pp. 127, 181.
41   Wright, *The Living City*, p. 82.
42   Wright, *The Living City*, p. 81.
43   Wright, *The Living City*, p. 148.
44   Wright, *The Living City*, p. 148.
45   Howard and Osborn, *Garden Cities of To-morrow*, p. 54.
46   Wright, *The Living City*, p. 69, 148.
47   Wright, *The Living City*, pp. 161–162.
48   Le Corbusier, *The Radiant City*, p. 149.
49   Le Corbusier, *The Radiant City*, p. 149.
50   Le Corbusier, *The Radiant City*, pp. 23, 86.
51   Le Corbusier, *The Radiant City*, p. 56.
52   Le Corbusier, *The Radiant City*, p. 96.
53   Le Corbusier, *The Radiant City*, p. 96.
54   Le Corbusier, *The Radiant City*, p. 86.
55   Le Corbusier, *The Radiant City*, p. 29.
56   Le Corbusier, *The Radiant City*, p. 143.
57   Le Corbusier, *The Radiant City*, p. 146.
58   Le Corbusier, *The Radiant City*, p. 61.
59   Le Corbusier, *The Radiant City*, p. 61.
60   Wright, *The Living City*, p.133.
61   Harrison, *The Economics of World War II: Six Great Powers in International Comparison*,
     pp. 1–42.
62   Le Corbusier, *The Radiant City*, p. 105.
63   Le Corbusier, *The Radiant City*, p. 344.
64   Le Corbusier, *The Radiant City*, p. 345.
65   Wright, *The Living City*, p. 131.
66   Wright, *The Living City*, p. 131.

67 Wright, *The Living City*, p. 220.
68 Wright, *The Living City*, p. 131.
69 Wright, *The Living City*, p. 131.

## Bibliography

Du Boff, R.B., 1967. The Introduction of Electric Power in American Manufacturing. The Economic History Review 20, 509. https://doi.org/10.2307/2593069

Harrison, M. (Ed.), 1998. The Economics of World War II: Six Great Powers in International Comparison, 1st ed. Cambridge University Press, Cambridge. https://doi.org/10.1017/CBO9780511523632

Howard, E., Osborn, F.J., 2001. Garden Cities of To-morrow, 11th Print. ed. MIT Press, Cambridge.

Le Corbusier, 1964. The Radiant City: Elements of a Doctrine of Urbanism to be Used as the Basis of Our Machine-Age Civilization. The Orion Press, New York.

Wright, F.L., 1958. The Living City. Horizon Press, New York.

### *Suggested Readings*

Cowan, R.S., Hersch, M.H., 2018. A Social History of American Technology, 2nd ed. Oxford University Press, New York.

Fishman, R., 1982. Urban Utopias in the Twentieth Century: Ebenezer Howard, Frank Lloyd Wright, and Le Corbusier, 1st MIT Press pbk. ed. MIT Press, Cambridge.

Gedion, S., 2013. Mechanization Takes Command: A Contribution to Anonymous History, First University of Minnesota Press edition. University of Minnesota Press, Minneapolis.

Marsan, J.-C., 1990. Montreal in Evolution: Historical Analysis of the Development of Montreal's Architecture and Urban Environment. McGill-Queen's University Press, Montreal.

Monkkomen, E., 2018. America Becomes Urban: The Development of U.S. Cities and Towns, 1780–1980. University of California Press, Place of publication not identified.

Peterson, J.A., 2003. The Birth of City Planning in the United States, 1840–1917, Creating the North American Landscape. Johns Hopkins University Press, Baltimore.

Pursell, C.W., 2007. The Machine in America: A Social History of Technology, 2nd ed. Johns Hopkins University Press, Baltimore.

Roberts, G.K., Steadman, P., 1999. American Cities and Technology: Wilderness to Wired City, The Cities and Technology Series. Routledge in association with the Open University, London; New York.

# 6  Food and Agriculture

While the Garden City, the Radiant City, and Broadacre City are often discussed as if they are primarily about cities proper, they provided a much broader vision than that – focusing on reorganizing entire social and political systems. This breadth necessarily included rural areas, agriculture, and food production. Howard, Le Corbusier, and Wright addressed these concerns in their works partly because the massive growth of cities and the depopulation of rural areas was to varying degrees at the core of their critiques of metropolitan areas. The population of London more than doubled from 2.7 million to 6.5 million from 1851 to 1901. Paris grew by nearly three times to 2.7 million in the same time period while New York City grew by over six times, from nearly 600,000 to just over 3.8 million. By 1921, London had grown by nearly an additional million people. Paris grew minimally from 1901 to 1921, but New York city more than doubled its 1900 population and grew to nearly 7.8 million people by 1920. For 70 years straight, Paris grew by an average of 72 people per day, London grew by 185 people per day, and New York City grew by 282 people per day.[1] The vast majority of these people came from the countryside. In 1850, the United States and Europe had similar percentages of people living in rural areas – 85 percent in the United States and 81 percent in Europe. By 1900, those percentages had dropped by 20 percent and by 1920 they had dropped by another ten. It is in this context that Howard envisioned London reduced to a fifth of its population, Le Corbusier thought that one million was an efficient population for Paris – roughly a third of its population at the time, and Wright thought that the only major cities which should exist would be adjacent to either mines or ports and those dramatically smaller than New York City which he described as "the biggest mouth in the world" and the

> prime example of the survival of the herd instinct, leading the universal urban conspiracy to beguile man from his birthright (the good ground), to hang him by his eyebrows from skyhooks above hard pavements, to crucify him, sell him, or be sold by him.[2]

In addition, though most thought and writing about cities since the earliest decades of the 20th century has ignored the importance of agriculture and

DOI: 10.4324/9781351053730-6

*Food and Agriculture*    101

food by treating food as just another commodity that arrives from somewhere else driven by the forces of an invisible hand, with no implications for the city itself, Howard, Le Corbusier, and Wright had no such delusions. In addition to seeing their proposals as providing a beneficial balance between urban and rural populations and life, they were ultimately concerned with the use of land for the common benefit and a society which would provide a good life for all people. They each holistically and rightly saw that they must account both for the affordable provision of good food to people living in cities and for a secure and pleasant life for the people who grew that food. Thus agriculture and the production of food played a significant role in their positions on land, capital, and labor as discussed in Chapter 4. They are also a significant component of the four works presented in Chapter 2. The history Marx tells of the development of capitalism begins with "the forcible driving of the peasantry from the land."[3] Henry George felt that great advances in productive technology had not lived up to its potential of "youth no longer stunted and starved."[4] Bellamy wrote, regarding the coach with which he illustrates the vast distance between the wealthy investment class and the poor laboring class, that "the driver was hunger" and that the lives of the laboring people who pulled the carriage of society were characterized by "agonized leaping and plunging under the pitiless lashing of hunger."[5] Lastly, Kropotkin stated that he was a utopian because he believed that the revolution should provide shelter, food, and clothes to all but that the middle class was displeased with this because "they are quite alive to the fact that it is not easy to keep the upper hand of a people whose hunger is satisfied."[6]

Howard, Le Corbusier, and Wright saw the revitalization of the countryside as critical to their overall project as well, though for very different reasons. The key conceptual cornerstone of Howard's entire project is the collective ownership of land and distribution of its use to benefit the entire community which would provide that agriculture would be profitable, food would be fresh and inexpensive for all, and the laborers necessary to grow food did not continue to leave the countryside and move to cities. He introduced his project with a statement that everyone across all political, religious, and other ideological spectrums agreed on one thing – namely that "it was deeply to be deplored that the people should continue to stream into the already over-crowded cities, and should thus further deplete the country districts."[7] He claimed that most people looking for a resolution to this issue posed the problem as if there were a necessary divide between areas of industrial production and areas of agricultural production, as if people's choice was either

> on the one hand, to stifle their love for human society – at least in wider relations than can be found in a straggling village – or, on the other hand, to forgo almost entirely all the keen and pure delights of the country.[8]

102    *Food and Agriculture*

Howard then claimed that the way to resolve the problem was to design a pattern of settlement which would reconfigure land use, urban life, agriculture, and industrial production so that all people would benefit from both the town and the country. He proposed that garden cities would resolve this problem and provide the attractions that would overcome the draw of large cities and at the same time "restore the people to the land."[9] It is worth noting that he felt that this model of life would be so powerful that it would drive the significant depopulation and subsequent reconstruction of London to hold a fifth of its then current population.

Le Corbusier also saw the depopulation of the urban areas as a key goal for cities and proposed a significant movement of population back to the countryside. First though, he saw that the distribution of land in the rural areas and the way that agricultural work was organized and remunerated needed a full reconstruction and furthermore that these deep changes in the countryside must precede any population movement in that direction. "We shall not," he wrote, "be able to empty the cities of their superfluous population until the land has been materially and spiritually redeveloped."[10] While he did not propose that the urban and rural populations would be integrated or that people would be able to live in new kind of environment that was the best of both the city and the country as did Howard, Le Corbusier did propose that instead of a stark disparity between the quality of life in the country and in the quality of life in the city it was necessary "to break down the dualism, the rivalry, the opposition, the inequality between these two factors that have created two classes, almost two different people's within the nation."[11] He felt that rural life and city life must hold equal opportunities for dignity, joy, and access to modern social amenities. Le Corbusier also felt that the proportion of work time to leisure time should be equivalent in the city and in the country, even if it were balanced on a daily basis in the city and on a seasonal basis in the country. Based on his travels through France and on looking down on it from airplanes, he stated that "we therefore have a pressing duty: to turn our thoughts to the peasant; to use our *reason* to help him; to use our *love* to make him into a brother and not an underprivileged enemy."[12] His paternalism such as is made clear in the previous statement will be discussed in Chapter 8 on freedom, cooperation, and authority.

Wright proposed the most radical reconstruction of the relationship between cities and agriculture, basing his utopian imagination of a truly democratic society on the distribution of land such that all people could support themselves through agricultural work if they so chose. This strategy was an explicit challenge to the power of capital. Giving people control over their own labor because they were not reliant on capital for their sustenance and housing meant that they were not beholden to whatever terms capital offered them. Wright saw his proposed pattern of the country neither as a balance to industrial production like Howard nor as an issue of justice between urban and rural populations as Le Corbusier. Rather, Wright's proposal would have so thoroughly remade the character of human settlement in contrast to existing urban

Food and Agriculture    103

and rural patterns at the time that one cannot imagine that he was arguing for revitalizing the countryside any more than he was arguing for revitalizing the city. While Howard felt that the Garden City would eventually lead to a partial reconstruction of London and Le Corbusier proposed a reconfigured city life at a higher site density though at a lower overall urban density, Wright was opposed to the existence of densely populated cities at all. He opened his book with a critique of the big city and claimed that if it continued to exist, "no man is going to be much more than a machine."[13] The person in the city had "traded his origins and native pastimes with streams, woods, fields, and animals for the ubiquitous, habitual to-and-fro; taint of carbon monoxide rising from him to his rented aggregations of hard cells on upended streets overlooking hard pavements."[14] In contrast to the city, and in contrast to the power structure of capital and rent that characterized human relations in the city for Wright and which for him denied both true community and the possibility of a genuine democracy, Wright proposed a radical decentralization of cities followed by a reintegration of social, economic, and political life. In his envisioned Broadacre City, people would predominantly live rural lives but with social and employment opportunities they chose to seek out readily available. While Howard and Le Corbusier projected a continued distinction between town or city and rural or country life, Wright projected a nation – which he referred to as Usonia – in which there was no distinction between city and country because there were no large dense human settlements to be found. "The city nowhere unless everywhere" he wrote.[15]

## Agriculture and Food in the Garden City

Howard's political vision was based on small integrated settlements equally reliant on agricultural and industrial production which would achieve health and economic security for all people as opposed to settlements in which economic activity is driven solely by industry or agriculture and only benefited the few who controlled access to land and means of production in either. Howard felt that a significant barrier to addressing the social problems of his day was the assumption that "crowded, unhealthy cities were the last word of economic science; and as if our present form of industry, in which sharp lines divide agricultural from industrial pursuits, were necessarily and enduring one."[16] The green belt around the Garden City, for which it is often superficially known, was Howard's strategy to unmake this divide between agricultural and industrial pursuits and all of the social and economic problems that came with it. Far from being a peripheral green belt around an isolated town which helped keep population densities from increasing and town borders from creeping outward, the agricultural and open space zone around the residential and industrial areas of the Garden City was both financially and politically integral to Howard's proposal in three ways.

First, the integration of town and country generated higher prices and regular markets for farmers so that agricultural producers would be lifted out

104   *Food and Agriculture*

of the state of poverty and uncertainty that motivated so many to leave the countryside for the cities. Stabilizing agricultural profitability was, for Howard, the first step in stabilizing population distribution. As Howard – writing from England – noted, "the American has to pay railway charges to the seaboard, charges for Atlantic transit and railway charges to the consumer" but "the farmer of Garden City has a market at his very doors."[17] On account of this benefit, he calculated that the farmers in the Garden City would be willing to pay rates for land higher than they would otherwise and that these rates would generate approximately 15 percent of the total income that the Garden City would collect. Both the economic and the nutrient cycle relationship between the agricultural estate and the Garden City as a whole situates the farmer in

> conditions so healthful and natural alike in a physical and moral sense, the willing soil and the hopeful farmer will alike respond to their new environment – the soil becoming more fertile by every blade of grass it yields, the farmer richer by every penny of rate-rent he contributes.[18]

This ability of the farmers to pay more for their land while still making enough profit to be financially stable is in part what allows for the provision of pensions and other benefits to the community such as ample and well-maintained roads and sites for parks, civic institutions like museums and libraries, and schools.[19] Farmers were not the only people that would benefit however. The proximity of agricultural production to the town settlements and their integration with the town would lower food costs and increase its quality for the consumer, offering them an economic benefit as well as an increase in quality of life.

Second, by bringing agricultural production into the same lease relationship with the incorporated body of the community as industrial production and residential property, agricultural land prices in the Garden City would stabilize and tenure would be secured, insulating farmers from the risk of eviction by large land holders or banks due to circumstances over which they had no control such as weather or market contractions. This long-term stability of tenure would in turn encourage farmers to make investments in soil health and other improvements to the property which would not only increase the profitability of the farm, further stabilizing them, but also result in more plentiful food for the city's residents. Howard pointed out on several occasions that, with regard to the expenditures of the Garden City and the establishment of rate-rents for land, "the farmer would have a share equal to that of every adult in the administration of such money."[20] Among other things, this means that the farmers themselves would be party to the contracts for the use of agricultural land. They did not get to hold tenure without performing for the community, however. Other potential farmers could approach the city with a proposal to take over leases from existing farmers, albeit on terms that would heavily favor the existing farmer. This was necessary so farmers, like business owners in the main shopping gallery, could be held accountable to the city. Howard considered both to be essentially well remunerated municipal servants and proposed that anyone wanting to take over tenure of an existing farm would have to pay the current farmer for the unrecovered cost of improvements as well as pay an increase in rate-rent of at least 10 percent. This ability of the farmer to not only partake of the benefits of society due to their proximity, have protected tenure contingent on contribution, and have an equal say in the decisions about such benefits is indicative of not only Howard's imagination for the integration of industry and agriculture into one system but also the integration of people who were engaged in both forms of production into the same polity.

Third, the Garden City ensured access to fresh air, nature, and open space by surrounding the civic core with farmland and other open space uses protecting the scale of town settlement through population limits which were enforceable due to the community ownership of land by the Garden City corporation. Not only did this belt of open land around the town proper hold the agricultural land which provided the primary source of food for the people in the town but also institutions such as agricultural colleges, convalescent homes, and asylums for the blind and deaf in addition to industries such as brickyards.[21] While we may rightly look askance today at the choice of institutions which Howard excluded from the town center to the countryside, we can certainly imagine for ourselves institutions that would be fitting in open country as a way to understand the benefit that this land distribution would offer. In addition, a significant function of the economic and institutional character of the open land around the town proper and its uses was to provide a means to resist the conversion of open space to additional residential and industrial uses. Howard proposes that, as a town would normally grow under the private ownership of land, "the agricultural land would be 'ripe' for building purposes, and the beauty and healthfulness of the town would be quickly destroyed."[22] However, since the inhabitants of the Garden City would own the agricultural land in common in the same way that they held all other land in common, he felt that "the people of the Garden City will not for a moment permit the beauty of their city to be destroyed by growth."[23] Because the land is owned by the city as a whole and all residents have a say in its disposition such that no individual is able to "secure to himself any undue share of the natural increment of land value which would be brought about by the general growth in the well-being of the town," there is neither avenue nor motivation for land speculation in the Garden City.[24] In typical developments, including many of those which have claimed to be drawing on Howard's proposal when they were only drawing superficially on its form, the residential areas pay to maintain open land around them. In most cases this has proven to be at best only an ineffective and temporary barrier to green field development and sprawl. The motivation to allow development on that land would be greatly reduced in Howard's proposal because the agricultural areas were, in contrast to most land development where land is not owned in common, integral to the town and supported the residential areas in a direct way.

106   *Food and Agriculture*

While Howard waxed poetic about things available in the countryside such as "beautiful vistas, lordly parks, violet-scented woods, fresh air" and "sounds of rippling water," he did not imagine that agricultural life was based on an ethos of engaging the world in significantly different ways than any other form of life – as would Le Corbusier and Wright.[25] Rather, he described agricultural life largely around his imagination that his proposal would make British agriculture profitable again and the security that his proposal for secure land tenure would give farmers. This relative lack of dogma allowed Howard to be more flexible in his imagination of the kinds of farming operations that will take place in the Garden City than Le Corbusier was in the Radiant City or Wright in Broadacre City. Howard projected the possibility of multiple ways in which farmers may organize themselves. Crops such as wheat which are best suited to large field operations may be undertaken by "a capitalist famer or a body of co-operators" and other crops which lend themselves to more personal care such as vegetables, fruits, and flowers may be best grown by individual farmers or small groups of farmers with "a common belief in the efficacy and value of certain dressings, methods of culture, or artificial and natural surroundings."[26] While farmers had a ready market within reach of easy transportation, they were also free to sell to any market nationally or internationally that they want. Discussing the merits of his proposal for the farmer, Howard pointed out that the local transportation system for food would not limit farmers in their choice of market but, "as in every feature of the experiment, … it is not the area of rights which is contracted, but the area of choice which is enlarged."[27]

Given the smaller scale of production and the proximity of it to the eating population, Howard imagined that the food available to people in the Garden City would be vastly different and improved. While Howard as we have seen was primarily interested in the financial implications for agriculture, this preoccupation leads him to believe – with significant justification – that farmers would be more likely to grow fruits and vegetables in the Garden City because of the ease of distribution of perishable high-value crops to the market at hand where they would fetch a premium. This is not only due to the proximity of the farm to the market but also the fact that this proximity has the potential to cut out the web of intermediate buyers and resellers between agricultural producers and consumers necessitated by greater distances which raised prices for consumers and decreased income for farmers. Howard discussed the economics and pragmatics of distribution of fruit and vegetables as well as milk, then followed with the conclusion that "the combination of town and country is not only healthful but economic."[28] It should not be misunderstood that he proposed a fully self-sufficient town. He noted that coffee, tea, tropical fruits, spices, and sugar would clearly not be provided by the farmers of Garden City. The food consumed would also change in quality and type for the families that chose to avail themselves of the opportunity to grow food in home gardens or in allotments available just outside the town. He noted that houses will have space for gardens and that some people may choose to garden cooperatively. He also included allotment gardens as the first ring of agricultural use outside the

Food and Agriculture     107

built areas of the town.[29] These allotments, where individual families would be able to grow for their own sustenance, further increased the amount of fresh produce available to people in the Garden City.

## Food and Agriculture in the Radiant City

While agriculture is philosophically central to Wright's political vision and economically and spatially central to Howard's, Le Corbusier did not hold a similarly conceptual centrality for agriculture in the daily life of the Radiant City. In fact, one of his several colorful disparagements of the Garden City came in the form of a criticism of new city developments in the USSR which, he opined, was

> also intent on dismantling its own cities, just as our own city authorities are all dreaming of sending out into the fields (their garden-cities) to scrabble earth around a lot of hypothetical onions and live out Jean-Jacques' eighteenth century fantasies (without his wit).[30]

In contrast to both Howard and Wright, Le Corbusier imagined a continued and perhaps even clarified distinction between urban and rural life. However, this is not to say that agriculture and rural concerns were not integral to Le Corbusier's overarching vision.

Le Corbusier gave little attention to the interaction between people who live in cities and people who live in rural areas and imagined that each style of life to be quite different. While in the city people were largely imagined to be leading lives of private contemplation blended with active and passive recreation in public and relying on large-scale mass services such as laundry and cooking, Le Corbusier imagined people in the country living lives that were much more intimately socially involved. His examination of the French countryside and the life of agriculturalists led him to propose a solution which was "composed of two clearly definable terms: The family farm at the center of a land allotment proportioned to it, and the co-operative village – the heart of the peasant community."[31] In both the city and the country, Le Corbusier imagined a balance between individual life and shared resources. The difference is that in the city, these shared resources were essentially anonymous and efficient commercial processes and in the country they were built on more personal and familial relationships. He proposed that these Radiant Villages would be centered around a co-operative silo and a club. The silo would "provide economic stability by safeguarding the individual peasant from speculators, money lenders and crooks."[32] The club would provide space for meetings, lectures, films, and contests but will also provide a place "where one can simply mingle with others who share the same local spirit, the spirit of that community."[33] In addition to other institutions in the town which relate primarily to the economic life and which he projected would be primarily co-operative in nature, the village hall would contain the Mayor's office and the community's labor

108    *Food and Agriculture*

union headquarters. This, he claimed, would be "the manifest symbol of the communal reality."[34] Le Corbusier's rural landscape would be comprised of architectural events "capable of charging its site with strong and positive emotional power."[35]

Unlike Howard, Le Corbusier attributed a high moral value to agricultural production, though he spent less time on the pragmatic economics of how agriculture fits into his proposed society. However, he claimed that both a technological and a spiritual revolution would be prerequisite to rural society achieving this value. The technological revolution involves modern equipment which would allow the agricultural peasant to work with "a body of mechanical and architectural equipment as impeccably efficient as the machinery that propels and sustains the aviator when his craft sweeps him up into the sky."[36] The spiritual revolution he proposed would bring the knowledge that agriculturalists gain from working the land into modern society. For Le Corbusier, this modern peasant was characterized by "that special and precious quality found only in people who are in permanent contact with nature."[37] There was a strong correlation for Le Corbusier between the ways in which agriculture in France was situated in local soil, its environmental attributes, and the need to respect local knowledge and tools.

This relationship between people and location also carried through into Le Corbusier's imagination of how buildings fit into farming landscapes. He proposed that prefabricated building elements, fitting modern life in the countryside, would improve the quality of rural life. Le Corbusier captioned one image of a radiant farm built out of prefabricated elements with the claim that it would be "a sort of geometrical plant as profoundly linked to the landscape as a tree or a hill, and as expressive of our human presence as a piece of furniture or a machine."[38] The prefabricated farm buildings Le Corbusier imagined would not be set up by local workers but were, rather, "erected by specialized teams of workmen, then put at the peasants' disposal" after being manufactured in urban centers, resulting in "a collaboration between the land and heavy industry."[39] It should be noted that is not clear, however, how much direction the peasants would have over the workmen in the actual arrangement of the housing and how it would fit to the place or the particularities of their lives.

Le Corbusier proposed that rural economies would be integrated within society economically as well as socially through transportation networks as discussed in the previous chapter. For Le Corbusier, these economies centered on the Radiant Village. While given the overall pattern of society, food would have to be transported much further in Le Corbusier's vision than in Wright's, the road network was a central component of each – in contrast to Howard's reliance on railways. Le Corbusier wrote that his concept for the radiant farm and village was developed in dialogue with an agricultural laborer named Norbert Bézard. While it was Bézard's poetic hope that the village would be on a hillside, bathed in sunlight and holding a commanding view across the countryside, Le Corbusier claimed that this is not possible because "the co-operative village too is fundamentally and inescapably a function of a transportation

Food and Agriculture 109

system, of storage needs, of merchandise handling problems" and that therefore the village could not be set on a hill but must be rather sited on level ground where transportation of heavily loaded trucks was best facilitated and where a branch road to the communal silo can be most easily connected to the national road network.[40]

Le Corbusier did not directly or indirectly propose that the kind of food that would be grown in the Radiant Village and eaten in the Radiant City would change significantly, only the efficiency of connection between farm and plate. He proposed that the communal provision of services like laundry and cooking integral to the basic living units should be modeled on cabins aboard luxury liners. Gone, as discussed in Chapter 4, are the small butchers, grocers, and dairies where Parisian people were accustomed to shopping. Instead, there would be centralized delivery to catering departments that occupy part of the communal service provision floor with space for dry, refrigerated, and frozen storage. The price of the goods would be lowered partly because, as Le Corbusier stated, "adequate refrigeration will assure storage without waste."[41] His proposed catering departments' operation were modelled on hotels and luxury liners as well. The menus would be distributed throughout the residential buildings in the morning and collected an hour later by catering staff. A system of special elevators would make it "possible to deliver hot meals in insulated containers to any apartment in a given block."[42] The novelty of this proposal at the time is illustrated for the modern reader, accustomed as they are to take-out and delivery meals, by Le Corbusier's perceived need to point out that people eat out in restaurants, on ships, in hotels followed by the observation that "eating in a restaurant does not necessarily cause instant death."[43]

## Agriculture and Food in Broadacre City

Wright opens *The Living City* with a long quote from Paracelsus, a Renaissance scientist, printed in red in which it is argued that there is an intimate relationship between true character and the ability to see the truth in nature. Wright closes the volume with a two-page appendix titled 'Ralph Waldo Emerson's Essay on Farming', also printed in red, which extols the primacy of the farmer in society and repeats the relationship between true character and working with the earth that Wright pulled from Paracelsus. This concept frames Wright's argument for a renewed democracy which he claimed was based on the Jeffersonian ideal of an aristocracy not bestowed "by heredity or privilege" but "now a matter of character."[44] An intimate relationship between people and nature was central to the development of individual character upon which true democracy rests for Wright. For him, only when people are engaged in harmonious relationships with Nature can the democratic spirit arise to create the "civilization of man and ground – really organic agronomy – democracy."[45]

Going further, Wright claimed that productive engagement with soil would save civilization from the city. "Of all the underlying forces working toward the emancipation of the city dweller," he wrote, "most important is the gradual

110  *Food and Agriculture*

reawakening of the primitive instincts of the agrarian."[46] The importance of the individual citizen's relationship to the land is also clear in Wright's imagination of schools and what they teach. The buildings of schools and their integration with the land around them would be "universally adapted to the uses of young life growing up in sunlight to cherish the ideals of freedom, love ground, love space and enjoy light."[47] Not only would students learn from observing and drawing elemental nature and listening to the sounds of flora and fauna in the open, but would also "learn the potentialities of soil" and the mysteries of the mind by "working on the soil and in it."[48] Not only the distribution of land but also the educational system would support the development of fully free citizens in Broadacre City. These citizens would be made free primarily by their intimate relationship with land through agricultural production and would belong "as hill-slopes, or the beautiful ravines and forests themselves belong" and with this new more natural sense of themselves attain both "physical and spiritual significance."[49]

The first and most pragmatic role that agricultural landscapes of Broadacre City played in Wright's political vision was that giving everyone the ability to opt out of employment and support themselves on their own acreage would allow them to be functionally independent citizens as described in Chapter 4. This connection between a healthy body politic and the ability for people to feed and house themselves without being beholden to employers and landlords is a critical logical armature upon which Wright's utopian proposal hangs. Democracy, for Wright, was only truly possible when people have the freedom to live the lives they authentically choose in their own homes on their own land and can therefore develop the intrinsic character that comes from an authentic and uncoerced engagement with land. The individual at home, he wrote, would be "organically related to landscape, to transport and distribution of goods, to educational entertainment and all cultural opportunity."[50] It is worthy of note, and also worthy of challenge, that Wright did not imagine anyone authentically choosing life in a dense urban condition which he tendentially described as living in "millions upon millions of little cavities ... a vast prison with glass fronts" and in which there was "forever a bedlam of harsh, torturing shrieks and roars."[51]

For Wright, economic equality came with independence. The previously poor would be "no longer enslaved to exercise himself as a soulless faculty of some machine-made producing system" but would be able to live "*with* the good ground *as a producer himself* not merely *on* it as a parasite of triple rent and hidden taxes."[52] He did not imagine that his proposal would only benefit the poor, however, and bring about a more equal society by raising their quality of life exclusively. He also proposed that it would improve the lives of people who were not financially constrained but who were no less hampered by the society and city of centralization. "The superfluous millions of white-collarites," he wrote, "now forever seeking and abandoning employment in the old cities would be happy independents in a beautiful life in beautiful country."[53] He

*Food and Agriculture*   111

felt that all people in all walks of life and at all socio-economic levels were oppressed and denied authentic forms of being by the city.

Wright also imagined that the freedom and independence of individual actors would be the foundation of a more genuine communal life – something often lacking in contemporary discussions of his proposal. A viable democracy, for Wright, would be characterized by "many free units developing strength as they learn to function and grow together in adequate space, mutual freedom a reality."[54] It was the interaction and cooperation between people, freely chosen, that Wright ultimately imagined as the true form of democracy. It must be remembered that Broadacre City was not only grounded on the independence of small production but also on common action and cooperation. Wright proposed that this new freedom and the distribution of land to small landholders would allow such arrangements as the common ownership of tractors and electrical utilities, communal forms of health insurance, and the production of cultural events which sprung from the people themselves. While Wright's emphasis was on the individual family home throughout, one of the two model layouts that he showed for how houses could relate to each other in Broadacre City is a diagram of four square lots with the four houses located at the intersections of the property lines, sharing common walls.[55] It is this possibility of common ownership and cooperation which conceptually spans the gap between Wright's insistence that every citizen have their own acre and his openness to the possibility that "well-designed farm life" may be "grouped…on units of five- ten- or forty-acre farms (or more)."[56]

Like Le Corbusier, Wright was also committed to prefabricated elements which small farm owners could use to assemble the home and farm buildings as they saw fit. He proposed that there would not be one type but rather "of as many types in various materials as there are bound to be endless modifications of the farmer's purposes and his ground."[57] Because all people were given equal footing, he proposed that there would not be a differentiation in quality of design or fabrication of these units. Whereas in the existing city "the workman has been thwarted by choice only of reactionary sentimentalities aborted by machine, and compelled to accept ugly machine-made things put into a boxing up by realtoristic bureaucracy," in Broadacre City, this same person would be "equal in quality of investment to anyone 'rich.'"[58] For Wright, the landscape of a farm itself was also demonstrative of agronomic values on which he felt the society would be firmly grounded. He imagined fields laid out in relation to natural and manmade features such as hedgeways, ravines, waterways, and well-placed roads. The whole ensemble, including contour plowing, would allow one to

> see the varied, multiple parts all thus contributing to a great dramatic whole in which you sense the repose of individual human contentment and the exuberance of plenty – the life of the imagination truly aesthetic … the national agronomy of our democratic future.[59]

## 112  Food and Agriculture

Wright similarly placed farms in relation to a road network. Individual farms were to be comprised of "well-placed buildings related to well-placed roads in suitable places" together being "rhythmic in relation to human use and movement."[60] His proposed markets, which he described as social features of urban integration, would likewise be set along the "interior roadways of the highways of the free city."[61]

Wright, like Howard, presumed that his proposal would significantly impact the food that people ate. Since food production was not primarily an economic activity undertaken at great length from center of population but was rather something undertaken by small units of production spread across the landscape in direct proportion to the population, he foresaw that fresh food would be readily available. He described highway-side markets through "which the citizens continually pass; picking up food continually fresh"[62] grown not only by people who had made agriculture their main occupation but also the families of industrial workers who chose to supplement their income by growing food to sell. He imagined that in Broadacre City "green-stuffs, produced fresh every hour" would be commonplace and that dairy, fruit, produce, meat, fowl, and eggs "in all of which freshness is a first consideration, will be the direct contribution of society to itself."[63] It is telling that he imagined the agricultural producers in Broadacre City would have an advantage over, and replace, the vast grain and beef producing operations of the West. This expectation of local, fresh food taking a significant part in daily life played out in his proposal for schools as well. Not only would working with soil and growing food be a part of children's education, but so would preparing and serving food. Indicative of the shared and graceful way in which Wright imagined people living in Broadacre City, children would learn not only how to prepare food but also "how to serve it charmingly to others."[64]

## Conclusion

As different as the Garden City, Radiant City, and Broadacre City proposals were regarding food and agriculture, there are three things that are consistent across all of them. First, the people who grew food in these visions were not impoverished or subject to the sudden loss of income common to capitalist organizations of food and agriculture. Farmers in the Garden City were protected by the markets close at hand and their political integration with the rest of the community. Farmers in the Radiant Villages were protected by their participation in cooperative silos and the cooperative social and political institutions associated with life in rural areas. Everyone in Broadacre City could be a farmer and everyone could grow food for themselves while not relying on the markets for income. Second, food was fresh and available in all three ideals. Food was produced close to consumers in both the Garden City and Broadacre City and efficient transportation systems delivered fresh food directly to refrigerated storage in the catering departments of the Radiant City. Lastly, quality food was less expensive for all people in each proposal. The proximity of

*Food and Agriculture* 113

the Garden City, as well as the increased soil quality and therefore productiveness due to free sewage as fertilizer in addition to the motivation of the farmer to make improvements in their practices due to secure tenure, kept food inexpensive in Howard's vision. Efficiency and the reduction of waste made quality food less expensive in the Radiant City. In Broadacre City, everyone could grow their own food on their own land so nobody could charge a premium beyond what someone would be willing to pay for convenience – keeping food as inexpensive as that margin of convenience implied.

## Notes

1 London data – www.demographia.com/dm-lon31.htm; New York data – www.demographia.com/db-nyuza1800.htm, Paris data – www.demographia.com/dm-par90.htm
2 Wright, *The Living City*, p. 24.
3 Marx, *Capital*, pp. 619–621.
4 George, *Progress and Poverty*, p. 14.
5 Bellamy, *Looking Backward: 2000–1887*, p. 12.
6 Kropotkin, *The Peter Kropotkin Anthology (Annotated): The Conquest of Bread, Mutual Aid: A Factor of Evolution, Fields, Factories and Workshops, An Appeal to the Young and The Life of Kropotkin*, p. 63.
7 Howard and Osborn, *Garden Cities of To-morrow*, p. 42.
8 Howard and Osborn, *Garden Cities of To-morrow*, p. 44.
9 Howard and Osborn, *Garden Cities of To-morrow*, p. 44.
10 Le Corbusier, *The Radiant City*, p. 197.
11 Le Corbusier, *The Radiant City*, p. 197.
12 Le Corbusier, *The Radiant City*, p. 322.
13 Wright, *The Living City*, p. 17.
14 Wright, *The Living City*, p. 18.
15 Wright, *The Living City*, p. 112.
16 Howard and Osborn, *Garden Cities of To-morrow*, p. 45.
17 Howard and Osborn, *Garden Cities of To-morrow*, p. 61.
18 Howard and Osborn, *Garden Cities of To-morrow*, p. 64.
19 Howard and Osborn, *Garden Cities of To-morrow*, p. 67.
20 Howard and Osborn, *Garden Cities of To-morrow*, p. 63.
21 Howard and Osborn, *Garden Cities of To-morrow*, p. 52.
22 Howard and Osborn, *Garden Cities of To-morrow*, p. 140.
23 Howard and Osborn, *Garden Cities of To-morrow*, p. 140.
24 Howard and Osborn, *Garden Cities of To-morrow*, pp. 62–63.
25 Howard and Osborn, *Garden Cities of To-morrow*, p. 47.
26 Howard and Osborn, *Garden Cities of To-morrow*, p. 56.
27 Howard and Osborn, *Garden Cities of To-morrow*, p. 56.
28 Howard and Osborn, *Garden Cities of To-morrow*, p. 61.
29 Howard and Osborn, *Garden Cities of To-morrow*, pp. 52–53.
30 Le Corbusier, *The Radiant City*, p. 136.
31 Le Corbusier, *The Radiant City*, p. 322.
32 Le Corbusier, *The Radiant City*, p. 323.
33 Le Corbusier, *The Radiant City*, p. 324.

114 *Food and Agriculture*

34 Le Corbusier, *The Radiant City*, p. 329.
35 Le Corbusier, *The Radiant City*, p. 337.
36 Le Corbusier, *The Radiant City*, p. 323.
37 Le Corbusier, *The Radiant City*, p. 323.
38 Le Corbusier, *The Radiant City*, p. 336.
39 Le Corbusier, *The Radiant City*, p. 330.
40 Le Corbusier, *The Radiant City*, p. 327.
41 Le Corbusier, *The Radiant City*, p. 116.
42 Le Corbusier, *The Radiant City*, p. 116.
43 Le Corbusier, *The Radiant City*, p. 116.
44 Wright, *The Living City*, p. 44.
45 Wright, *The Living City*, p. 25.
46 Wright, *The Living City*, p. 62.
47 Wright, *The Living City*, p. 188.
48 Wright, *The Living City*, p. 188.
49 Wright, *The Living City*, p. 214.
50 Wright, *The Living City*, p. 78.
51 Wright, *The Living City*, p. 56.
52 Wright, *The Living City*, p. 153.
53 Wright, *The Living City*, p. 163.
54 Wright, *The Living City*, p. 83.
55 Wright, *The Living City*, p. 151.
56 Wright, *The Living City*, p. 163.
57 Wright, *The Living City*, p. 162.
58 Wright, *The Living City*, p. 153.
59 Wright, *The Living City*, p. 93.
60 Wright, *The Living City*, p. 93.
61 Wright, *The Living City*, p. 163.
62 Wright, *The Living City*, p. 125.
63 Wright, *The Living City*, pp. 155, 161.
64 Wright, *The Living City*, p. 189.

## Bibliography

Bellamy, E., 2018. Looking Backward: 2000–1887. DIGIREADS COM, Place of publication not identified.

George, H., 2016. Progress and Poverty. Aziloth Books, United Kingdom.

Greater London, Inner London & Outer London Population & Density History, n.d. Demographia.

Howard, E., Osborn, F.J., 2001. Garden Cities of To-morrow, 11th Print. ed. MIT Press, Cambridge.

Kropotkin, P., 2020. The Peter Kropotkin Anthology (Annotated): The Conquest of Bread, Mutual Aid: A Factor of Evolution, Fields, Factories and Workshops, An Appeal to the Young and The Life of Kropotkin. CSA Publishing, Coppell.

Le Corbusier, 1964. The Radiant City: Elements of a Doctrine of Urbanism to be Used as the Basis of Our Machine-Age Civilization. The Orion Press, New York.

Marx, K., Engels, F., Moore, S., Aveling, E.B., Untermann, E., 2017. Capital. Volume 1. Digireads, USA.

Food and Agriculture    115

New York Urbanized Area, n.d. Population and Density from 1800 (Provisional). Demographia.

Ville de Paris, n.d. Population & Density from 1600. Demographia.

Wright, F.L., 1958. The Living City. Horizon Press, New York.


## Suggested Readings

Belasco, W.J., 2006. Meals to Come: A History of the Future of Food, California Studies in Food and Culture. University of California Press, Berkeley.

Bell, D., Valentine, G., 1997. Consuming Geographies: We Are Where We Eat. Routledge, London; New York.

Estabrook, B., 2011. Tomatoland: How Modern Industrial Agriculture Destroyed Our Most Alluring Fruit. Andrews McMeel Publishing, Kansas City.

Fishman, R., 1982. Urban Utopias in the Twentieth Century: Ebenezer Howard, Frank Lloyd Wright, and Le Corbusier, 1st MIT Press pbk. ed. MIT Press, Cambridge.

Gumpert, D.E., 2013. Life, Liberty, and the Pursuit of Food Rights: The Escalating Battle Over Who Decides What We Eat. Chelsea Green Publishing, White River Junction, Vermont.

Hart, J.F., 2003. The Changing Scale of American Agriculture. University of Virginia Press, Charlottesville.

Kneen, B., 1989. From Land to Mouth: Understanding the Food System. NC Press, Toronto.

Morgan, D., 2000. Merchants of Grain: The Power and Profits of the Five Giant Companies at the Center of the World's Food Supply. iUniverse.com, Inc., Lincoln.

O'Connell, D.J., Peters, S.J., 2021. In the Struggle: Scholars and the Fight against Industrial Agribusiness in California, 1st ed. New Village Press, New York.

Patel, R., 2012. Stuffed and Starved: The Hidden Battle for the World Food System, 2nd ed. Melville House Pub, Brooklyn.

Roberts, P., 2008. The End of Food, 1st Mariner Books ed. Mariner Books, Boston.

Steel, C. (Ed.), 2013. Hungry City: How Food Shapes Our Lives. Vintage Books, London.

Zeunert, J., Waterman, T. (Eds.), 2018. Routledge Handbook of Landscape and Food, Routledge Handbooks. Routledge, Taylor & Francis Group, London; New York.

# 7 Leisure

The Garden City, the Radiant City, and Broadacre City were all intended as models in which all people could live joyful and satisfying lives. For each writer, time and accommodations for leisure activities played a significant role in their underlying imagination of the good life. Howard imagined people spending their leisure time primarily in passive recreation outside or in social activities. While Le Corbusier emphasized leisure hours spent in sport as is well known, he also placed great emphasis on passive recreation like sunbathing and walking amongst flowers as well as creative works of the mind. Wright foresaw that people in his utopian vision would primarily spend their leisure time pursuing aesthetic production, social activities, and community forms of entertainment. The discussion about the balance between time for leisure and hours of required work that one finds in these three proposals was situated in open public debate at the time – Howard, Le Corbusier, and Wright were not outliers in this regard. It is worth noting that the contemporary workweek typical in most countries allows significantly more time for leisure than did the typical workweek of the late 19th and early 20th century. Depending on occupation and season, most workers around the turn into the 20th century worked from 55 to more than 80-hour weeks as a matter of course – with manual industrial laborers working the most. While the push for an eight-hour workday began as early as the 1870s in the United States and even earlier elsewhere, a five-day work week did not become common until the 1930s and the 40-hour work week did not become common until after that and is still not universal within or between countries. Howard, Le Corbusier, and Wright all imagined that our workdays could be cut even shorter if the benefits of machine production were distributed fairly across society and each one proposed urban resolutions for the use of leisure time which were consistent with the overall goals of the rest of their projects.

Howard listed 'excessive hours' as one negative characteristic of the town and 'long hours for low pay' as one for the countryside. One benefit that he offered as indicative of his Garden City proposal was 'no sweating,' a labor practice in which work, particularly for the textile industry in Britain at the time, was contracted to people as piecework who finished the product in very poor conditions for extremely low payment, often at home.[1] Howard never explicitly

DOI: 10.4324/9781351053730-7

stated that the residents of the Garden City would have more leisure time but did argue that the benefits of his proposed reformulation of the city would lead to "a higher and better form of industrial life" and provided extensive landscapes and public institutions for recreation and social intercourse. Not treating one's employees "with proper consideration with regard to hours of labour" was one reason that Howard imagined business owners may fall out of favor with the Garden City administration and thereby endanger the lease to the space necessary to their business.[2] It is also worth noting that "parks and gardens, orchards and woods ... planted in the midst of the busy life of the people, so that they may be enjoyed in the fullest measure" throughout England was among the benefits Howard expected that the new city form and land ownership model would bring about.[3] This all clearly implies that Howard expected there to be a higher number of hours available for leisure to all members of society than were available to the laboring classes of his time who often worked 10- or 12-hour days at least six days a week.

Le Corbusier stated that people would have significantly more leisure time in the Radiant City because "the workers' hours of obeisance to the machine are reduced to five or six."[4] Once industrial society had been thus organized, each person would have a quota of industrial production to perform to provide for the basic needs of society followed by time dedicated to physical culture, mental activities, family, and sleep.[5] In much the same way that the efficiencies of machine production generated leisure hours, the efficient prefabricated house —referred to as domestic equipment – would also generate leisure hours by relieving its occupants of unpleasant tasks. The house would then become "a genuine source of happiness, for happiness is liberty, time saved, freedom from unpleasant tasks."[6] The central concern which he proposed the Radiant City addressed is the fact that after accounting for these few hours of work, sleep, and other necessities, there would still be 11 unoccupied hours. He proposed that the city must be redesigned because "we cannot leave millions of men, women, and young people to spend seven or eight hours a day in the streets."[7] These unoccupied hours represented, for Le Corbusier, a "gaping void awaiting the modern age, that imminent danger: leisure."[8] In fact, he credited the birth of the idea of the Radiant City to years spent thinking about how cities ought to provide for this leisure time. Rather than leisure being restricted to occasional daytrips to the seaside, he proposed a city organized around the idea that leisure would become renamed "the daily activities of modern man."[9] While sport and physical activity played a significant role in his proposal, they did not exhaust his imagination for the use of leisure time. Rather, he defined recreation more broadly as time to take part "in projects no longer implacably subjected to the laws of money."[10] He proposed that we reconsider the term 'leisure' and instead imagine it "as the normal work of people in the machine age" after five hours or so are given over to tasks necessary to the "nourishment and maintenance of the social body."[11]

Wright also stated that people would have more leisure in his proposed reorganization of the city and society. This expanded number of leisure hours

118  *Leisure*

that residents of Broadacre City enjoyed were the result of two things; the use of machines in production and the reduction of time commuting to work. He claimed that once machine power was "decentralized and better distributed, more directly and simply applied to humane purposes," there would be a "universal margin of leisure" and "greater rational freedom for the individual than any known by previous civilizations."[12] The leisure he imagined was not necessarily what we think of as leisure today, though it does include free time for recreation and social entertainment. As for Le Corbusier, leisure time for Wright meant simply the time that was not focused on daily necessities or on working for money. Immediately preceding his design for a new motor car, Wright claimed that "the time and money that the white-collarite now spends going to and from work" would instead be "spent in the diversified colorful activities in the workman's widened margin of leisure in happier circumstances."[13]

Each of the three writers had a different sense of how they imagined people would use the new-found leisure hours derived from their political reorganization of the landscape and proposed landscape resolutions which reflected that imagination. These recreational uses were significant drivers of the landscapes each proposed and provision for recreation can be looked to as a key component of their political imagination of the good life. The landscapes of the Garden City are focused on parks and other outside spaces which provide for recreation in the natural world. Le Corbusier included much open space for similar activities, but also included a significant emphasis on the availability of sport. Wright provided landscapes for many social and community activities but, given his emphasis on leisure as aesthetic production and the importance of home, his approach to personal homes and landscapes should also be understood as space for leisure.

## Leisure in the Garden City

Howard's more spiritual goal regarding daily life was the integration of the experience of nature with the social benefits of towns which was aligned with his pragmatic goal of integrating agriculture and industry. His diagram for the Garden City was organized around this integration of town and country and centered on the leisure enjoyment of both. Introducing *Garden Cities of To-Morrow*, Howard wrote that "the town is the symbol of society" while "the country is the symbol of God's love and care for man."[14] The country was, in his view, "the source of all health, all wealth, all knowledge."[15] However, the full benefits of the country could not be enjoyed widely as long as "this unholy, unnatural separation of society and nature endures."[16] Society was characterized for Howard by the expectation of "mutual help and friendly co-operation" as well as "broad, expanding sympathies" and the arts, science, religion, and culture.[17] His belief that a new civilization, as well as a new life and a new hope, would come of the union of the town and country is clear in how he imagined the town, symbolized by the organization of the town center. He organized his diagrammatic plan for the Garden City around providing close access to open space for passive recreation, space for social interactions in all seasons, and a centrality of civic and entertainment institutions.

Howard represented his town-country magnet as a walk from center to perimeter. The central figure of Howard's plan is not a building or a monument but rather a "beautiful and well-watered garden" of five and a half acres surrounded by civic and entertainment institutions.[18] Just outside this ring of public buildings is another larger park representing an additional 145 acres. This park, encircled by the Crystal Palace, includes "ample recreation grounds within very easy access of all the people."[19] One passes next through two residential districts comprised of individual house and garden lots separated from each other by Grand Avenue. In contrast to the housing available to most people at the time, houses with "nice little gardens" would be readily available to all in the Garden City – including those within the laboring class then living in the slums of the large industrial cities.[20] Grand Avenue is 420 feet wide and Howard noted that it "constitutes an additional park of 115 acres … within 240 yards of the furthest removed inhabitant."[21] While 40 acres of this park would be given over to trees and shrubs planted along the roadside, he proposed that "much of the park space would probably be left in a state of nature."[22] In addition to providing manicured open space, wild areas, and sites for public buildings such as churches and schools with their playgrounds, Grand Avenue also contains spaces for active outdoor recreation such as cricket fields, tennis courts, and playgrounds. He proposed that clubs using these grounds would likely be called on to contribute to the expense of upkeep.[23] Walking past the last ring of housing, one would pass through a belt of factories and workshops before reaching a zone with garden allotments available to residents of the town and then finally the outer area of rural agricultural production and institutions that Howard felt best suited to being placed in rural settings. Summarizing his proposal, he wrote that the Garden City was laid out such "that, as it grows, the free gifts of Nature – fresh air, sunlight, breathing and playing room – shall be still retained in abundance."[24] The reader should note the alignment of fresh air and sunlight with room to breathe and play.

Howard did not foresee these benefits being impinged upon as the Garden City matured. He imagined that as the Garden City became successful, people would naturally want to move there to enjoy the benefits of the town but because the people in the city would be so attached the outdoor and social spaces of the city, they would not allow these benefits to be lost to additional buildings. Securing this easily accessible open space is one of the primary reasons for Howard's proposal that land should be owned in common in the Garden City. Since no individual landowner could sell land for profit, nobody could be motivated by personal benefit to fill in the open spaces which provided the entire community access to the natural and social spaces for leisure that characterized life in the Garden City. This is a direct contrast to the crowded cities of his day which, he claimed "were the best which a society based on selfishness and rapacity could construct."[25] Howard foresaw a network of garden cities – each maintaining the same balance of open space for recreation and

## 120    *Leisure*

agriculture to population and built structures – grouped around one Central City such that each inhabitant in all the cities "would enjoy all the advantages of a great and most beautiful city; and yet all the fresh delights of the country – field, hedgerow, and woodland – not prim parks and gardens merely … within a few minutes' walk or ride."[26]

Howard's expectation about life in London after the wide success of the garden city concept expanded regionally also includes spaces for leisure. Once the vested interests of landownership in London accepted the inevitable loss of the monetary value of their land to competition with the benefits of the landownership model of the Garden City, the equally inevitable reconstruction of London would begin. The simple fact that so many people would leave London for these new garden cities would mean that the rent which landlords could charge would drop and nobody would be willing to live in slums. The landowners of London as a whole would have no choice but to effectively match the benefits of the garden cities if they were to maintain any population in London at all, and therefore even modest income from their property. Howard predicted that thus the slums would be replaced with "parks, recreation grounds, and allotment gardens."[27] Of the future of London he writes that "elsewhere the town is invading the country: here the country must invade the town."[28]

Outdoor activities were not the only recreational activities that the Garden City accommodated. Howard imagined a ring of public buildings directly outside the Garden City's central garden. While one of these is the town hall and another is a hospital, the rest are all institutions which offered cultural entertainment directed primarily toward the life of the mind – the town's primary concert and lecture hall, a theatre, a library, and a museum, and art gallery. These facilities, in addition to the central pleasure garden, emphasize the centrality of leisure to the social life of the Garden City. As he stated, his proposal was intended to join with the benefits of the country the "advantages of the most energetic and active town life."[29] The fact that the institutions which hold the center of the diagram are all typical to progressive ideologies of social and personal uplift further supports the mildly sedate and cultured image that one senses of Howard's imagination of life in the town.

Encircling the large park just beyond these public buildings is Howard's proposed Crystal Palace. This large facility was intended to serve not only as the main site of commerce in which "that class of shopping which requires the joy of deliberation and selection is done" but also – being much larger than the commercial needs of the town would indicate – as a public space that would draw people to the center of the town.[30] The Crystal Palace would be, Howard wrote, "in wet weather one of the favourite resorts of the people, whilst the knowledge that its bright shelter is ever close at hand tempts people into Central Park, even in the most doubtful of weathers."[31] As he noted in his diagram, the Crystal Palace would not have been more than 600 yards from any residence. In the same way that Howard imagined the town protecting its open space from development, he imagined that the town would protect the use of the Crystal Palace for social recreation. It was imagined to be so well loved and highly used that one of the impediments to allowing multiple competing retailers into the town was that the people of the town would prefer that "none of the space devoted to these recreative purposes" be unnecessarily given over to additional retail space.[32] While Howard himself made it clear that his diagram of the town is circular for reasons of argument and presentation and not because he expected that it would be the final form of the town, it is worth observing that the centrality of leisure in natural and social settings to the Garden City provided the driving clarity of his diagram.

## Leisure in the Radiant City

Le Corbusier opened the section of his book titled 'Leisure' with the statement that "as soon as production is reorganized, the leisure time made available by the machine age will suddenly emerge as a social danger: an imminent threat."[33] His approach to accommodating these leisure hours was primarily, but not exclusively, through the provision of large outside spaces to give people access to the natural world. Le Corbusier explicitly contrasted the role of nature in the Radiant City with its role in the Garden City which he equated with commuter suburbs. While this contrast may be unfair to Howard's full proposal, it may not be not unfair relative to the many developments which have claimed Howard's ideas as foundational but have failed to include the common land ownership and other social and structural organizations which would have made the Garden City much more than a commuter suburb. Le Corbusier described the garden city as an "illusory solution" and a "palliative conceived in panic" which offered "the fallacious benefits of an illusory countryside."[34] He proposed instead that society must "eliminate the suburbs, eliminate and ban these garden-cities with their mock nature" and build Radiant Cities which he described as genuine green cities into which nature has been brought.[35] This nature, he wrote, was "neither more nor less artificial than that of the garden-cities, but useful inside the city."[36] The artificial nature which he proposed to bring into the city would be the site of two of the three forms of leisure activities he expected to characterize life in the Radiant City – sport and passive outdoor recreation.

Le Corbusier also contrasted the Radiant City with the historic city which he described as "merely a blighted crust pierced by deep ditch-like streets."[37] He claimed that his proposed change to typical urban landscapes would "be able to accommodate leisure activities, the most imminent phase in the evolution of our modern machine age."[38] These leisure activities were framed by what Le Corbusier referred to as life's basic pleasures – "sun, greenery, and space."[39] He listed sun, sky, and trees as basic materials of city planning and proclaimed that in his proposal for Algiers, for example, the benefit of his proposed city plans would have been that all people would have access to these basic pleasures of the natural world.[40] Much of his claim to have designed a classless city is based on this idea that open space for recreation and the enjoyment of nature would

## 122  *Leisure*

be available to all people – not just those who can afford vacations or homes in leafy neighborhoods.

While Le Corbusier's emphasis on sport is well known, the simple ability to spend time outdoors and experience the benefits of fresh air is an important component of Le Corbusier's proposal as well. He expected that his proposed "reconstitution of the natural environment," would provide the benefits of "living air, greenery and sky and the desired dose of sun on the skin; and, in the lungs, the living air of wide-open spaces."[41] Since all buildings would be lifted off the ground, if someone wanted to get out of the rain or the sun and not use the "walks, shady avenues, and lawns" that spread across the landscape and provide "limitless opportunities for walking," they could "cross the entire residential area from end to end, in any direction … entirely sheltered from sun and rain."[42] The rooftops would also be recreational spaces with large beaches, pools, open-air hydrotherapy establishments, flowers, shrubs, and trees. The rendering titled "Anywhere in the residential city" which accompanies his proposal for Antwerp illustrates how this use of the landscape dominates the human experience at the ground level.[43] One can also see the value he placed on life lived in the open in his perspectives of housing blocks at Algiers where each unit has a large outdoor living space and the interior street is open to the elements.[44] The dominance of areas for walking and other forms of passive recreation within his proposal can be seen throughout the plans, sections, and sketches of the Radiant City.

As noted earlier, Le Corbusier stated that sport was the driver for his Radiant City concept. Given the newly found time for physical recreation, he claimed that "sport should be a daily matter and it should take place directly outside the houses."[45] One can see spaces for football fields, swimming pools, tennis courts, and other field sports – he also mentions basketball, tennis, races, and watersports – in addition to playgrounds and extensive pedestrian networks in many of his plans.[46] He proposed that these sports were necessary to not only physical health but also to fully develop and express our mental and emotional characters. Le Corbusier asserted that sport would give people an outlet for mental capacities such as natural aggression, drive to performance, sense of competition, teamwork, initiative, character, and discipline while also giving them a chance to develop their bodies in terms of strength, speed, flexibility, initiative, and decisiveness. In addition, he stated that the ready availability of space for daily partaking in sport would fill people "with joy and optimism."[47] These "profoundly human values" around which Le Corbusier proposed to organize the entirety of the new city are in contrast with his observations regarding the human experience of his contemporary society in which he saw "the human animal was being crushed, subjugated, torn apart, denatured by its subjection to the machine" and that "everything that lies at the very heart of human nature, the primordial level of man's being, had been trampled on."[48]

Le Corbusier also drew a distinction between his proposal for sport as an urban amenity and the development of sport as a professional spectator activity in which the vast majority of people are mere voyeurs. He was critical of sport

*Leisure* 123

characterized by stadiums and arenas in which 30 or fewer athletes perform for thousands of spectators "who have assembled to live a vicarious dream of valor."[49] Rather than catering to only the privileged few who play professional sports, Le Corbusier proposed that "modern city planning will accomplish the miracle of putting the crowds themselves on the playing field."[50] His ideal was that people come home, take off their jackets, and participate in sporting activities directly outside their homes because sport is "a food as indispensable as bread itself."[51] This reinforced his claim to have designed a city for a society based on equality in the same way as open space and fresh air would be available to all, not just those who could afford to retreat to the mountains or the seaside.

Sport was not, however, the only form of recreation that would be part of the "disappearance of the proletariat" Le Corbusier predicted.[52] Not only was maintaining bodily health central to the benefits of the Radiant City in his imagination, but also "the cultivation of the mind and spirit on every level (clubs and education)" as well as the "manifestations of initiative (handicrafts without thought of profit.)"[53] Instead of spending time working in order to be able to purchase what Le Corbusier referred to as useless consumer goods, he proposed that people would make things for themselves using the freedom that they should have now that machines could "produce ten or twenty times as much as we ourselves" allowing people "to work at least five or ten times less."[54] He saw craft and study as ways to productively fill time freed up from obeisance to machines. This, for Le Corbusier was the true work of a machine age civilization in which people had "reconquered their freedom" such that their "freely chosen forms of work would be carried out in joy as *leisure activities.*"[55] To illustrate his sense of this work, he listed Pasteur's advances in chemistry, Marconi's work with electricity and radio waves, and his own book, as well as someone "playing about with some piece of cabinetmaking or an idea."[56] These activities were not imagined by Le Corbusier as benefitting only the individual freely taking them on – he was not proposing that people pick up what we refer to today as hobbies. These activities, as made clear by his examples, were "creative impulses directed toward the public good."[57]

Lastly, meditation as another use of leisure time comes up sporadically throughout Le Corbusier's book in relation to improved overall health. The house in the Radiant city, modelled on a cell or a cabin and described by Le Corbusier as domestic equipment, is "a vessel for silence and lofty solitude."[58] Leisure for Le Corbusier spans a wide range of activity from those directed toward the health of the body as well as the mind to creative work which benefits the public as a whole. He concluded the section of his book titled "Leisure" with the proclamation, "A healthy body maintained in that state. Meditation. Civic Activity."[59]

## Leisure in Broadacre City

In contrast to both Howard and Le Corbusier, Wright imagined leisure activities primarily focused on active engagement of the mind in creative and social

124   *Leisure*

activities. His projected use of leisure is intimately tied to the development of aesthetic lives and to the ability to live intimately with land. He stated in the forward to *The Living* City that the book was "written in firm belief that true human culture has a healthy sense of the beautiful as its life-of-the-soul: an aesthetic organic as *of* life itself, not *on* it; nobly relating man to his environment."[60] The natural aesthetic which would follow on the free inhabitation of ground and use of leisure time to develop one's aesthetic sense is, for Wright, a necessary foundation to a civilization worthy of being aspired to. In a section subtitled 'Land and Money,' he claimed that "when economic liberation of land and money is duly effective, none may say how far man's cultural liberation may go with greater aesthetic uses of his ground."[61] Regarding the increase in hours for leisure that he predicted would occur in Broadacre City, he claimed that this wider margin of leisure did "not mean more or less employment for anyone but more time to spend as the independent workmen may like to spend time."[62] In addition to small scale production of goods for household use and sale, Wright also imagined leisure time being taken up with social activities and cultural forms of entertainment such as theatre and music.

While Howard did not seem to imagine leisure beyond recreation in nature and time spent in social activities and Le Corbusier imagined leisure time being taken up by a balance of sport, passive recreation, and creative explorations of various kinds, Wright proposed that the increase in leisure time would be spent primarily in workshops, studios, and other creative outlets. This freedom from the machine and rent would also, in Broadacre City, lead to the prevalence of "arts and crafts of eager, growing, young work-life more conveniently established wherever willed by the citizens" and a wide distribution of small independent workshops and artists' studios.[63] In the final section of his book, he directly tied the increase in leisure to the capacity of people to find for themselves the basis of happiness – claiming that "no other secure basis for happiness is as intelligent as good *use* of good ground."[64] This search for happiness would be successful because the workman citizens of the nation would be free on their own ground and able to succeed by their character, skill and – importantly for our understanding of his imagination of leisure – "voluntary labor."[65] Describing what people would do with the time reclaimed from commuting as made possible by many aspects of his decentralized plans, he claimed that life would be spent in "more spacious, comfortable free establishments where whole families play and work" where they may grow food for home consumption or sale at road stands and modern farms.[66]

In addition to leisure time spent in creative activities and engaging productively with soil, Wright imagined that the citizens of Broadacre City would lead rich and involved social lives. He described the small market as an "additional festive social feature" of the new landscape organized around independent small-scale production.[67] While Wright saw the beginnings of these markets in the expanding highway service stations of his day, it is important to note that he imagined these markets developing distinct local characters that would be sought out and enjoyed for their variety – not the consolidated corporate chains we are accustomed to in our day. He noted that these markets would have the character of county fairs in which people not only displayed and exchanged their commodities and goods but also engaged in cultural events and entertainment. They would have included spaces for open-air concerts, cabarets, cafes, theatres, and restaurants as well as motels for travelers. Community centers were another important feature of the imagined social and leisure life of Broadacre City. These would be spaced throughout the landscape and contain a wide range of cultural facilities from art museums to golf courses, from libraries to planetariums, from operas to racetracks. These community centers "would catch, retain, and express the best thought of which growing American democracy is available" and each would be "a respected, respectful place – a place for quiet comradeship suited to inspection, introspection and good company concerning both people and things."[68] The large fold-out map included in the front cover of *The Living City* shows a broad variety of spaces for social events including a baseball field, a music garden, a zoo, an arboretum, and athletic clubs. While he clearly included spaces for sports and physical recreation, they were was not the focus of his imagination of leisure time and he did not write about people specifically engaging in such activities.

He did, however, write at length about people engaging in artistic production. One especially telling aspect of the role of leisure in the life of the residents of Broadacre City is theatre as Wright imagined it. "Wherever," he claimed, "a phase of Nature will have been raised by society to the level of greater Nature there we will find the Theater and find the people themselves owner and producer."[69] His proposal for theatre is consistent with his critique of centralization in society. Rather than entertainment produced primarily by large studios with a profit motive, theatre in Broadacre City would develop out of an organic relation of people to their place and would be produced in cooperative and creative community. The theatre would not only be radical and inspirational he claimed, drawing on problems of people's present daily lives, but it would also be put on by the community itself. He proposed that "inhabitants of the whole country would probably become performers themselves in preference to employed entertainers."[70] In Wright's imagination, the market for traveling theatre stars and companies – a commonplace of his time – would wither since most people would prefer local theatre authentically related to their lives as opposed to productions which he described as either peep-shows or soapbox speeches. Wright proposed that film and music would be similarly driven by popular interest – "taken from the marketeer and having the people now for producer (or sponsor)."[71] Film and music would be distributed through circulating libraries maintained by the community and free of the influence of the "salesmanship for big production" and "any monopolizing commercial element whatever."[72] He claimed that music would become similarly enlivened and connected to daily life, not only over radio but also in the home. "The chamber music concert would naturally become a common feature at home;

126   *Leisure*

players growing up until it amounted to a home culture beyond mere enter-tainment."[73] As in all other forms of aesthetic production that Wright imagined, music would be something people engaged in personally rather than something they consumed – and it was intimately tied to the family home made possible by the redistribution of access to land and the leisure time that it freed up.

## Conclusion

All three utopian proposals were intended as models of the good life, and in each case this included a significant focus on leisure time filled by individually chosen activities. Each writer imagined landscapes which support their imagin-ations of leisure and clearly indicate how they imagined this good life for the inhabitants of their proposed cities. Howard provided open space in parks as well as places left wild that would accommodate strolling and social interactions as well as sports of various kinds. This kind of leisure activity was clearly so important to his vision that he included an immense facility to allow for social leisure in a garden within close proximity to all residences. Le Corbusier stated that his entire proposal was based on accommodating the hours of leisure that would follow a redistribution of benefits of machine production such that people would need to work less than half the hours that a typical industrial worker of his day worked. In the Radiant City, sports fields would be avail-able immediately outside all residences. But his imagination of leisure was not limited to sport. The majority of his city as proposed and drawn was dedicated to more passive forms of leisure such as walking and sunbathing. He went to great lengths to describe the unimpeded access that his proposal would afford the pedestrian. Wright also provided landscapes that provided for his imagination of leisure including social activities and entertainment but primarily focused on freely chosen aesthetic production. Wright imagined that these forms of leisure would happen at home – from engaging with soil to playing music – and so offered fewer public grounds and spaces for social interaction than did Howard and Le Corbusier. These are not absent though, and he included many instances of landscapes that accommodate social interaction as well.

In each vision, as well, the capacity for leisure was deeply embedded in the revised relationship between capital, labor, and land as described in Chapter 4. For all three – from Le Corbusier's emphasis on shared landscapes to Wright's emphasis on private ones – the concept of putting land to use for the common good is foundational. One can, of course, challenge their understanding of this common good and even more specifically how the common good is decided on. While Howard, Le Corbusier, and Wright offered landscapes which accommodated what they each imagined people would freely choose as leisure activities, they also each imagined fairly narrow visions of what those choices would entail. While each emphasized the importance of freedom in their own way, they also each closed off some choices that people could make. This issue of freedom and authority with regard to the definition of the good life will be taken up more directly in the next chapter.

# Notes

1 Howard and Osborn, *Garden Cities of To-morrow,* p. 46.
2 Howard and Osborn, *Garden Cities of To-morrow,* p. 98.
3 Howard and Osborn, *Garden Cities of To-morrow,* p. 151.
4 Le Corbusier, *The Radiant City,* p. 64.
5 Le Corbusier, *The Radiant City,* p. 191.
6 Le Corbusier, *The Radiant City,* p. 96.
7 Le Corbusier, *The Radiant City,* p. 64.
8 Le Corbusier, *The Radiant City,* p. 85.
9 Le Corbusier, *The Radiant City,* p. 152.
10 Le Corbusier, *The Radiant City,* p. 65.
11 Le Corbusier, *The Radiant City,* p. 68.
12 Wright, *The Living City,* p. 86.
13 Wright, *The Living City,* p. 125.
14 Howard and Osborn, *Garden Cities of To-morrow,* p. 48.
15 Howard and Osborn, *Garden Cities of To-morrow,* p. 48.
16 Howard and Osborn, *Garden Cities of To-morrow,* p. 48.
17 Howard and Osborn, *Garden Cities of To-morrow,* p. 48.
18 Howard and Osborn, *Garden Cities of To-morrow,* p. 53.
19 Howard and Osborn, *Garden Cities of To-morrow,* p. 53.
20 Howard and Osborn, *Garden Cities of To-morrow,* p. 79.
21 Howard and Osborn, *Garden Cities of To-morrow,* p. 55.
22 Howard and Osborn, *Garden Cities of To-morrow,* p. 85.
23 Howard and Osborn, *Garden Cities of To-morrow,* p. 86.
24 Howard and Osborn, *Garden Cities of To-morrow,* p. 127.
25 Howard and Osborn, *Garden Cities of To-morrow,* p. 146.
26 Howard and Osborn, *Garden Cities of To-morrow,* p. 142.
27 Howard and Osborn, *Garden Cities of To-morrow,* p. 156.
28 Howard and Osborn, *Garden Cities of To-morrow,* p. 156.
29 Howard and Osborn, *Garden Cities of To-morrow,* p. 45.
30 Howard and Osborn, *Garden Cities of To-morrow,* p. 54.
31 Howard and Osborn, *Garden Cities of To-morrow,* p. 54.
32 Howard and Osborn, *Garden Cities of To-morrow,* p. 98.
33 Le Corbusier, *The Radiant City,* p. 64.
34 Le Corbusier, *The Radiant City,* p. 149.
35 Le Corbusier, *The Radiant City,* p. 107.
36 Le Corbusier, *The Radiant City,* p. 106.
37 Le Corbusier, *The Radiant City,* p. 272.
38 Le Corbusier, *The Radiant City,* p. 272.
39 Le Corbusier, *The Radiant City,* p. 86.
40 Le Corbusier, *The Radiant City,* p. 13.
41 Le Corbusier, *The Radiant City,* p. 43.
42 Le Corbusier, *The Radiant City,* p. 115.
43 Le Corbusier, *The Radiant City,* p. 284.
44 Le Corbusier, *The Radiant City,* pp. 247, 293–294.
45 Le Corbusier, *The Radiant City,* p. 65.
46 Le Corbusier, *The Radiant City,* p. 163.
47 Le Corbusier, *The Radiant City,* p. 65.

128  *Leisure*

48  Le Corbusier, *The Radiant City*, p. 66.
49  Le Corbusier, *The Radiant City*, p. 66.
50  Le Corbusier, *The Radiant City*, p. 66.
51  Le Corbusier, *The Radiant City*, p. 65.
52  Le Corbusier, *The Radiant City*, p. 191.
53  Le Corbusier, *The Radiant City*, pp. 190–191.
54  Le Corbusier, *The Radiant City*, p. 68.
55  Le Corbusier, *The Radiant City*, p. 68.
56  Le Corbusier, *The Radiant City*, p. 68.
57  Le Corbusier, *The Radiant City*, p. 67.
58  Le Corbusier, *The Radiant City*, p. 67.
59  Le Corbusier, *The Radiant City*, p. 68.
60  Wright, *The Living City*, p. 9.
61  Wright, *The Living City*, p. 85.
62  Wright, *The Living City*, p. 217.
63  Wright, *The Living City*, p. 125.
64  Wright, *The Living City*, p. 217.
65  Wright, *The Living City*, p. 217.
66  Wright, *The Living City*, p. 125.
67  Wright, *The Living City*, p. 163.
68  Wright, *The Living City*, p. 176.
69  Wright, *The Living City*, p. 177.
70  Wright, *The Living City*, p. 178.
71  Wright, *The Living City*, p. 178.
72  Wright, *The Living City*, p. 178.
73  Wright, *The Living City*, p. 178.

## Bibliography

Howard, E., Osborn, F.J., 2001. Garden Cities of To-morrow, 11th print. ed. MIT Press, Cambridge.

Le Corbusier, 1964. The Radiant City: Elements of a Doctrine of Urbanism to be Used as the Basis of Our Machine-Age Civilization. The Orion Press, New York.

Wright, F.L., 1958. The Living City. Horizon Press, New York.

### Suggested Readings

Carr, E., 1999. Wilderness by Design: Landscape Architecture and the National Park Service. University of Nebraska Press, Lincoln.

Cranz, G., 1982. The Politics of Park Design. MIT Press, Cambridge.

Czerniak, J., Hargreaves, G., Harvard University (Eds.), 2007. Large Parks. Princeton Architectural Press in association with the Harvard University Graduate School of Design, New York; Cambridge.

Danks, S., 2010. Asphalt to Ecosystems: Design Ideas for Schoolyard Transformation. New Village Press, Oakland.

Dulles, F., 1965. A History of Recreation: America Learns to Play, 2nd ed. Appleton-Century-Crofts, New York.

Fishman, R., 1982. Urban Utopias in the Twentieth Century: Ebenezer Howard, Frank Lloyd Wright, and Le Corbusier, 1st MIT Press pbk. ed. MIT Press, Cambridge.

Low, S.M., Taplin, D., Scheld, S., 2005. Rethinking Urban Parks: Public Space and Cultural Diversity, 1st ed. University of Texas Press, Austin.

Olmsted, F.L., Sutton, S.B., 1997. Civilizing American Cities: Writings On City Landscapes, 1st Da Capo Press ed. Da Capo Press, New York.

Solomon, S.G., 2005. American Playgrounds: Revitalizing Community Space. University Press of New England, Hanover.

Souter-Brown, G., 2015. Landscape and Urban Design for Health and Well-Being: Using Healing, Sensory and Therapeutic Gardens. Routledge, Abingdon; Oxon.

Tate, A., 2015. Great City Parks, Second edition. ed. Routledge, Abingdon; Oxon; New York.

# 8 Freedom, Cooperation, and Authority

One of the most striking similarities between these three utopian projects is the ardency with which each writer believed that they were proposing a future of greater freedom for all people. Each proposal for greater freedom has much to do with the corresponding proposal for a reconstructed relationship between capital, labor, and land as discussed in Chapter 4. However, the content of the good life and the freedom central to each vision is radically different. These differences play out not only in the content of the freedoms themselves but also in the relationships between freedom, cooperation, and authority. Embedded within each relationship between freedom, cooperation, and authority, one also finds a duality which varies greatly across the three proposals – namely, the relationship between the individual and the collective. In the Garden City, freedom and authority are equally derived from cooperation. Howard imagines that the individual in the Garden City has freely chosen to be a member of a collective body. Authority provides the foundation for freedom in the Radiant City, but the freedom offered also justifies the fact that authority requires certain forms of cooperation. The collective body of the Radiant City takes precedence over any individual choices which, in Le Corbusier's imagination, would reduce the basic freedoms the city makes available to all. Broadacre City is organized around the proposal that household economic freedom allows for the uncoerced cooperation upon which the minimal authority needed for Wright's imagination of an ideal society is grounded. The individual in Broadacre City takes precedence over any form of collective body, but Wright clearly states that a healthy collective social body is the ultimate aim. It is worth noting that the writings by Marx, George, Bellamy, and Kropotkin which were examined in Chapter 2 are all centered on proposals for right relationships between freedom, cooperation, and authority as well.

Discussions about freedom, cooperation, and authority in utopia get right to the heart of the squeamishness about authoritarianism that underlies many of the prejudices against utopian thinking. This concern is certainly not unwarranted. Thomas More's proposal for utopia is deeply and troublingly authoritarian and relies on not only a strict social hierarchy but also slavery, as discussed in Chapter 1. However, the Garden City, the Radiant City, and Broadacre City – while perhaps not as perfectly classless as they were imagined by their

DOI: 10.4324/9781351053730-8

Freedom, Cooperation, and Authority 131

creators – do not contain the same brutal inequalities that More felt necessary to ground his vision. Though their visions and the equity within them are obviously open to challenge, each writer's stated intention is to make good lives available equally to all. It is also true that the 20th century certainly saw grave crimes against humanity committed by authoritarian states with the intention of creating a perfect society. While these actions by authoritarian governments are sometimes used to discredit utopian thinking, it would be anachronistic to use them to criticize the intentions of Howard, Le Corbusier, and Wright even if it may be a fair concern to draw forward in any evaluation of the potential outcomes of their ideas. It is worth remembering that Howard, Le Corbusier, and Wright had developed at least the significant core of their ideas prior to these atrocities which come so readily to mind for readers in the 21st century. All three of them, however, would have been aware of the brutality of the authoritarian rule of monarchies. Moreover, it is also worth considering that they were all responding directly to the many unjust and brutal impacts that industrial capitalism's near total control over society had on people.

Regarding these concerns about authoritarianism and utopia, the productive question is not, however, whether attempts to achieve utopia *could* result in authoritarian forms of control. History shows us that democratic states are not immune to authoritarian turns, so utopian thinking is not the only path to authoritarian abuses of power. The question with regard to utopia's relationship to authoritarianism is whether the link is either *certain* or *likely*, or at least more certain or more likely than any other vision of society. As stated in Chapter 1, the challenge of this book regarding utopian visions is whether we can achieve the benefits of any model without having to accept its drawbacks. In that vein, this chapter lays out the role of authority each writer thought necessary for their imagination of the good life characterized by the freedoms their proposal offered as well as the cooperation this relationship entailed. This discussion also gets to the heart of the role of landscapes as political media as presented in Chapter 2. Howard made use of existing land ownership rights to provide landscapes across which people have the capacity to cooperate more fully and more fruitfully. Le Corbusier stated that the ultimate logic behind the authority which drives the Radiant City is the provision of landscapes reflective of a new political organization of the benefits of industrial production. Wright imagined an intertwining of genuine democracy with landscapes of individual freedom because the landscapes he proposed allow for the development of individuality which, for him, is the foundation for genuine democracy.

## Cooperation, Freedom, and Authority in the Garden City

Howard consistently referred to the Garden City as an invention or an experiment and proposed that "in every feature of the experiment, it will be seen that it is not the area of rights which is contracted, but the area of choice which is enlarged."[1] He argued that in all progressive communities there will be found "societies and organizations that represent a far higher level of public spirit

132    *Freedom, Cooperation, and Authority*

and enterprise than that possessed or displayed by such communities in their collective capacity."[2] He saw the Garden City as one of these organizations on the forefront of developing a more cooperative and therefore more just and equitable society. He proposed that the Garden City would be implemented as pioneering pro-municipal work undertaken by "those who have not a merely pious opinion, but an effective belief in the economic, sanitary, and social advantages of common ownership of land."[3] While Howard imagined that these individuals would be advocating for positive changes at a national scale, he also imagined that they would be impatient with national political processes and be "impelled to give their views shape and form as soon as they can see their way to join with a sufficient number of kindred spirits."[4] While the cooperation inherent in commonly owned land is the critical foundation to the budgetary and functional proposal that Howard put forward, cooperation between people who share beliefs in progress and equity – including the original investors willing to put money into the initial land purchase for only a charitable rate of return – precedes the cooperative ownership and management of land. It should be noted, however, that for all Howard's emphasis on the common ownership of land as the way forward, he still relied on existing laws regarding property rights associated with owning land and does not propose to change the legal framework of land, only the ownership of land within that framework. Howard was merely proposing that within that existing framework of land rights, there is a way to voluntarily cooperate which would lead to different results. In fact, it is specifically the extensive set of rights that comes with the ownership of land that, for instance, allows the corporate body of the Garden City to take such actions as limiting the number of certain kinds of shops within the city – something a publicly chartered town could not do – in order to balance the needs of residents with the needs of shop owners.

### Cooperation Is the Foundation of Freedom

At the most fundamental level, the common ownership of land allows for cooperation in the Garden City because it removes the barrier of competition over the use of and benefit from land. This cooperation in turn grounds the freedoms that are the intent of Howard's Garden City model. Because no one person can individually benefit from the sale of land or its conversion to another use, the population as a whole is freed from competition. While the phrasing, 'freed from competition,' may strike the reader as a concerning instance of newspeak at first take, pragmatic examples of this freedom may mitigate that concern. To be freed from competition regarding the use of land as individuals in a municipal body is to be freed from the speculative increases in property value which led to extreme crowding in Victorian cities and the construction of slums as a rational solution to maximizing profit for landowners at the expense of tenants. The collective ownership of land also means that no political decisions regarding land use within the Garden City could benefit any one person – politician, friend, or family – by increasing the value of their

Freedom, Cooperation, and Authority 133

land either directly or indirectly. Similarly, the denial of selling land for private profit underlies and is requisite to the freedom to participate in the social and economic life of the industrial city while also enjoying the benefits of intimate experiences of the natural world close at hand that was central to the Garden City. Not only could people not sell or lease residential land for profit, but nobody could sell the open land which the community relied on for recreation and food production which was within easy reach of industrial land either – preserving it for the use of the people in the Garden City as was described in Chapter 7 on leisure and Chapter 6 on food and agriculture. Arguing that the residents of the Garden City would not allow the city's open land to be built upon, Howard stated that the health and beauty of the town would be protected because the land is "not in the hands of private individuals: it is in the hands of the people: and is to be administered, not in the supposed interests of the few, but in the real interests of the whole community."[5]

The second major area of freedom which cooperation in the Garden City provides is the freedom to experiment with social form by way of public investment in infrastructure and other potential public goods. Howard did not draw a firm line between the appropriate spheres for municipal and private action in the Garden City. In fact, he explicitly left the issue open to experimentation by the residents themselves through a cooperative political process. Whether such things as water systems are private or municipal, Howard argued would ultimately be "measured simply by the willingness of the tenants to pay rate-rents, and will grow in proportion as municipal work is done efficiently and honestly, or decline as it is done dishonestly or inefficiently."[6] This willingness to pay rate-rent, Howard's proposal for a combined payment which covers both rent and taxes, is expressed by the residents largely through the election of officers to the Central Council and to the departments which are in control of the municipal utilities and other shared actions.

### *Authority Is Derived from Cooperation*

The authority for the operations of the Garden City derives from two things; first the fact that it is privately incorporated and not a true public municipal government, and second that it is organized based on common land ownership. Residents hold shares in the corporation as well as voting rights with regard to its administration. Typical public bodies' ability to raise taxes and spend revenue was constrained by Acts of Parliament and therefore they were not able to undertake the same kinds of experiments with infrastructure and social benefits nor were they able to limit individual action to the same degree. By freely joining the Garden City, and also because they do not freehold property individually and so cannot appeal to property rights law at a national level, people agree to give the corporation this level of authority and the Garden City's Central Council could therefore "exercise on behalf of the people those wider rights, powers and privileges which are enjoyed by landlords under the common law" because "the private owner of land can do with his land and with

134 *Freedom, Cooperation, and Authority*

the revenue he derives from it what he pleases so long as he is not a nuisance to his neighbor."[7] The ways in which this authority is organized by Howard is particularly telling regarding his vision for the town. The constitution of the Garden City is to be

> modelled upon that of a large and well-appointed business, which is divided into various departments, each department being expected to justify its own continued existence – its officers being selected, not so much for their knowledge of the business generally as for their special fitness for the work of the department.[8]

The Board of Management of the Garden City consists of a Central Council and the departments. Rather than voting for political leadership which appoints directors of the technical services and departments of the city, the voting members of the Garden City would select the people to run particular departments based on their perceived ability and expertise within that specific area of work. The Central Council is comprised of the Chairmen and Vice-Chairmen of three departments which are voted for directly by the residents of the Garden City. The Garden City's functions are organized into three departments: public control, engineering, and social purposes – offering insight into Howard's imagination of the city as a technical and scientific problem. He opens his chapter on the administration of the Garden City with a long quote from Albert Shaw's 1895 book *Municipal Government in Great Britain* in which Shaw claimed that

> the so-called problems of the modern city are but the various phases of the one main question: How can the environment be most perfectly adapted to the welfare of urban populations? And science can meet and answer every one of these problems.[9]

The public control department handles issues of finance, law, assessment, leases, and inspection. The engineering department oversees transportation systems including roads, public buildings other than schools, open spaces and parks, power, lighting, and all things having to do with water. The social purposes department manages education, libraries, baths and wash-houses, music, and recreation. There are three areas for which the Central Council collectively maintains responsibility: the general plan of the estate including the preservation of the open space and agricultural lands, "the amount of money voted to each of the various spending departments," and oversight of the departments necessary to maintain "a general unity and harmony, but no more."[10] The authority to do all these things is dependent on the cooperation of people who freely join the Garden City thereby accepting its organization and procedures for collective decision making, as well as the cooperative model of land ownership. It is this, Howard claimed, which allows the Garden City model to bring about "the long-sought-for means of reconciliation between order and freedom."[11]

### The Individual Is a Free Member of the Collective

Howard opened his chapter titled 'Some Difficulties Considered' with a response to some of the conceptual objections he imagined being raised against the Garden City as an idea, beginning with a long quotation from an unattributed 1894 article published in the *Daily Chronicle*. From this article he quoted that

> the future probably lies with those who, instead of pitting against one another, Socialism and Individualism, will seek to realize a true, vital, organic conception of Society and of the State in which both Individualism and Socialism will have their proper share.[12]

He stated that the reason the majority of previous social experiments had failed was that they assumed that human nature was best fit to either one or the other. Howard, on the other hand, proposed that the ideal is a mediated position between the two. He used the analogy of the orchestra and stated that it relies on both joint and individual practice. "That society," he wrote, "will prove the most healthy and vigorous where the freest and fullest opportunities are afforded alike for individual and for combined effort."[13] He expanded on this concept later in his book when he wrote that his proposal bound both individualistic and socialistic reform ideas "with a thread of practicality" – and that by individualistic he meant "a society in which there is fuller and freer opportunity for its members to do and to produce what they will, and to form free associations" and by socialistic "a condition of life in which the well-being of the community is safeguarded, and in which the collective spirit is manifested by a wide extension of the area of municipal benefit."[14] It is important to note that one of the things that maintained the freedom of the members of the society at large in his model is their eventual ability to join the garden city of their choosing. While he imagined that the success of the Garden City idea would eventually depopulate London as people left en masse to join garden cities across the country, he did not imagine that the garden cities from which they would have to choose would be uniform in character. While Howard was convinced that the right answer to the proper scope of municipal governance was neither fully individualistic nor fully socialistic, where the answer rested in the middle – he felt could – "only to be gained by experiment" and would "differ in different communities and at different periods."[15]

## Authority, Freedom, and Cooperation in the Radiant City

Of the three projects we are concerned with in this book, Le Corbusier's proposal places by far the most emphasis on authority. He stated on the title page of the book that his work was dedicated to AUTHORITY. However, this dedication is complicated by other statements such as his declaration that "the cornerstone of all modern urbanization is absolute respect for the freedom of the individual."[16] The simple narrative of Le Corbusier's alignment with

136    *Freedom, Cooperation, and Authority*

authoritarianism is also complicated by a deep examination of the sources of that authority and how it is grounded. A more nuanced examination of the freedoms that he proposed people should hold as basic rights, as well as a similarly nuanced examination of the grounding of the authority to which he dedicated his volume, is warranted before considering whether or not the Radiant City is necessarily authoritarian. The Radiant City relies heavily on the production of a plan – not only for the city, but for industrial production as will be discussed. For Le Corbusier, authority did not make the plan but followed it. This plan was generated through the resolution of technical problems and motivated by the basic freedoms, among others, that the Radiant City offered. Le Corbusier supported his plan with an appeal to nature as well as to what he referred to as a natural hierarchy grounded in trade syndicates. Only once the plan was realized could the freedoms Le Corbusier proposed be had. Cooperation, in particular limiting industrial production to useful goods, was to be organized by authority. For Le Corbusier, broad individual liberty was subservient to collective liberty which allows individuals to have specific freedoms and basic rights.

### *Authority and Where It Comes from*

While Le Corbusier emphasized the role of authority throughout his book, he made it clear that "authority will follow the plan, not precede it."[17] He imagined the plan to be the application of modern building techniques to solve biological problems such as providing exact air, open public space for the health of the body, and serene private space for the health of the mind. Le Corbusier proposed that a despot is needed to realize the promise of what he referred to as the second machine age. However, he stated that "the despot is not a man. The despot is the *Plan*. The *correct, realistic, exact* plan, the one that will provide your solution once the problem has been posited clearly, in its entirety, in its indispensable harmony."[18] The plan, he proposed, would not be produced in political offices or based on the input from the electorate. He decried both the weakness of the current authorities and "democratic inertia."[19] Rather it was to be produced by "serene and lucid minds" and take account of human truths as opposed to current regulations and laws. Le Corbusier stated that this plan, once produced, would plead its own cause and reply to any objections as well as overcome private interests, customs, and regulations and "create its own authority."[20] In his conclusion, he affirmed "that it is on the 'Plan' that the Authority we need will be founded."[21] While the plan was not put together with public processes that we expect today, it was intended to benefit all people. "Total city-planning for the good and dignity of all" he wrote.[22] Whether or not readers of this book decide that Le Corbusier's vision of the Radiant City is authoritarian, it is unavoidably paternalistic – something he in fact claimed directly in several places throughout his text.

The reason that Le Corbusier was confident that the plan would produce good outcomes for all people was that it would be based on biological needs,

*Freedom, Cooperation, and Authority* 137

which for Le Corbusier also included needs of the mind. He wrote that the plan was "*a biological creation destined for human beings and capable of realization by modern techniques.*"[23] Throughout his work, he referred back to the needs of bodies and minds as a basis for particular outcomes – whether it is the landscapes for recreation or the size and equipment of dwelling units. Of course, supreme authority based on a plan drawn up by technicians which takes into account facts about the physical, mental, and emotional needs of people without their input provides an easy target for accusations of authoritarianism since, of course, people have different bodies, different minds, and different emotional needs. However, it would be an interesting exercise for anyone making this claim to go through the facts of bodies and minds that Le Corbusier draws on and challenge each of them to see what opportunities for variation of needs are, or are not, allowed for within the basics he presents. For instance, his very narrow and particular definition of exact air may be an easy thing with which to find fault, but can anyone argue against planning cities and designing building so that, for instance, everyone can breathe clean air throughout their daily lives?

Le Corbusier's imagination of how authority is held within society, and by whom, is also of interest. He argued that a natural hierarchy based on trades would result in a person or persons holding supreme authority in society. While he acknowledged that it may "entail the most violent struggles," Le Corbusier proposed that this natural hierarchy would develop first within each of the trades which would then nominate a qualified deputy to join an inter-union conference.[24] The very real question of who is excluded from these trades and therefore from positions of higher authority within society is not addressed by Le Corbusier. At this level, "the main problems of economic interdependence are hammered out and a state of balance achieved."[25] A supreme authority which will concentrate on the higher purposes of the country – represented as multiple dots not a singular figure in his diagram – is nominated from within this conference. It is critical to note that in the triangular diagram Le Corbusier used to illustrate this natural hierarchy with the supreme authority on the top and the trades at the base, information flows from the supreme authority down to the trades at the base but control runs the opposite way – from the trades which form the base of the hierarchy up to the supreme authority at the apex.

### Cooperation Required by Authority

Le Corbusier intended that the plan which founded authority and which authority implemented would be much more than the physical layout of the Radiant city. The plan which was the foundation of his proposal would be heavily dependent on not only a program of constructing buildings and landscapes which make up the physicality of the Radiant City but also a program for machine production which would reduce the number of hours spent in industrial work. While the cooperation that Le Corbusier imagined is not the same kind of self-selected cooperation that Howard imagined as the basis of the Garden City, cooperative work toward shared ends is still a central

138    *Freedom, Cooperation, and Authority*

component of the Radiant City. Le Corbusier ranted throughout his book against useless consumer goods and the wasted time to produce them. "It is recognized," he wrote, "that industry is submerging us with products that are irrelevant to our happiness."[26] Not only was producing what he referred to as useless consumer goods a source of unnecessary industrial labor, but so were all the types of effort that go into the competition to sell them – travelling salesmen, advertising, and exhibitions for example. Replacing these goods with useful consumer goods would require "a program for *the production of useful consumer goods*" which would redirect industry

> onto a path towards its true aims; with providing work for all and guaranteeing every man his daily hours of freedom; and with providing physical sites and quarters designed to permit the man of today to enjoy this new freedom without constraint.[27]

No longer would society allow "the masses to manufacture no matter what, *for their own misfortune*" in the Radiant City.[28] In contrast to the current modes of production in which Le Corbusier felt that "there is no harmony at all," this redirection of production toward only things that are necessary, along with the intensification of machine production, is what would allow people to contribute no more than four hours working to provide "properly equipped cities, new housing, and the countryside (at last!) accessible to the wind of spiritual change that we have taken as the standard of all our efforts."[29] When population density allowed for the expansion of communal services which Le Corbusier imagined to be part of daily life in the Radiant City, such as cooking and laundry, to everyone, "then genuine freedom can be achieved in the heart of family life, freedom instead of domestic slavery."[30] The direct result of this reduction in industrial effort and the reduction in drudgery of housework is the free time for leisure which is the basis for the landscapes and built form of the Radiant City.

### Authority and Cooperation Are Justified by the Freedom They Make Possible

The primary freedoms that Le Corbusier sought to gain for humanity are what he referred to throughout his book as basic pleasures. "Modern techniques (steel, reinforced concrete, etc.)," he wrote, "have brought *vast new measures of freedom to the city dweller; we may call them the 'basic pleasures.'*"[31] Of course, these construction techniques could only bring this freedom and these basic pleasures to people if the land was put to common use and the Radiant City could be built. Le Corbusier described city life of the time as "a glimpse of purgatory" with its noise and dust and soot, its traffic at a standstill, its residential areas with their "torrid canyons of summer heat," and the claustrophobia of looking out one's windows to only ever see other windows with other people looking out of them back at you.[32] He asked, "Where is the freedom here?"[33] In contrast, he proposed that people should have the freedom "to live, to laugh, to be master in one's own home, to open one's eyes to the light of day, to the light of the sun, to look out on green leaves and blue sky."[34] He referred to the basic pleasures – for people in cities as well as in farms – throughout the book, in slightly different formulations but always as some variation on "sun in the house, sky through their windows, trees to look at as soon as they step outside."[35]

However, one can see in his attack on suburbs, which he often conflated with Howard's Garden City, that these basic freedoms were not sufficient unto themselves. The suburbs offered sun, sky, and trees but, he observed, in order to access them people needed to be "whisked out of the city on steel rails."[36] While they had little houses surrounded by greenery awaiting them, they were socially isolated in evenings and days off and so would, according to Le Corbusier, "still tick off the hours without living and without laughter" unless they chose to spend their free time getting back on the train to access the social life of the city. One has to wonder if Howard, looking at life in suburbs that were built without the social and economic integration achieved through the common ownership of land central to his Garden City proposal would not have agreed.

Next to the basic freedoms of sun, sky, and trees, Le Corbusier sought to secure for people the freedom to do meaningful, self-chosen work by which he does not mean merely that everyone gets to select the paying job that they would most prefer. Le Corbusier tied the lack of this freedom directly to the private ownership of land. "The impossibility of doing the kind of work that makes men free, and that makes creative enthusiasm, civic trust and collective action practicable" was founded on the laws which guard private property.[37] These laws, he proposed, maintain a city such that people led a "robot-like existence every day of the year and every day of their lives."[38] By reorganizing the city for efficiency and incorporating the benefits of machine production for all of society not just the few capitalists, he proposed that what we call work now would become "five hours per day that must of necessity be given over to the nourishment and maintenance of the social body as a sort of normal tax on our time."[39] This would leave time for self-directed engagement with creative and productive work whether it was a book, a body of scientific discovery, or fine cabinetry. This he described as "true work, the work of the machine civilization" in which people "have reconquered their freedom."[40] He called this individual liberty the "unalterable, indisputable, essential foundation, the only true basis for any attempt at social organization."[41]

### Collective and Individual Freedom

While Le Corbusier claimed that individual freedom was the foundation for all modern urbanization, this individual freedom was in turn for him dependent on collective order. He captioned an image of a contemporary city with skyscrapers, with "Everything here is paradox and disorder: individual liberty destroying collective liberty. Lack of discipline."[42] His belief that a communal order is necessary to individual freedom is repeated often throughout his book. For instance, following a description of the role of authority he wrote that

## 140  *Freedom, Cooperation, and Authority*

"when the collective functions of the urban community have been organized, then there will be individual liberty for all. Each man will live in an ordered relation to the whole."[43] It is not only the actions and choices of individuals taken unto themselves that concerned him. He was also concerned with the individual's freedom to participate in collective bodies. Though one could argue with the accuracy with which he impugns Howard's theory, it is in this sense that he claims that the garden city is "an attack on freedom" which leads to "an enslaved individualism" and the "sterile isolation of the individual" as well as the "destruction of the social spirit, the downfall of the collective forces" and the "annihilation of the collective will."[44] The reader can also see this relationship between the individual and the collective noted above with regard to useless and useful consumer goods. The collective freedom necessary for individuals to enjoy the basic freedoms of sun, sky, and trees trumps the individual freedom to manufacture, sell, or buy whatever consumer goods they see fit just as the right to organize landscapes and their use for the collective good trumps the right to personally profit from land.

## Freedom, Cooperation, and Authority in the Broadacre City

The foundational principle of Broadacre City is that the financial autonomy of households made possible by an equal distribution of land to all people would allow them the option to be self-sufficient. This distribution of access to land also allows people to be free of rent to landlords, reinforcing their freedom from the need to sell their labor to employers on the employers' terms. Wright did not imagine, however, that Broadacre City would be a society of isolated individuals or households. The freedoms it offered were, in Wright's mind, the foundations for genuine cooperation specifically because the cooperation would not be coerced. While he did not specifically address the mechanism of authority for the infrastructure that Broadacre City relies on, he made it clear that he felt planning the new city was a necessity. He also did not do away with all forms of governance and specifically proposed that some county seats remain in place functionally and physically, even if he felt that their number could be dramatically reduced. While the individual and their freedom from coercion was the prime motivating principle of Broadacre City, an authentic democracy was Wright's ultimate goal and the role of the individual in this collective body was critically important to his imagination of human flourishing.

### *Freedom Leads to Cooperation*

Under a heading "Democracy: Gospel of Individuality," Wright stated that only by desiring "deeply to live on harmonious terms with Man and Nature…can the democratic spirit of man, individual, rise out of the confusion of communal life in the city to a creative civilization on the ground."[45] He continued by equating the civilization of man and ground, which he called organic agronomy, with

*Freedom, Cooperation, and Authority* 141

democracy and stated that if people "live in the free city of democracy" they would "not fail to make communal life richer for all the world."[46] The contrast Wright drew between the confusion of communal life in the city and creative civilization on the ground brings forward the conceptual relationship between his proposed redistribution of land, the freedom that this offered, and a healthy and democratic society. While his arguments for decentralization are often at the forefront of discussions of Broadacre City, reintegration was just as critical to his vision of a healthy society. Countering the imperative of centralized cities – whether driven to centralization by kings, capital, or machines – which compelled people to "revolve as closely as possible around an exalted common center," Wright proposed a decentralization of all aspects of the city followed closely by a reintegration of life centered around individuality.[47] He defined this reintegration in many ways, but one which emphasized the cooperative aspect is his expectation that there would be "many free units developing strength as they learn to function and grow together in adequate space, mutual freedom a reality."[48] Wright's imagination of changes to factory production illustrate this concept of reintegration. Large factories, he proposed, would also separate into smaller units driven by the need to move closer to workers who live in a more disparate urban pattern. This is in contrast to the then-current factories with their "exaggeration of size due to overcentralization and the imprisoning of factory workers in 'housing.'"[49] The reintegration he referred to was industrial production reintegrating with the lives of people in opposition to people having to center their lives around industrial employment.

The cooperation Wright imagined would take place once people were not beholden to capital for their sustenance was well expressed in his imagination of the industrial production of houses in particular. Writing about what would become of the poor in Broadacre City, after they are given subsidized transportation from the city to their newfound freedom on their own land, he argued that as they sustain themselves with their chosen combination of growing their own food and some level of employment in agriculture, craft, or industry they would also slowly be able to build their own home which would "do no outrage to the landscape but ... be roomy and cheap enough for the consumer."[50] Since people would not be beholden to large manufacturers for wages and the profit from industry would no longer go "to the big producer to increase production" such that "quantity soon wipes out quality," the cost savings of modern mass production would benefit the workers with good pay for reasonable work as well as with quality goods at affordable prices.[51] The house would be equipped with modern appliances and accompanied by outbuildings which would stand on the family's land "among shade trees, fruit trees, berry bushes, vegetables and flowers in the garden."[52] This is all the result of the cooperation made possible by the freedom grounded in owning land and the resulting potential for self-sufficiency. "Under these better, more co-operative conditions," he wrote, "machinery could produce a good house for him more economically than his automobile."[53]

142    *Freedom, Cooperation, and Authority*

### Authority Derived from Freedom and Cooperation

Authority and freedom within Wright's proposal are also worth considering with a bit more nuance, especially for those who equate his proposal with exurban development. While his proposal does spread across the countryside, it is – as he imagines it – far from the speculative and unproductive sprawl that currently mars so much land. Just as Le Corbusier's emphasis on authority was counterbalanced by a clear commitment to freedoms, Wright's emphasis on freedom is counterbalanced by a framework of planning and concerted action. Wright clearly felt that the nation should be able to organize itself for peace to the degree it had for war. In fact, he claimed that because the forces of peace had "never been truly organized…the freedom guaranteed by the Constitution of the USA has not only never been achieved but seldom understood."[54] The organization he proposed was specifically focused on not only redistributing the ownership of land to achieve equality and give people true freedom, but also on planning the new city. "What," he asks, "will the nation that is an organic comprehensive new city be like if we would thus design and build it instead of letting it, as now, haphazard, build itself?"[55] While he grounded his proposal for the new city on decentralization, he was not proposing that this decentralized growth be left without coordination – noting that the free city of decentralization was already building itself but that it was happening "without our help or any wise planning."[56] For Wright, "*organic reintegration* must follow decentralization" and "planning is the factor that will develop the new city and keep the city economical and beautiful."[57] Similarly, after discussing the decentralization of factories in Broadacre City, Wright proposed that offices and office districts will follow suit to be close to the factories they support. He observed that this movement had already started and then asked "Why not accomplish this by good planning rather than let it happen haphazard? Efficient conservation of time and energy by the worker, the manufacturer and the farmer (all as co-operating citizens) will benefit the producer and consumer alike."[58]

His disdain for centralizing forces of kings, socialism, and capital does not mean that he sees no role for government in Broadacre City, as is clear in his maintenance of the political and spatial organization of county seats. He proposed some county seats would continue given their current placement at existing transportation intersections. These county seats with "offices for public officialism, petty or major" would include things like police stations, fire stations, and district courts of law.[59] Given the increased efficiency of transportation and the reduced load on the court system due to the simplifications of law resulting from a reduction in disputes over land and money, he proposed that half to two-thirds of the county seats could be demolished and replaced with grass and trees. His imagination of these county seats is telling of his imagination of the role that government would serve. Governmental offices such as were still needed would not "be found in braggadocio buildings, the exaggerations now customary, because such official functions are really not grand but merely *utilitarian*."[60]

Wright also relied on large systems of infrastructure which would require significant authority to implement. Broadacre city could only function as he imagined with a highly developed and efficient transportation system ranging from local roads, along which those passing by could procure the goods of daily life from roadside farmstands and community centers, to a network of highways that span the country with high-speed options for freight and personal travel. He proposed that the network of railway rights-of-way be converted to accommodate truck and bus lanes. Further clarifying that Wright saw significant areas for collaborative action requiring the authority to plan, these converted rights-of-way would "naturally enough...belong to the people."[61] The transportation system was not the only thing that Wright felt would be publicly owned. He also proposed that the apartment towers that will exist in Broadacre city for those who chose not to live on their own land – those "untrained urbanites desiring to enjoy the beauty of the country but yet unable to participate in creating or operating it" – would be not only cooperative apartment houses, but semi-public buildings which he called out as county buildings.[62]

Wright specifically stated that power would no longer be "in the control of vicarious officialism at public expense."[63] In contrast with "strong-arm enforcements of authority" used by the elites in society to maintain the status quo at the time, Wright proposed that creative artists are the natural leaders of society who would lead by example.[64] He proposed that such individuals are "by nature (and by office) the qualified leader in any society, natural, native interpreter of the visible forms of any social order in or under which we choose to live."[65] Wright described this leader toward a native culture as a way-shower and relied on the expectation that people will rationally see what was in their best interests and follow this lead. It should be noted that Wright was not referring to people whose profession is in the fine arts exclusively. Rather, he thought of artists as people who create out of a deep and embedded life with soil and/or craft and solve daily problems organically and with beauty. He wrote in his forward that the book was "written in firm belief that true human culture has a healthy sense of the beautiful as its life-of-the-soul: an aesthetic organic, as *of* life itself, not *on* it; nobly relating man to his environment."[66] The artist in Wright's imagination would be driven by interior discipline and the pursuit of ideals in their own home and on their own ground. This ability of the artist to pursue such ideals is the link Wright saw between the household ownership of land and a healthy democracy.

### *Individual Dominant Concern but Aim Is Healthy Collective Body*

Wright's distinction between individualism and individuality offers an insight into his understanding of the relationship between the individual and the collective. He referred to individualism as "cowardly selfishness" and "mere personality."[67] He disdained the 'rugged individualism' of the captains of industry and the vicarious power by which they operate what he referred to as plutocratic capitalism. Individualism, for Wright, was characteristic of centralized urban

144    *Freedom, Cooperation, and Authority*

life in which the citizen had become "a broker of profit-system ideas, a vendor of gadgetry, a salesman dealing for profit in human exaggeration. A speculator in frailties…an avid spectator" and a "puller of levers, pusher of the buttons of vicarious power."[68] Illustrating the unanimity and position of people in the modern city, he captioned an image of a city shrouded in smoke through which one can just make out buildings and the occasional skyscraper with an instruction to the reader to "find the citizen."[69]

Individuality, on the other hand, was not only Wright's ideal for human life but also for him the foundation of democracy. He equated individuality with the character that develops from the organic engagement of daily life in coordinating with good ground. He claimed that creative ability is the first concern of democratic individuality and that "conversely, Individuality must ever be the concern and success of creative ability."[70] This individuality, equated with organic democracy, was a genuine form of self-expression and for Wright synonymous with character. This self-expression is not a vapid and flamboyant display of personality – which is his imagination of individualism – but rather a genuine expression of a self that is organically grounded in the authentic and free self-direction of daily life. It is this individuality – the development of internal character based on organic, free choices allowed by the land distribution in Broadacre City – that allows for the society to be healthy in Wright's imagination. The nation would be indestructible, he wrote, because each citizen would be a "true exponent of a man's true relationship to his fellow-men because he *is* his fellow-man."[71] The entire citizenry of Broadacre City, he proposed, would be committed to ensuring for all the freedom they personally value highly and "out of independence such as his a new ideal of man emerges. He co-operates because it is for him to say either 'Yes' or 'No' and say so *as his own conscience dictates!*"[72]

## Conclusion

Each writer proposed a utopian vision of a social and built form that reinforced visions of particular kinds of freedom. These freedoms, in turn, held particular relationships to cooperation and authority. It is in particular the role of authority in these proposals but also the preservation of some freedoms at the expense of others which leads to concerns about abuses of authority and the process by which these trade-offs are made. However, we must remember that each writer was responding to a pervasive and deep lack of freedom in the cities of capitalist industrial society around them as well as what they saw as an unjustified authoritative role in society held by those who controlled capital and land at the expense of the majority. Each one, though in different ways, saw that the society in which they lived was organized in a way that precluded human flourishing and individual autonomy. All three saw that people in cities were restricted to lives that denied them ready access to clean air, open space, and experiences in the natural world on a regular basis. All three saw people spending their lives in frustration and poverty as they worked long hours at

*Freedom, Cooperation, and Authority* 145

dangerous jobs only to enrich others who did not work. All three saw an organization of industrial society around them – in both social and physical form – that was unjust. In response, each one proposed what they thought would be a resolution to those problems. The question for the reader is whether the worlds these three proposed – including the relationship between freedom, cooperation, and authority inherent to each – is better in some way than the world they see around them today. A subsequent question is how might the visions of Howard, Le Corbusier, and Wright be improved upon and what pieces could or should be implemented in whole or in part. The next chapter will take this question up directly following a discussion of three more concepts which are pertinent to both the visions this book examines and questions about progress toward human flourishing today – namely nature, history, and agency.

## Notes

1 Howard and Osborn, *Garden Cities of To-morrow*, p. 56.
2 Howard and Osborn, *Garden Cities of To-morrow*, p. 104.
3 Howard and Osborn, *Garden Cities of To-morrow*, p. 106.
4 Howard and Osborn, *Garden Cities of To-morrow*, p. 106.
5 Howard and Osborn, *Garden Cities of To-morrow*, p. 140.
6 Howard and Osborn, *Garden Cities of To-morrow*, p. 91.
7 Howard and Osborn, *Garden Cities of To-morrow*, p. 92.
8 Howard and Osborn, *Garden Cities of To-morrow*, p. 92.
9 Howard and Osborn, *Garden Cities of To-morrow*, p. 89.
10 Howard and Osborn, *Garden Cities of To-morrow*, p. 93.
11 Howard and Osborn, *Garden Cities of To-morrow*, p. 151.
12 Howard and Osborn, *Garden Cities of To-morrow*, p. 112.
13 Howard and Osborn, *Garden Cities of To-morrow*, p. 114.
14 Howard and Osborn, *Garden Cities of To-morrow*, p. 131.
15 Howard and Osborn, *Garden Cities of To-morrow*, p. 90.
16 Le Corbusier, *The Radiant City*, p. 9.
17 Le Corbusier, *The Radiant City*, p. 154.
18 Le Corbusier, *The Radiant City*, p. 154.
19 Le Corbusier, *The Radiant City*, p. 249.
20 Le Corbusier, *The Radiant City*, p. 154.
21 Le Corbusier, *The Radiant City*, p. 342.
22 Le Corbusier, *The Radiant City*, p. 343.
23 Le Corbusier, *The Radiant City*, p. 154.
24 Le Corbusier, *The Radiant City*, p. 192.
25 Le Corbusier, *The Radiant City*, p. 192.
26 Le Corbusier, *The Radiant City*, p. 68.
27 Le Corbusier, *The Radiant City*, p. 69.
28 Le Corbusier, *The Radiant City*, p. 104.
29 Le Corbusier, *The Radiant City*, p. 177.
30 Le Corbusier, *The Radiant City*, p. 38.
31 Le Corbusier, *The Radiant City*, p. 272.
32 Le Corbusier, *The Radiant City*, p. 91.

146  *Freedom, Cooperation, and Authority*

33  Le Corbusier, *The Radiant City*, p. 91.
34  Le Corbusier, *The Radiant City*, p. 91.
35  Le Corbusier, *The Radiant City*, p. 86.
36  Le Corbusier, *The Radiant City*, p. 92.
37  Le Corbusier, *The Radiant City*, p. 10.
38  Le Corbusier, *The Radiant City*, p. 67.
39  Le Corbusier, *The Radiant City*, p. 67.
40  Le Corbusier, *The Radiant City*, p. 68.
41  Le Corbusier, *The Radiant City*, p. 90.
42  Le Corbusier, *The Radiant City*, p. 129.
43  Le Corbusier, *The Radiant City*, p. 152.
44  L Le Corbusier, *The Radiant City*, p. 38.
45  Wright, *The Living City*, p. 25.
46  Wright, *The Living City*, p. 25.
47  Wright, *The Living City*, p. 83.
48  Wright, *The Living City*, p. 83.
49  Wright, *The Living City*, p. 165.
50  Wright, *The Living City*, p. 149.
51  Wright, *The Living City*, p. 149.
52  Wright, *The Living City*, p. 152.
53  Wright, *The Living City*, p. 152.
54  Wright, *The Living City*, p. 131.
55  Wright, *The Living City*, p. 132.
56  Wright, *The Living City*, p. 137.
57  Wright, *The Living City*, p. 137.
58  Wright, *The Living City*, p. 165.
59  Wright, *The Living City*, p. 165.
60  Wright, *The Living City*, p. 166.
61  Wright, *The Living City*, p. 114.
62  Wright, *The Living City*, pp. 122–124.
63  Wright, *The Living City*, p. 216.
64  Wright, *The Living City*, p. 145.
65  Wright, *The Living City*, p. 145.
66  Wright, *The Living City*, p. 9.
67  Wright, *The Living City*, pp. 46–47.
68  Wright, *The Living City*, p. 17.
69  Wright, *The Living City*, p. 30.
70  Wright, *The Living City*, p. 46.
71  Wright, *The Living City*, p. 208.
72  Wright, *The Living City*, p. 214.

# Bibliography

Howard, E., Osborn, F.J., 2001. Garden Cities of To-morrow, 11th Print. ed. MIT Press, Cambridge.

Le Corbusier, 1964. The Radiant City: Elements of a Doctrine of Urbanism to be Used as the Basis of Our Machine-Age Civilization. The Orion Press, New York.

Wright, F.L., 1958. The Living City. Horizon Press, New York.

## Suggested Readings

Agamben, G., 2017. The Omnibus Homo Sacer, Meridian, Crossing Aesthetics. Stanford University Press, Stanford.

Arendt, H., Kohn, J., 2005. The Promise of Politics. Schoken Books, New York.

Fishman, R., 1982. Urban Utopias in the Twentieth Century: Ebenezer Howard, Frank Lloyd Wright, and Le Corbusier, 1st MIT Press pbk. ed. MIT Press, Cambridge.

Mitchell, D., 2003. The Right to the City: Social Justice and the Fight for Public Space. Guilford Press, New York.

Ostrom, E., 2015. Governing the Commons: The Evolution of Institutions for Collective Action, Canto Classics. Cambridge University Press, Cambridge.

Rawls, J., Kelly, E., 2001. Justice as Fairness: A Restatement. Harvard University Press, Cambridge.

Rousseau, J.-J., Cole, G.D.H., 2005. The Social Contract, A Discourse on the Origin of Inequality, and A Discourse on Political Economy. Digireads.com Publishing, Stilwell.

Sen, A., 2001. Development as Freedom, 1st ed., 6th Print ed. Borzoi Book. Alfred A. Knopf, New York.

Shiva, V., 2015. Earth Democracy: Justice, Sustainability, and Peace. North Atlantic Books, Berkeley.

# 9 History, Nature, Agency; and So, What Next?

In response to the increased technological capacities of society alongside the highly visible and accelerating inequality between people, Howard, Le Corbusier, and Wright all saw their proposals for a reorganization of landscapes and cities as well as the social and political relationships they embodied as the rational next stage in human civilization. All three foresaw a better and more just way to organize industrial and agricultural work and distribute its benefits – including newfound time and space for leisure – and based their proposals on a redistribution of access to land that stridently opposed the foundational principles of capitalism and private profit from land. All three portrayed their imagined societies as inevitable or nearly inevitable given where they understood themselves within history. Each, however, made different claims about what was natural – in particular, what was natural to a thriving human life. In addition, each of them imagined agency located differently in the society they foresaw as a resolution to the conundrum of poverty in the face of progress, and in particular the location of agency as it controlled land. Each location of the agency responsible for their vision is closely aligned with implementing their imagination of human thriving, which is tied in turn to how each understood human nature.

If we are to take the Garden City, the Radiant City, and Broadacre City as more than interesting concepts to be read in passing as we survey the history of ideas about cities and landscapes, and more specifically if we are to take up the challenge for ourselves of proposing cities and landscapes which contribute to societies which are more just – then we too must ponder the same questions. What historical processes are we in the midst of and which can we inflect toward a better future world, which should be accentuated, and which should be brought to end? If we accept that there is something natural about the ideal of human flourishing – what is the practical range of what it can mean to thrive and how are decisions made within a society about the inevitable trade-offs that ideal requires? Finally, what is the role of agency in this resolve toward a better world and who should hold it? Given that the audience for this book is largely comprised of people who design or will design landscapes, cities, buildings, and policies that aim toward a better world for the lives of others, what is the de facto role in this construction toward a better future for which we cannot avoid responsibility? Or, what should our role be as we design armatures toward a better and more just future, if it

DOI: 10.4324/9781351053730-9

*History, Nature, Agency; and So, What Next?* 149

should be more expansive than the unavoidable minimum? What are the limits and responsibilities of *our* agency, and what should they be? While simple and comprehensive answers to these questions are likely not available, examining the aspects of history, nature, and agency within the proposals put forward by Howard, Le Corbusier, and Wright serves as a conclusion to this jumping off point to begin investigating our own commitments to the world and to our work in it.

## Nature

There are two inter-related aspects of the concept of nature relevant here. The first is an understanding of nature as the non-human world. Each of these three writers called to nature in this register by way of justification or explanation of the ideal that they propose will support thriving human lives. All three were convinced that human life is deeply improved by intimate and daily interaction with nature understood as the non-human world. But in addition, and at least as interestingly for us, each also makes claims – implicit and explicit – about what *human* nature is and each proposal rests heavily on these claims. On one hand, the concept of human nature as a unitary idea is easy to abuse and has often been so. Presuming that a way of being in the world particular to one person or small, often already privileged, group is indicative of the best way of being in the world for all people has done great violence to those for whom that one way did *not* support a life of wellbeing and delight. As such, the concept could potentially be dismissed as one that necessarily does violence to difference. On the other hand, the physical built world of landscapes and cities serves many different people at any given time and also persists beyond individual human lives for decades if not centuries. How can one design a physical place intended to be experienced with joy, delight, and belonging by many people without some concept of what those people share in their definitions of the good life? While one may choose to use a different term than 'human nature' for the things that people share as foundational agreements about what supports the good life, the basic concept of trying to find a resolution to the built environment that supports the thriving of all people seems to require just such a conjecture. The trick, as hinted at in the introduction with Ruth Levitas' proposal for utopian thought and method, is to hold this understanding in a way that respects radical difference. We may not agree with how Howard, Le Corbusier, and Wright understand nature and human nature – and in fact we cannot agree with all of them simultaneously since they hold conflicting views – but thinking through how they understand these issues and how their understandings are related to the proposals for the built environment they put forward is valuable as a way to challenge and sharpen our own thoughts.

### Nature and Human Nature in the Garden City

Howard stated that the base problem his proposal resolved was how to balance the benefits of town and country so that people have simultaneous access to the

150  *History, Nature, Agency; and So, What Next?*

natural world and society in a direct and daily manner. He defined this problem as a question of

> how to restore the people to the land – that beautiful land of ours, with its canopy of sky, the air that blows upon it, the sun that warms it, the rain and dew that moisten it – the very embodiment of Divine love for man.[1]

Proposing that town and country must be joined because "human society and the beauty of nature are meant to be enjoyed together," he claimed that this beauty "is the inspiration of art, of music, of poetry," and that the country is "the source of all health, all wealth, all knowledge."[2] The garden cities he imagined would provide people with a wide range of typologies of outdoor recreation and access to the natural world ranging from what he described as a beautiful and well-watered garden at the center of the town to the open spaces left unmanaged toward the perimeter. Spread throughout these landscapes from center to periphery are spaces for several forms of recreation as well as churches and schools. For Howard, access to the natural world is critical to leading a fulfilling human life, but only in combination with easy and simultaneous access to society.

Unlike Le Corbusier and Wright, Howard did not project a theoretically intertwined understanding of nature and human nature. However, this does not mean that both aren't equally critical to Howard's imagination of the future. In presenting an argument for why he thought that his social experiment would succeed where so many others had failed, he claimed that "probably the chief cause of failure in former social experiments has been a misconception of the principal element in the problem – human nature itself."[3] He consistently argued against the kind of society that is produced by an emphasis on individual attainment of wealth, "a society largely based on selfishness and rapacity," throughout his text.[4] However, he also argued in parallel against communism and socialism because they are based on an incomplete vision of human nature – one that emphasizes people's altruism at the expense of recognizing the "love of independence and initiative."[5] Howard insisted on leaving the question of a right balance between collective and individual action up to the residents themselves to negotiate through the governing structure of garden cities as shareholder corporations. His claim was not merely that *he* could not project the right balance, but that there was no *one* right resolution to be had of the right balance between these two sides of human nature for all people or times. He was adamant that the garden city idea was an experiment which would continue to be modified by its users throughout time.

However, there is one area where Howard did assume a consistency to human nature across people – namely that each person has some level of altruistic motivation. Proposing that taxation or other uses of force by the state to implement his vision would backfire because the wealthy will resist through all means possible and that his scheme should instead be advanced through the example of social benefit, he stated that "the average wealthy man is no more

History, Nature, Agency; and So, What Next?    151

an unmixed compound of selfishness than the average poor man" and that "in every man there is some measure of the reforming instinct; in every man there is some regard for his fellows."[6] Even the most hardened individual, once they see the benefits that the garden city model provided for all people and especially the impoverished, would according to Howard, even when "these natural feelings run athwart his pecuniary interests," be willing to sacrifice their position of wealth for the greater good.[7] It is this seed of compassion for other people which Howard counted on to motivate not only the initial investors in the first Garden City as well as the first inhabitants, but also what he counted on – once the first example has been shown successful – to bring ever more people into "voluntary collective efforts similar to those adopted in the Garden City experiment" until the whole of England, including London, was reconstructed along lines in which there would be no profit to be had in land speculation or the exploitation of labor.[8] This same assumption about human nature is behind Bellamy's use of the fictional novel *Looking Backward: 2000–1887* to try to inspire change as described in Chapter 3. Bellamy was clearly calling to the same altruistic part of human nature that Howard assumed was universal, as was indicative of the progressive movement of which they were both a part.

### Nature and Human Nature in the Radiant City

Human nature was more closely bound to nature for Le Corbusier than it was for Howard, to the point that they were perhaps inseparable. The suffering and lack of joy that Le Corbusier saw in the world around him, which he proposed could be alleviated with the Radiant City, he set at the feet of the fact that people had been "seduced away along a path contrary to that of nature" and subsequently claimed that "we must now return to the path of nature, and listen to her voice again."[9] Human nature, for Le Corbusier, was to follow the laws of nature. He ws convinced that not doing so, explicitly as a society, denies our true selves and leads to all the miseries of the first machine age. Nature was not, for Le Corbusier, fundamentally the physicality of the non-human world. Rather, nature for him was a set of processes and laws which instantiate in physicality. He claimed that "in nature life follows the seasons – birth, maturity and death, spring, summer, fall and winter – and each year nature cleans up, throws out and buries" while people have maintained streets and houses that are outdated "under obsolete laws, ruled by a system that is like a dead branch fallen from the tree of life."[10] He repeatedly called to the rhythms of seasons and cycles of organisms from life to death as well as the cycles of the sun and the moon as the right basis for all harmonious human action. In contrast to the production of what he referred to as useless goods and the persistence of pre-machine urban forms, Le Corbusier stated that "life is precise, strict, and economical. The law of nature makes it so."[11] He illustrated his understanding of life, and nature, with a description of an organism developing out of a collection of cells which form at first only "an amorphous, quivering, but purposeless mass" until "an intention appeared, an axis began to form in the center of this

## 152 History, Nature, Agency; and So, What Next?

motionless agglomeration. A current, a direction became apparent. An organism was born."[12] Life, he claimed, follows "its natural impulse towards *organization*. This impulse toward organization exists throughout nature."[13] While nature is wholly mathematical for Le Corbusier, he claimed that people see only chaos. To save ourselves from this chaos and make life bearable, people have "projected the laws of nature into a system that is a manifestation of the human spirit itself: *geometry*."[14] For Le Corbusier, society and the city should be directed by the laws of nature in the same way.

It is this understanding of nature, which it is human nature to follow toward happiness, which underlies Le Corbusier's proposal for the Radiant City. He claimed that people are the product of nature, created by the laws of nature, and that if they become aware of these laws, obey them, and harmonize their lives with them, then they will achieve "a conscious sensation of harmony that will be beneficial."[15] This harmony, for Le Corbusier, is not harmony on an individual basis however – not the romantic notion of an individual consciousness in alignment with nature in solitude portrayed by Caspar David Friedrich in Wanderer Above the Sea of Fog. Rather, this harmony is to be found in collectively following nature in its imperative toward organization. Criticizing deurbanization, garden cities, and satellite cities of all types he stated that in them

> the laws of nature had been stood on their heads: men are creatures born to live in groups, to live closely with one another, to collaborate; it is nonsense to try and make them into hermits living in the depths of the woods.[16]

This understanding of human nature aligning with the laws of nature also underpins his critique of money as the primary motivator in society. "From the conquest of money," he wrote, "which merely spurs on individuals, we wish to press on towards achieving a harmony in this age of ours that will summon all of us to the great task and bring satisfaction to everyone."[17] He continued to claim that participation in this task of society would require following "nature, which is all discipline, the logic of cause and effect."[18] If the forces of machine production were harnessed according to the laws of nature, Le Corbusier predicted that everyone would receive their share of society by which he meant "the right to eat, the right to expect a serene end to a life that has been filled with fruitful labors, and the right to know the reasons for all the daily activities we are obliged to perform."[19]

### Nature and Human Nature in Broadacre City

While nature and human nature, for which Wright used the word 'organic' somewhat interchangeably, were as interwoven for him as they were for Le Corbusier, Wright's understanding of them was radically different. Whereas Le Corbusier saw collective order and strict geometry, Wright saw individuality and growth from the interior. Wright stated that Laotze "preached the sense of Individuality as a reflex of the organic unity of the Cosmos" and

*History, Nature, Agency; and So, What Next?* 153

made similar claims about the teachings of Buddha and Jesus in support of his understanding of the relationship between nature and human nature.[20] He went on to claim that

> our own democratic ideal of the social state seems originally conceived in some such unit. That is to say, Democracy was conceived as a free growth of humane individuality, mankind free to function together in unity of spirit (their own skill in the making); by nature thus averse to formalism and so to institutionalizing.[21]

Arguing that we must be able to plan for the new time-scale made available by electricity and modern mechanisms of mobility, as opposed to the old space-scale, he claimed that we must eliminate "tyrannical major and minor axes in order to be free to plan according to Nature. Here we have at last the elimination of the insignificant."[22]

Wright told a story about the beginnings of humanity divided into two conflicting human natures – that of the cave-dweller and that of the nomad. The cave-dweller was the conservative who relied on static defenses – cave, then cliff, then city – and on things saved and stored. The nomad was the wanderer who relied on distance and agility for security and moved dwelling to resources, relying on what they could do rather than what they could control. It is the latter human nature, that of the nomad, which Wright saw as the future of humankind with its newfound mobility and capacity to communicate at a distance. Only when people follow this path and become "as native as trees to the wood, as grass to the floor of the valley," would "the democratic spirit of man, individual, rise out of the confusion of communal life in the city to a creative civilization of the ground" which would be "intrinsically superior to the more static faiths of the past lying now in ruins all about him."[23] When land was redistributed so that all people have security of residence and sustenance and are therefore free to follow the instincts of the nomad, then would people be able to in spirit belong "even as hill-slopes, or the beautiful ravines and forests themselves belong and as the bees and trees and flowers in them."[24] No longer would people place their faith in "arbitrary hangovers of Roman law" but rather would go "deeper to the organic law beneath."[25]

It is important to remember that for all of Wright's emphasis on individuality and freedom to fit into the landscape and society as the individual desired, his imagination of the civilization, as his imagination of human nature, was not restricted to individualized pursuits. If people "were to live in a free city of democracy" as he proposed that Broadacre City would be, they "would not fail to make communal life richer for all the world" because they had "true individual independence – by natural growth of a natural conscience."[26] While Le Corbusier referred to the organization that underpins life, Wright referred throughout his book to life as the inter-relatedness and fitness between organisms and between organisms and land. This included the relationships between people in Broadacre City as they cooperated on a truly authentic

154    *History, Nature, Agency; and So, What Next?*

foundation of free choice. For Wright, the freedom of the nomad allowed people to develop individuality, their true human nature, by freely embedding themselves in the natural world. Only then would they be able to engage in an authentic, organic form of democracy natural to human thriving because only then would that engagement be uncoerced.

## History

Howard, Le Corbusier, and Wright all saw their projects as a fulcrum in the history of civilization, as well may be tautologically true of any utopian proposal. Each saw the society around them as having reached a point at which the fulcrum they proposed was not only feasible due to advances in technology but also necessary for the equitable establishment of human flourishing in the modern world, though their understandings of this flourishing varied significantly. As described in Chapter 5, they found themselves in a whirlwind of accelerating social and material transformation as a result of dramatic increases in the capacity of machine production as well as stunning advances in communications and transportation technologies. However, dramatic increases in inequality between people and the dislocation of power from everyday life to the abstract forces of capital was equally as evident and was as concerning to them as the technological advances were exhilarating. These disparities were most evident in the explosive growth of cities and the lives people lived in them, particularly the poor and the laboring classes, but were also visible in the deepening poverty of rural areas for those who chose to look. That this awareness was widely felt is evident not only in the works of Howard, Le Corbusier, and Wright but also in the wide public appreciation of the works by Henry George and Edward Bellamy as described in Chapter 3. Howard, Le Corbusier, and Wright each proposed a future society in which people made use of technological advances that were occurring around them, put to the common good instead of private gain, but also returned people to what each imagined as a previous state of life enriched by being intimately embedded in the natural world.

### The Garden City in History

Howard described his proposal for the Garden City as an experiment that would advance society in the same way that experiments in the generation and control of power advanced mechanical production. "There have in the past," he wrote, "been inventions and discoveries on the making of which society has suddenly leaped upward to a new and higher plane of existence."[27] By way of example, he offered the development of steam power and the great advances that it allowed. However, he claimed that, "the discovery of a method for giving effect to a far greater force than the force of steam – to the long pent-up desire for a better and nobler social life here on earth – will work changes even more remarkable."[28] The Garden City was this method, he proposed, and in this passage made it clear how he situated the project in

History, Nature, Agency; and So, What Next?   155

history. He continued that the garden city experiment, once proven successful, would show that there

> is a broad path open, through a creation of new wealth forms, to a new industrial system in which the productive forces of society and of nature may be used with far greater effectiveness than at present, and in which the distribution of the wealth forms so created will take place on a far juster and more equitable basis.[29]

It is worth emphasizing here that the garden city idea is explicitly a proposal about *industrial* society – in contradistinction to the many projects which have referenced the formal and largely residential component of his proposal alone and produced twee residential neighborhoods centered around bourgeois shopping districts.

Howard also imagined that the flow of history is one of progress toward a state of universal human wellbeing. This is made most clear not only in the quotation above referencing the design for a better social life but also by the projection of the future of London with which he concluded his work. Once the first garden city had been proven successful and additional garden cities began to take hold with their new means of communication, new means of distribution which raise profits for producers and reduce costs for consumers, "parks and gardens, orchards and woods" planted within easy access of all people, homes for those previously housed in slums, and when "work is found for the workless, land for the landless," there will be found that

> a new sense of freedom and joy is pervading the hearts of people as their individual faculties are awakened and they discover … the long-sought-for means of reconciliation between order and freedom – between the well-being of the individual and of society.[30]

This awakening would subsequently lead to London itself being revitalized and see its slums replaced with parks and playgrounds; nature invading London to the point that life there offered the same benefits and pleasures as life in the garden cities that had been constructed across England. While he was imagining a forward progress in forms of both technology and social form, this ultimately included a return to a social frame in which people were immersed in the natural world – readers may recall his goal of returning people to the land as described earlier. However, readers should also recall that Howard was not predicting a stable, unitary, end to history. As described above in the section on nature, the experimentation with a balance between individual and collective action would continue in garden cities and indeed vary between them. He imagined a future state in which that experimentation itself could flourish as people found for themselves the balance between initiative and cooperation they personally sought. While it may be hard to imagine one of Howard's temperament reading Agamben's *Means without Ends*, his social imagination is not unaligned.

156   *History, Nature, Agency; and So, What Next?*

### The Radiant City in History

Le Corbusier, likewise, sought a proposal which would maintain the benefits of modern industrial and technological society and distribute them more equitably while returning people to a closer interaction with nature. The Radiant City was a concept in which he imagined people as "members of a species developed over thousands and thousands of years (both biologically and psychically) according to established relations with the sky, with fresh air, with the sun, with greenery, with water, with physical activity" who had been "torn out of that framework and are wasting away in an entirely unnatural environment" could have both the benefits of industrial society and simultaneously return to a life of the basic pleasures of sun, sky, and greenery.[31] He claimed that this work was the *"restitution of freedom which has been lost."*[32] The technological advances with which he proposed to achieve this balance and restitution were "the marvelous fruits of a century of toil, the harvest of the first era of the machine age," tools which provided "the means of labor that allow us to begin putting the world in order."[33] The result of this putting the world in order would be "the second era of the machine age; the era of harmony. Man and nature."[34] Much if not all of the existing cities would need to be replaced in order to achieve this.

Le Corbusier described the existing infrastructure of society including houses, cities, streets, farms, and "the arbitrary distribution of property" as "premachine-age equipment."[35] He made clear how little he cared for the historical continuation of the form and elements of city when he commented on a critique of his ideas for Paris that they did not respect the fact that it was once a Roman city. He dismisses this argument by pointing out the fact that "a brick wall in Cluny gardens, ivy-covered and crumbling, proves that Paris was once Roman" while he was more concerned about a million people who lived in the slums of the historical city and another million forced to live "in the difficult conditions of the suburbs."[36] He argued that Paris, based on current trends, would inevitably be demolished and become "an enormous asphalt hole" and that "eventually, we shall have to plant it full of carrots and onions."[37] Instead of allowing the current processes to continue with the great loss of opportunity and money, he proposed the Radiant City and that Paris should be demolished "quietly, section by section, rationally, with calm good sense" as the Radiant City is constructed in its place.[38] This would "provide the machine-age man with a full and fruitful life" and, thus, "Paris, the *City of Light*, will go on."[39] The obstacle to this vision, Le Corbusier claimed is what he refers to as a premodern "form of land tenure, which is invested with private rights antagonistic to the public right."[40]

### Broadacre City in History

Like both Howard and Le Corbusier, Wright saw his proposal for a new form of life as one in which people would be able to reclaim a previous life closer to the natural world but at the same time avail themselves of the benefits of

*History, Nature, Agency; and So, What Next?* 157

modern technology. He wrote that the close connection between people and the earth was severed by "any big city centralization has built."[41] In the narrative of the cave-dweller and the nomad discussed previously, the new modern and democratic society based on intuitions of the nomad is bound to replace the old society of hierarchy and centralized cities resting on the inherited conservatism of the cave-dweller who became the city-builder. "Centralization itself is the old social principle," Wright wrote, "that made kings an appropriate necessity" and which had "degenerated to a force we call communism."[42] Not only is this historic city at odds with an authentically democratic society for Wright, but also at odds with technological advances in transportation and communication. While the medieval city was "conveniently enough spaced" for life in that era, contemporary mobility rendered that urban form obsolete "like some hopelessly inadequate old boat or building."[43] While the ancient city fit human life and needs at the time and "was not opposed to the course of normal human life in relation to natural beauty of environment," Wright observed that, "those ancient civilizations have perished."[44]

The new city, one based on decentralization, was not only already coming to be but also, Wright felt, inevitable. He observed that this new city was "happening now upon the very ground whereon we stand; forced by circumstances we fail to recognize as advance agents of decentralization."[45] Wright described this new city as inevitable in a number of locations in his text, and in his conclusion stated that the rubbish-heaps of urban obsolescence should undergo a "wholesome destruction."[46] He admonished young architects to accomplish this wholesome destruction by

> learning how to help the inevitable natural city to go on building itself: the right kind of buildings, built the right way in the right place for the right people – this, and the right kind of city will grow for us.[47]

It is not only the technological advances in transportation and communication that Wright saw leading to people escaping the city however, but also social and economic facilities. For example, Wright had high expectations for the service stations which supplied gasoline to support mobility in the nascent stage of decentralization he saw around him. He imagined that they "are probably the beginning of future collateral cultural centers" which may be "the beginning of the future humane establishments we are now calling the free city."[48] He projected that these would expand to become wayside markets which would include facilities for cultural activities such as live theatre and dining as well as shopping for everything from locally grown produce to wares sold by department stores. While this has clearly not happened, we must remember that without the redistribution of access to land and the subsequent reintegration of industrial and agricultural society resulting in wide household self-sufficiency within which Wright's vision of the future of service stations was set, we cannot claim with any intellectual rigor that this particular imagination has failed.

158    *History, Nature, Agency; and So, What Next?*

# Agency

Agency is the thorniest of issues not only in the realm of utopian proposals, but in the built environment generally. Philosophically speaking, agency is a vast and complicated topic which has spawned an even more vast and more complicated body of literature. Covering that wide range of thought is well beyond the scope of this project and so we will work with a rather simplistic understanding of agency as follows: agency is the ability to select not only the ends of action but the means with which to attempt their attainment. With regard to these utopian proposals, there are two levels of agency worth considering. First is the agency required for the initiation of the conditions of the utopian ideal writ large. Second, the agency required for implementation of the vision is also critical – including not only who holds agency but what they hold agency for. Both levels of agency are embodied in landscapes as they take the role of political media presented in Chapter 2. It should be noted that agency is also closely related to authority and so reading Chapter 8 will add much to the consideration of agency introduced in this chapter.

## *Agency Required as the Preconditions of Utopia*

All three utopian proposals required significant changes in the foundations of social form in broad terms before the physicality of their proposed organization could be initiated. While Howard's proposed change was far more modest than that of either Le Corbusier or Wright, it also has not come to pass though it came the closest to partial realization in some few places – perhaps because it was the least systemic but perhaps also because it was the easiest for the forces of capital to subvert. The agency required to set up the preconditions for the Garden City did not need to be generated – it existed in the society Howard saw around him, which was one of the reasons he felt so sure his experiment would succeed. There were many people with the wealth who could have chosen to invest in garden city idea on the basis of an altruistic return – people of "responsible position and of undoubted probity and honour" as he described them.[49] Howard did not require a change in the legal structure of land. In fact, he relied quite explicitly on the rights of land-ownership for the power that would allow the incorporated garden cities he described as "*quasi* public bodies" to enforce the common good over private gain.[50] Individual people also had the agency within society at the time to be able to move to any garden city that was established as long as they could afford the move, the change of habitation from place to place was neither restricted nor uncommon at the time. Likewise, manufacturers and other industrialists could move their operations to garden cities and provide work for the residents of the city. However, all of these agents would have needed to act in concert for the garden city idea to get off the ground as a holistic experiment – which in turn would have required a significant level of trust between actors. It was not a lack of agency which kept the garden city from becoming the norm as Howard imagined it would, it was a lack of will and trust between actors.

*History, Nature, Agency; and So, What Next?* 159

The Radiant City, on the other hand, required a massive act of agency as its precondition. Whereas Howard relied on existing frameworks of owning land, Le Corbusier argued that the existing laws regarding land ownership were the direct and most significant barrier to his vision. In terms of the definition we are using for agency; Le Corbusier identified the ends necessary as a first step toward the Radiant City, but not the means to achieve those ends. While he stated that "in order to provide liberty for the individual and all the benefits of collective action, on both the material and the spiritual plane, contemporary society must have the entire land surface of the country at its disposal," he also equivocated that this did not mean doing way with property and that we should "let the lawyers find a way."[51] He further sidestepped the question of how to set up the preconditions of his utopian proposal by stating that "mobilization does not mean nationalization. It means solidarity!" without putting forward any depth of discussion about how that solidarity is to be arrived at.[52] The other significant precondition for Le Corbusier's proposal is the reorganization of industrial production such that nobody had to work more than a few hours a day to support themselves. While this precondition was part of the plan that would be put forward by Authority as described in Chapter 8, his sketch of how authority was generated is left somewhat bare. The question of why he assumed that people would follow that authority, even once installed, he left unasked. However, it must be remembered that his intent was not to provide a political program for achieving the Radiant City but rather to offer it as a vision of how life could be, if the political will were found to attain it.

Wright shared with Le Corbusier the precondition of redistributing land for the common good as a basis for utopia. He wrote that "our growing dissatisfaction with autocratic power or bureaucracy of any kind requires wisdom" and that this wisdom which was simultaneously ancient and modern "recognizes this new democratic concept of man free in life wherein money and landlaws are established as subordinate to the rights of human beings."[53] This subordination of land law to the rights of people in order that an acre of land could be distributed to all people is the first step toward his utopian vision. However, he wrote even less than did Le Corbusier about how this might be achieved except to say on one hand that the vested interests of society "will never voluntarily agree to the loss of their immediate quarry which lies in some form of rent" and on the other hand that our system of "free enterprise, so called" will inevitably fall as had monarchies and despotisms.[54] It should be noted that Wright also, like Le Corbusier, was more interested in proposing a vision to which society should aspire – both in contrast to Howard who imagined himself laying out a meticulous plan by which his utopian vision could be achieved within existing forms of society.

### Agency Required for the Implementation of Utopia

Once the preconditions for the Garden City were in place – funding and the commitment from all the actors that would need to simultaneously commit

160  *History, Nature, Agency; and So, What Next?*

to the experiment – agency would be held by the residents who made their decisions through a practice of deliberative democracy with all of the potential for inclusivity as well as for exclusion that we understand today this process implies. As described in Chapter 8, they would vote not for political leaders who would then assign technical tasks of physical and social infrastructure to departments but rather would vote for the leaders of the technical departments responsible for social and physical infrastructure who would subsequently collaborate as political leadership to protect the overall form and intent of the Garden City. Not only would the residents make their views known through this process of selecting this technical leadership, but they could change their views and expectations through the same process based at least in part on whether they felt the leadership was able to meet their expectations. Howard felt that their collective will would be "measured simply by the willingness of the tenants to pay rate-rents."[55]

The residents of the Garden City, through their power as a collective landowner, would not be restricted in Howard's mind to making determinations regarding the infrastructures of the city however. Even though he argued against doing so, he did note that the municipality would have "the *power* of dealing in the most drastic manner possible with the liquor trade" and choosing to forbid the sale of alcohol.[56] He also argued that people in the garden city would have the collective agency to deny the sale of goods produced with inequitable labor practices. The residents of a garden city would also have the collective agency to go beyond the installation and operation of infrastructure and the forbidding of practices that run afoul their collective conscience. He noted that bakeries and laundries have a very close relationship to health and therefore "a very strong case might be made out for municipal bakeries and municipal laundries," or at least their very close public supervision.[57]

Le Corbusier saw only obstacles and inaction in the kind of process that Howard relied on. Because the authorities then in political power were afraid to act and unwilling to overturn centuries of ideas which "are incompatible with a normal and harmonious evolution" as well as being "ignorant of the technical facts of the matter," Le Corbusier observed that "a democratic inertia reigns over the nation, a nonsensical situation causing anxiety, disturbances, rebellion and sadness."[58] He was consistent throughout his text that the agency to implement the Radiant City should be held by an authority which is created by the plan. This plan would define not only the built form of the city – its infrastructure, open spaces, and buildings – but also the allowable goods for industrial production and one can presume other aspects of life in the Radiant City. The plan, in the way of which stands the democratic inertia he decried, was to be "drawn up by a technician."[59] Yet even the technician was imagined by Le Corbusier as having less free agency than one might at first think.

Le Corbusier imagined that the technicians would draw up the plan taking "account of nothing but human truths."[60] These truths derived largely from nature in two ways. The first of these was the biology of human life – Le Corbusier referred back to the concerns of the body throughout his proposal.

*History, Nature, Agency; and So, What Next?* 161

The second was the motivation of nature toward organization, and the implications that has for human nature and human thriving, as described in the section on nature earlier in this chapter. The agency for making the plan which will then give authority its charge to build the city is largely one of applying "serene and lucid minds" to modern problems with nature as a guide in order to produce a plan which is "an emanation of modern society, an answer to its needs, an urgent necessity. It is a product of technology."[61] Of course, this locating of agency with technicians as if there were one right technical resolution to the problems of society runs into a whole phalanx of challenges with regard to who the technicians are and how their identities, personal histories, and idiosyncratic intuitions inflect their interpretation of not only the needs of modern society, but also the nature of nature itself. I have written elsewhere about the problems with practical arguments and technical solutions.[62]

Once the foundational structure of a redistributed land rights was in place for Broadacre City, Wright conceptually avoided both the problems with deliberative democracy on one hand as well as the problems with singular technical solutions on the other. It must be admitted, however, that he did this, in part, by stepping lightly over decisions like which county seats to keep and which to replace with grass and how the right-of-ways along which train, truck, and bus traffic would run as well as how other forms of civic infrastructure are located and managed. He noted at multiple points in his text that the city ought to be planned – that "planning is the factor that will develop the new city and keep the city economical and beautiful" but did not locate the agency with which that planning would be achieved, in either philosophical or pragmatic terms.[63] We are left to presume that once people had gained their self-sufficiency through engagement with land and could participate authentically in democracy as Wright imagined it, these decisions would be made through some form of consensus – though it must be admitted that one is left with a distinct feeling from his writings that voting as a deliberative process to determine shared action would likely rankle Wright's sensibilities and fall under his contempt for "external compulsions, personal or official" that "were never more than weakness continually breading weaknesses."[64]

The primary landscape of Broadacre City was the home farm and therefore the primary form of agency in Broadacre City rested, of course, with the individual and the household. Not only was this agency focused on whether to take paid employment or not as has been mentioned in previous chapters, but it was also focused on the home and farm itself. The basis of individuality for Wright, and therefore the basis for democracy, was the ability of the individual to fit themselves and their life to the land. This was not only evident in how they used their land – whether they chose to grow their own food or grow some food for sale at the roadside markets – but also in the homes themselves. "Every true home," he wrote, "should be actually bound to grow from within to dignity and spiritual significance: *grow* by the right concept and practice of building into a pervasive social circumstance."[65] This growth from within had much to do with the availability of quality prefabricated dwelling components

162   *History, Nature, Agency; and So, What Next?*

as described in Chapter 5 and would lead "the small home-farm-building to take the place of promiscuous farm buildings and the tenement."[66] As much as he relied on people returning to the land, good ground, as their birthright, he wrote little about the actual uses and organizations of those household landscapes. However, it was people living with land and installing their own dwellings in harmony with it which would lead to the goal he stated in his forward: a true human culture with "a healthy sense of the beautiful as its life-of-the-soul: an aesthetic organic, as *of* life itself, not *on* it; nobly relating man to his environment."[67]

## So, What Next?

So what does having this perspective on the Garden City, the Radiant City, and Broadacre City proposals imply for our own action going forward toward positive change? How should we think about what it means for us as we engage in the world, bringing our commitments toward justice and equity into our work? What is utopian thinking good for now? I propose that there are two different ways to begin thinking about answering these questions – though I feel I should make it clear that I think no such answers can be final or comprehensive. The best we can do, if we are honest about ourselves and the scope of human knowledge and foresight, is to provide provisional answers to guide explorations into action and maintain for ourselves the right of reevaluation as well as hold ourselves accountable to a periodic review not only of our commitments but also how we are going about meeting them. Using the framework for understanding agency as given earlier in this chapter, we are responsible for the ends we seek and also the means by which we attempt to attain them. Those ends may well be to support the needs toward and expectations of good lives held by others, but that does not change that we have chosen *that* as our ends and that we are individually responsible for the means by which we choose to act to achieve them.

The first level of consideration regarding what to do with this book about three utopian proposals and the particular thread of thought it foregrounds within each is to ask what these things lead us to think regarding the change *we* want to make in the world, and what arena that desire for a contribution to positive change leads us to play in. Clearly none of us are going to be able to single-handedly enact change at the deeply systemic level of disrupting the legal and financial distribution of rights to land as broadly as these three thinkers thought would lead to a better world and with which, if the reader hasn't yet guessed, this author firmly agrees. Even Howard foresaw that the ultimate change he wanted to propose for all of England – networks of garden cities spread across the land to become the dominant typology of urban life and human experience – would require the broad, nearly universal, use of eminent domain. But let's suppose for a moment that anyone did aspire to directly contribute to that level of change. What career path would put one in a position to do so? What field of practice would allow one to develop not only the skills but

*History, Nature, Agency; and So, What Next?* 163

the social position to be able to accomplish that? Even intending oneself toward positive change at a much less comprehensive level should lead one to ask the same questions: What career path leads to the development of the capacity for agency to contribute to the change one want to see in the world? What skills, connections, experiences, and positions does one need to gain to be able to do that? If one is not on that path now, what path should one be on or how does one inflect the current path in that direction? It is critical to note that not every intention to contribute to positive change lies along a professional path, and that there are many valid reasons for choosing a professional path in addition to using it as a lever to make change. It may well be that it is most productive to act as an engaged citizen through formal and/or informal processes of civil society and governance. This first level of consideration about what to do with utopian thinking lies at the broader frame of life choices, philosophy, and looking at the world around one holistically.

The second level of consideration about what to do with utopian thinking lies at the level of a project or program. How does one take one's commitments toward change in the world into this work? While one obvious answer is that we seek much community input and try to meet the needs of the people who will be most directly impacted by the project, and that is our responsibility, that does not absolve us of the agency central to our work. We take community input – but we have to make a judgment about whether we are getting everyone's input equally. We have to make a judgment about what to do with conflicting input. Even when we present, as we often do, multiple options for additional feedback – there are inevitably *innumerable* options based on also equally adequate interpretations of the original feedback which we don't present. We make judgments at every step of the process, and – ultimately – we draw lines which become translated into real, solid material and write words which become actual, implemented rules and regulations. These then impact people's lives in real ways. It is our hope that they lead to a world which supports lives of joy, delight, and beauty for all people, but we can never pretend that our personal and professional agency did not play a significant role. The challenges to Le Corbusier's technocrats who draw plans, ultimately, apply to us no matter how well intentioned and conscientious about community input we are.

What is it that this analysis of utopian proposals adds to our ability to effectively navigate these concerns? I propose that there are at least four components that it offers. First, we have to identify who holds agency in the project or program and understand how we can influence that agency in ways that we believe – guided by as much input by potential users as we can collect - will make the world a more just, more equitable, and more delightful place – even if that agency is a client. There may be cases in which all the agency necessary for a project is held by only people who will put that first on their agenda, taking this step off our plate – but this is rarely the case. Second, once we understand the roles of agency in a given setting and have a plan to influence them as needed, we should look at what relations between people and between people and landscapes will or could be impacted by the work at hand. Chapter 2 which

164  *History, Nature, Agency; and So, What Next?*

presents a theory of landscapes as political media is intended to help frame these relationships which we influence. The topical chapters are intended to flesh out some of the considerations regarding those relationships which we can take into account – from issues as pragmatic as in food and agriculture to issues as ephemeral as freedom, cooperation, and authority but no less consequential for that ephemerality. Third, we should consider the relationships between people and between people and landscapes that extend beyond the direct site or program parameters of our work but which are impacted by the work nonetheless. We should then ask how to bring the importance of those relationships into the consideration of the lines and words we use to direct actual change in the real world. Lastly, considering all of these concerns, we should ask what should be our role relative to our commitments in the world – not just as professionals but as people. Does a given project and the implications it holds imply that we should take our knowledge and commitments outside the professional role of the work and into thinking and acting as citizen advocates? Are there others already doing that work that we should support?

Our last consideration is how these approaches to action in the world support action that leads to what Ruth Levitas' work was used to introduce at the beginning of this volume – holistic thinking about holistic futures which support human flourishing, acknowledging that of course human flourishing also implies the flourishing of the ecologies in which we live. I propose that we use utopian thinking in this way: not to propose utopias as states of the world but to propose utopian work as building and reinforcing webs of actions and relationships that contribute to justice, beauty, equity, and delight. I find it insightful, and hopefully also inciteful, that all three of the utopian projects presented in this volume rely heavily on landscapes of embedded cooperation – even if the content of that cooperation and its relation to freedom and authority were quite different. Every project or program we are involved in should look for links into other places and areas with which it can connect and build or reinforce these things, and I propose that the links we make will be the more robust for the degree which they rely on and support cooperation. I think of utopian action in the world akin to cultures with which one starts a ferment such as kimchi or sourdough. The projects or programs we are involved have the most impact if they not only have an internal stability but also are able to reach out into the medium – in our case the landscape – where they are placed and begin to convert materials and processes around them. Utopia then becomes a living, variable, self-actualizing trajectory – as long as it continues to be fed the raw materials it needs. To stretch the analogy even a bit more thinly, these raw materials are hope, respect , cooperation, and a commitment to justice, equity, diversity, and inclusion held alongside a belief in the value of beauty, delight, and joy. The utopian proposals put forward by Howard, Wright, and Le Corbusier provide visions of what the world could be and serve as an instigation for us to use as a basis for the possibility of utopian inoculations of the world by providing footholds from which we can challenge our own world and our work in it.

# Notes

1 Howard and Osborn, *Garden Cities of To-morrow*, p. 44
2 Howard and Osborn, *Garden Cities of To-morrow*, p. 48
3 Howard and Osborn, *Garden Cities of To-morrow*, p. 113
4 Howard and Osborn, *Garden Cities of To-morrow*, p. 146
5 Howard and Osborn, *Garden Cities of To-morrow*, p. 115
6 Howard and Osborn, *Garden Cities of To-morrow*, p. 149
7 Howard and Osborn, *Garden Cities of To-morrow*, p. 149
8 Howard and Osborn, *Garden Cities of To-morrow*, p. 149
9 Le Corbusier, *The Radiant City*, p. 196.
10 Le Corbusier, *The Radiant City*, p. 8.
11 Le Corbusier, *The Radiant City*, p. 76.
12 Le Corbusier, *The Radiant City*, p. 81.
13 Le Corbusier, *The Radiant City*, p. 81.
14 Le Corbusier, *The Radiant City*, p. 83.
15 Le Corbusier, *The Radiant City*, p. 83.
16 Le Corbusier, *The Radiant City*, p. 84.
17 Le Corbusier, *The Radiant City*, p. 176.
18 Le Corbusier, *The Radiant City*, p. 176.
19 Le Corbusier, *The Radiant City*, p. 176.
20 Wright, *The Living City*, p. 45.
21 Wright, *The Living City*, p. 45.
22 Wright, *The Living City*, p. 138.
23 Wright, *The Living City*, p. 25.
24 Wright, *The Living City*, p. 214.
25 Wright, *The Living City*, p. 214.
26 Wright, *The Living City*, p. 25.
27 Howard and Osborn, *Garden Cities of To-morrow*, p. 128.
28 Howard and Osborn, *Garden Cities of To-morrow*, pp. 128–130.
29 Howard and Osborn, *Garden Cities of To-morrow*, p. 130.
30 Howard and Osborn, *Garden Cities of To-morrow*, p. 151.
31 Le Corbusier, *The Radiant City*, p. 67.
32 Le Corbusier, *The Radiant City*, p. 37.
33 Le Corbusier, *The Radiant City*, p. 18.
34 Le Corbusier, *The Radiant City*, pp. 340–341.
35 Le Corbusier, *The Radiant City*, p. 76.
36 Le Corbusier, *The Radiant City*, p. 13.
37 Le Corbusier, *The Radiant City*, p. 141.
38 Le Corbusier, *The Radiant City*, p. 141.
39 Le Corbusier, *The Radiant City*, p. 141.
40 Le Corbusier, *The Radiant City*, p. 139.
41 Wright, *The Living City*, p. 17.
42 Wright, *The Living City*, p. 31.
43 Wright, *The Living City*, p. 50.
44 Wright, *The Living City*, p. 68.
45 Wright, *The Living City*, p. 87.
46 Wright, *The Living City*, p. 222.
47 Wright, *The Living City*, p. 222.

# 166 *History, Nature, Agency; and So, What Next?*

48 Wright, *The Living City*, p. 168.
49 Howard and Osborn, *Garden Cities of To-morrow*, p. 51.
50 Howard and Osborn, *Garden Cities of To-morrow*, p. 93.
51 Le Corbusier, *The Radiant City*, p. 189.
52 Le Corbusier, *The Radiant City*, p. 189.
53 Wright, *The Living City*, p. 26.
54 Wright, *The Living City*, pp. 81,83
55 Howard and Osborn, *Garden Cities of To-morrow*, p. 91.
56 Howard and Osborn, *Garden Cities of To-morrow*, p. 102.
57 Howard and Osborn, *Garden Cities of To-morrow*, p. 101.
58 Le Corbusier, *The Radiant City*, p. 249.
59 Le Corbusier, *The Radiant City*, p. 249.
60 Le Corbusier, *The Radiant City*, p. 154.
61 Le Corbusier, *The Radiant City*, p. 154.
62 Beck, *John Nolen and the Metropolitan Landscape*, pp. 144–154.
63 Wright, *The Living City*, p. 137.
64 Wright, *The Living City*, p. 208.
65 Wright, *The Living City*, p. 209.
66 Wright, *The Living City*, p. 61.
67 Wright, *The Living City*, p. 9.

## Bibliography

Beck, J., 2013. John Nolen and the Metropolitan Landscape. Routledge, London; New York.
Howard, E., Osborn, F.J., 2001. Garden Cities of To-morrow, 11th Print ed. MIT Press, Cambridge.
Le Corbusier, 1964. The Radiant City: Elements of a Doctrine of Urbanism to be Used as the Basis of Our Machine-Age Civilization. The Orion Press, New York.
Wright, F.L., 1958. The Living City. Horizon Press, New York.

### Suggested Readings

Ackerman-Leist, P., 2013. Rebuilding the Foodshed: How to Create Local, Sustainable, and Secure Food Systems, The Community Resilience Guide Series. Post Carbon Institute, Chelsea Green Pub, Santa Rosa, White River Junction.
Bookchin, M., 2007. Social Ecology and Communalism. AK Press, Oakland.
Bregman, R., 2018. Utopia for Realists: How We Can Build the Ideal World. Back Bay Books, New York, Boston, London.
Busbea, L., 2012. Topologies: The Urban Utopia in France, 1960–1970. MIT Press, Cambridge, London.
Callenbach, E., 1981. Ecotopia Emerging. Banyan Tree Books: Distributed by Bookpeople, Berkeley.
Carlisle, L., 2015. Lentil Underground: Renegade Farmers and the Future of Food in America. Gotham Books, New York.
Derr, V., Chawla, L., Mintzer, M., 2018. Placemaking with Children and Youth: Participatory Practices for Planning Sustainable Communities, 1st ed. New Village Press, New York.

## History, Nature, Agency; and So, What Next? 167

Eckersley, R., 2004. The Green State: Rethinking Democracy and Sovereignty. MIT Press, Cambridge.

EcoArts, Geffen, A., Rosenthal, A., Fremantle, C., Rahmani, A. (Eds.), 2022. Ecoart in Action Activities, Case Studies, and Provocations for Classrooms and Communities, 1st ed. New Village Press, New York.

Fishman, R., 1982. Urban Utopias in the Twentieth Century: Ebenezer Howard, Frank Lloyd Wright, and Le Corbusier, 1st MIT Press pbk. ed. MIT Press, Cambridge.

Fleming, R., Roberts, S., 2019. Sustainable Design for the Built Environment. Routledge/Taylor & Francis Group, London, New York.

Forester, J., 1989. Planning in the Face of Power. University of California Press, Berkeley.

Fullilove, M.T., 2013. Urban Alchemy: Restoring Joy in America's Sorted-Out Cities, 1st ed. New Village Press, Oakland.

Gorz, A., 1980. Ecology as Politics. South End Press, Boston.

Hamin, E.M., Abunnasr, Y., Ryan, R.L. (Eds.), 2019. Planning for Climate Change: A Reader in Green Infrastructure and Sustainable Design for Resilient Cities. Routledge, New York.

Harvey, D., 2000. Spaces of Hope, California Studies in Critical Human Geography. University of California Press, Berkeley.

Hester, R.T., 2006. Design for Ecological Democracy. MIT Press, Cambridge.

Hou, J. (Ed.), 2013. Transcultural Cities: Border-Crossing and Placemaking. Routledge, New York.

Ladner, P., 2011. The Urban Food Revolution: Changing the Way We Feed Cities. New Society Publishers, Gabriola Island.

Manuel, F.E., Manuel, F.P., 1979. Utopian Thought in the Western World. Belknap Press, Cambridge.

Miles, M., 2008. Urban Utopias: The Built and Social Architectures of Alternative Settlements. Routledge, London, New York.

Pitzer, D.E. (Ed.), 1997. America's Communal Utopias. University of North Carolina Press, Chapel Hill.

Redzepi, R., Zilber, D. 2018. The Noma Guide to Fermentation. Routledge, Taylor & Francis Group, London; New York.

Wark, M., 2019. Capital Is Dead. Verso, London; New York.

Winne, M., 2009. Closing the Food Gap: Resetting the Table in the Land of Plenty. Beacon Press, Boston.

Wright, E.O., 2010. Envisioning Real Utopias. Verso, London; New York.

Wright, E.O., 2019. How to be an Anticapitalist in the Twenty-First Century. Verso, London, Brooklyn, NY.

Zamalin, A., 2019. Black Utopia: The History of an Idea from Black Nationalism to Afrofuturism. Columbia University Press, New York.

# Afterword

All worthwhile projects open vistas of more work to be done, and it is my hope that this book is no exception. While by far the most interesting and valuable work that awaits is the utopian construction of the world by people who design places, write policies, and engage citizens in envisionings of the future as part of their daily working toward a world that is more just and more beautiful as described in the last chapter, there are a great number of other – perhaps more academic – projects that this work makes available. First, while for a number of reasons I did not make use of or bring to bear any secondary literature on Ebenezer Howard, Le Corbusier, or Frank Lloyd Wright – or on the Garden City, the Radiant City, or Broadacre City for that matter – this decision regarding scope does not imply that I do not feel that there is a value to secondary literature. The bibliography of this secondary material would take up a full volume itself, and there is much of interest while also, to be honest, much chaff. The main reason for not including works from this wide though sometimes shallow body of literature was that adjudicating between competing analyses, argumentations, and claimings-of-mantles-of-authority would distract from the narrative I wished to draw forward into the early 21st century regarding the anti-capitalist foundations of these utopian ideals. But that adjudication, especially in light of the material I have presented herein which, I hope, will be heartily challenged by some if not many is work that I propose we need to do to come to terms with the history of our professions and their alignment with the imperatives of capital.

Similarly, while I did not look for connections between the biographies of these three individuals and their ideas, that does not imply that digging into those connections wouldn't be fruitful. One of the most tantalizing historical bits that I came across in the writing of this book was Marx's observation that Swiss watchmaking families resisted capitalist industrial production longer than most. This is relevant, of course, because Le Corbusier was born Charles-Edouard Jeanneret-Gris into a Swiss watchmaking family. Personally, I find it less of interest to look at their individual psychologies as a way to understand the trajectory of their work and more of interest to look at the historical facts and trajectories into which they lived to understand how broader social, political, and economic frames of being impacted not only their work but the work

DOI: 10.4324/9781351053730-10

of those around them. This is why I found it valuable, if a bit of a detour, to look at the work of Marx, George, Bellamy, and Kropotkin. Not because those individuals impacted Howard, Le Corbusier, and Wright as personalities, but rather because of the breadth of public reception that the former authors enjoyed and the impact that reception had on the environments into which the latter authors thought. Of course, this of my personal predispositions, like all other predispositions, is open and ready for challenge.

Secondly, this is the first official foray of the theory of landscapes as political media onto the open road, and I feel much remains to be done to extend, sharpen, challenge, and develop that proposal. This is particularly true of the third manner in which I argue that landscapes operate as political media – that aligned with Agamben's theory of form-of-life and its place in his politics of means which resists the establishment of ends. Along that trajectory, thinking about how the foundations of these ideas has played out in the history of theories about and proposals for landscapes and cities is of great interest. Why have the professions that take on landscapes, cities, and buildings drawn the line between what is included in and what is excluded from their professional range in the way that they have with regard to politics? How, and why, have those boundaries shifted over time? How have they been different in different cultural or national traditions? Why have capital and the power of privilege inherent in it not been more successfully and directly challenged in the name of equity and justice from within these professions?

Lastly, what are the utopian visions to be made now that will inspire discussion in a future century in the way that these utopias from roughly a century ago draw us into thinking about our contemporary world? Howard, Le Corbusier, and Wright all had similar observations about what was wrong with their world and offered beatific visions for changes that would resolve the suffering and pain they saw around them. Their utopias were grand and remain unrealized. But they stir the imagination still. They challenge the world yet. As we look around us, and see the same challenges they saw and more – what utopian visions do we have to offer which will stir the imagination and challenge the world in the beginning of the 22nd century? While the work of improving the world on a daily and immediate basis is critical and very much needed, the work of inspiring the future by envisioning it differently is just as critical to the pursuit of equity, joy, justice, and delight.

# Index

Abrams, David 31
Agamben, Giorgio 21, 32, 35, 155
agency: as ability to select ends and means of action 158, 162; assessing who will be affected by our actions and how 163–164; agency for initiation and agency for implementation 158; career paths for accomplishment of change 162–163; citizen engagement 163, 164; identifying key holders of agency in projects 163; personal agency unavoidable in project work 163; utopian action in the world 164; *see also* utopian thinking
agency required for implementation of Utopia: agency held by residents of GC 159–160; individuals and households as primary agents in BC 161; planning agency for BC left unspecified by Wright 161; "serene and lucid minds" of technicians as ultimate agency for RC 160–161, 163
agency required as precondition for Utopia: already in existence for GC 158; existing land ownership laws, BC incompatible with 159; existing land ownership laws, RC incompatible with 159; lack of will and trust, as main obstacle to GC 158; means of realizing for BC, unexplained by Wright 159; means of realizing for RC, unexplained by Le Corbusier 159
agriculture and food in Broadacre City: agrarian education for children 110, 112; agronomic landscape aesthetics 111; common ownership and cooperation in agricultural life 111; cooking lessons for children 112; fresh food readily available 112; prefabricated elements in farm buildings 111; productive engagement with soil, redeeming for civilization 109–110; road networks, farms in relation to 112; self-sufficient acreage for every person 9, 76, 77, 102, 110, 112, 113
agriculture and food in Garden City: agricultural greenbelt 4–5, 67–68, 103; agricultural land prices and tenure stabilized by community ownership 104, 106, 113; allotment gardens 106–107, 119; farmers held accountable to city 104–105; food quality, improved by local growth 106; freedom of farmers to sell to any market 106; fruit and vegetable farming, stimulated by local market 106, 112; large field operations 106; local markets for local farms 67, 89–90, 103–104; reintegration of agriculture and industry 103, 105; sewage recycling 5, 69, 113; small-scale farming 106; speculation, greenbelt protected against 69–70, 105
agriculture and food in Radiant City: communal provision of cooking services 109; family-unit farms and cooperative villages 72, 107–108, 112; prefabricate rural buildings 108; rural–urban distinction sharply maintained 107; technological revolution in agriculture 108; transportation networks for produce 108–109, 112
anarchist communism 54; *see also* Kropotkin, Peter
Arendt, Hannah 17–19, 32
authority *see* freedom, cooperation, and authority

Balmori, Diane 27
Barnett, Jonathan 25
Bellamy, Edward *see Looking Backward*

*Index* 171

Broadacre City *see* agency required for implementation of Utopia; agency required as precondition for Utopia; agriculture and food in Broadacre City; building technology; capital in Broadacre City; electricity; freedom, cooperation, and authority in Broadacre City; history, Broadacre City in; labor in Broadacre City; land in Broadacre City; leisure in Broadacre City; nature and human nature in Broadacre City; transportation; urban growth; war technology

Buckingham, James S. 68

Buddha 153

building technology: design and harmony in BC 94; low-rise, low-technology buildings in GC 93; minimum houses in RC 95; prefabricated materials and components in BC 93, 141, 161; prefabrication crucial in RC 94–95; steel-and-concrete crucial in RC 94; "sun, greenery and space" aesthetic in RC 95

Calthorpe, Peter 25

*Capital* (Marx): land, expropriation of 44, 48, 62, 101; land as means of production through rent 45; means of production, capitalist expropriation of 43–44; surplus value, capitalist expropriation of 43, 62; publication of 42; reduction of laboring skill levels 44; returning means of production to common control 45; rural domestic industry, destruction of 44; urban growth 45; vicious exploitation of labor 44

capital in Broadacre City: economic activity as cultural activity 80; non-profit banks 79; public markets as civic institutions 79–80; public ownership of infrastructure 143; small businesses, proliferation of 79, 80; true capitalism 79

capital in Garden City: capital investment for construction of GC 65; collective control of capital investment 64; Crystal Palace 120; cooperative building societies 64; municipal control of commerce 64–65; true work, as remedy for capitalist oppression 64

capital in Radiant City: communal provision of goods and services 73, 109; honest money 74; planned efficiencies, supply-driven economy replaced by 73–74

capitalism: contemporary unthinkability of radical questioning of 41; domination of forms of life 17; harms currently inflicted by 2; Howard's critique of 64, 150; inequality intrinsic to 3; "invisible hand" 22, 101; Le Corbusier's critique of 6, 70–71, 72–74, 152; as primary organizing force of built environment 3; profit-seeking land ownership as foundational problem 3, 6; Wright's critique of 8–9, 75–76, 77–78, 78–79; *see also* industrial revolution

*Carrot City* 26

Central City, network of garden cities and 120

Central Park, NYC 20

Christo (Vladimirov Javacheff) 31

City Beautiful movement 19, 29

Cleveland, Horace 21–22

climate change 1

*Conquest of Bread*: *see* Kropotkin, Peter

cooperation *see* freedom, cooperation, and authority

Deming, M. Elen 32

democracy: democratic inertia 160; harmonious relationship with nature fundamental to 109, 110, 140–141; household autonomy as elemental basis of 8, 161; individuality crucial to 8, 9, 144, 153; Jeffersonian aristocracy of character 109; organic democracy dependent on lack of coercion 154; voting as deliberative process 161

Denes, Agnes 30

Duisburg-Nord 35

electricity: air conditioning in RC 88; electrical utility in GC 87; electronic communication in BC 88–89; elevators in RC 88; factory production electrified in GC 85; gradual advance of in twentieth century 87; pollution reduced by in GC 87

Emerson, Ralph Waldo 77, 109

environmental degradation 1, 84, 86, 87

farm-cities 24

*Fields, Factories, and Workshops*: *see* Kropotkin, Peter

Finlay, Ian Hamilton 31

forms-of-life (Agamben) 21, 32–35, 169

freedom, cooperation, and authority in Broadacre City: county seats, partial

172   *Index*

retaining of 142, 161; creative artists as natural leaders 143; freedom as basis for cooperation with minimal coercion 130, 140–141; individualism vs. individuality 143–144; planning for organic reintegration 142–143, 161; reintegration of life centered around individuality 141
freedom, cooperation, and authority in Garden City: administrative structures 134, 160; authority derived from cooperation 130, 133–134; collective and individual endeavour, harmonizing of 135; common land ownership frees cooperation from competition 132; cooperation as basis of justice and equality 132; cooperation as foundation of freedom 130, 132–133; existing property law, reliance on 132, 158; freedom for public experiments in social form 133, 135, 150; freely chosen membership of collective body 130, 134; private incorporation, legal authority based on 133–134, 158
freedom, cooperation, and authority in Radiant City: freedoms, authority justified by achievement of 138–139; biological needs, plan based on technicians' elaboration of 136–137; authority as foundation of freedom 130; collective body's precedence over individual choice 130; cooperation required by authority 137–138; freedom as basic pleasures 138–139; freedom as meaningful self-chosen work 139; individual freedom dependent on collective order 139–140; natural hierarchy based on trades 137; paternalism 136; plan, authority's subordination to 136
Friedrich, Caspar David 152

Garden City *see* agency required for implementation of Utopia; agency required as precondition for Utopia; agriculture and food in Garden City; building technology; capital in Garden City; cooperation, freedom, and authority in Garden City; electricity; history, Garden City in; labor in Garden City; land in Garden City; leisure in Garden City; nature and human nature in Garden City; transportation; urban growth; war technology

George, Henry *see Progress and Poverty*
Goldsworthy, Andy 31
Gorz, André 18

Haymarket Riot 50
High Line, NYC 34
Hirschfeld, C.C.L. 28–29
history, Broadacre City in: centralization as outdated principle 157; gasoline service stations as sign of nascent decentralization 157; industrialized return to nature as restitution of lost freedom 156–157; inevitability of decentralization 157
history, Garden City in: as epoch-making experiment 154–155; flow of history as progress toward universal wellbeing 155; future progress as flourishing of experimentation 155; as proposal about industrial society 155
history, Radiant City in: first and second machine ages 85, 136, 151, 156; industrialized return to nature as restitution of lost freedom 156; industrial present as deviation from natural history of humanity 156
Hitchmough, James 34–35
Holt, Nancy 31
Howard, Ebenezer *see* Garden City
human nature as unitary idea 149
Hunt, John Dixon 31, 35

industrial revolution, social harms of 3, 8, 10, 17, 70, 96; *see also* capitalism
inequality: current increase of 1, 12; exacerbated by technology 84, 148, 154; expropriation of land, as source of 48, 54, 62, 75; inherited investments as basis of 154; intrinsic to capitalism 3, 14, 44, 154; industrialization as cause of 8, 84; landscape architecture as means of redress 3, 24; in More's *Utopia* 11–12, 131; need for systemic solution to 1; in neighborhood amenities 19; potential for technology to eliminate 84; resolvable by cooperation 53; utopian discussion of 3

Jefferson, Thomas 109
Jekyll, Gertrude 34
Jesus 153

Kropotkin, Peter: anarchist communism 54, 55; common ownership of land 55, 63;

## Index    173

division of labor, critique of 5, 36, 55–56; Howard influenced by 64; re-integration of agriculture and industry in small cooperative units 53–54, 56–57, 63–64; spontaneous cooperation as natural condition of society 53, 63; State, need for as superstition 55; syndicalization 56; violent expropriation of land, as source of poverty and inequality 54

labor in Broadacre City: agricultural labor, emphasis on 78, 109–110; democracy, freely chosen employment crucial to 77, 110; decentralization, proximity to employment options created by 78; factories, separation into smaller units 141; freedom to pursue meaningful work 78; machine power for provision of basic goods 78, 84; reduced workday 78; self-sufficiency, employment rendered voluntary by 9, 77, 78, 79, 102, 110

labor in Garden City: addressing rural–urban labor imbalances 65–66; local farms growing for local markets 5, 67, 89–90, 112; sweated labor, absence of 116; town-country magnet 66, 102; wages and conditions supported by community control of tenancy 67, 117

labor in Radiant City: machines, increasing capacity of 74; reduced workday 6–7, 73, 74; true work 74–75; waste and inefficiency, labor hours reduced by elimination of 74; land in Broadacre City: decentralizing distribution of 8, 9, 77, 78; communal distribution of benefits of land 76; landlaws subordinate to rights of human being 76; publicly owned apartment towers 143; self-sufficient acreage for every person 9, 76, 77, 102, 112

land in Garden City: agricultural greenbelt 4–5, 67–68; central public gardens 4, 119; common ownership of land 4, 67, 70, 101; eminent domain, proposed use of 64, 162; established on land bought at agricultural prices 65, 69; homes with gardens for all laborers 4, 68; outer band of industrial land 68; planned efficiencies in use of 69; rate-rent used for communal benefit 68, 69, 101, 104; speculation and competition, absence of 69–70, 105, 119, 132

land in Radiant City: diversified agriculture 72; family-unit farms and cooperative villages 72; material and spiritual redevelopment of land use 71; mobilization of land for common good 5–6; pedestrianization 71; sports and recreation facilities interspersed among residences 7, 71, 74

landscape architecture: Cleveland's conception of 3, 22, 27; one of several disciplines that design landscapes 27; potential role in addressing inequality 3

landscape: contribution to more just societies 148; definition of 20; of embedded cooperation 164; foundational political medium 2; as things lived 2–3

landscapes as political media: deep reorganization vs. amelioration of social problems 24–26; distribution of and access to resources through landscape 19, 20, 21–27; forms-of-life 21, 32–35, 169; as foundational political media 2; inequality in neighborhood amenities 19; political imagination, landscape as medium for 21, 27–32; public art and statuary 19, 28; relations of people and things 20, 27, 31; relations of people 19, 27; *see also* politics

landscape urbanism 25, 27

Laotze 152

Laugier, Marc-Antoine 33

Le Corbusier *see* Radiant City

leisure in Broadacre City: aesthetic lives, development of 124, 126, 143, 162; arts and crafts 124; community centers 125; commuting reductions, leisure increased by 118, 124; film and music 125–126; home as center of 125–126; machine production, leisure increased by 118; productive engagement with soil 124; small roadside markets as social hubs 80, 124–125, 157; sports facilities 125; theatre 125; as voluntary labor 124

leisure in Garden City: allotment gardens 119; central public gardens 4, 119, 126, 150; Crystal Palace 120–121; cultural entertainment 120; green spaces throughout city 4, 117, 119, 126, 150; increase of leisure hours 117; integrating experience of nature with social benefits of towns 118, 119–120; public institutions for recreation 117, 119, 150

174 *Index*

leisure in Radiant City: efficient prefabricated houses, leisure hours increased by 117; green and open spaces for passive leisure 71, 95, 121–122; machine production, leisure hours increased by 117, 121, 123, 126; meditation, houses as vessels for 123; professional spectator sports, discouragement of 122–123; sports and recreation facilities throughout city 7, 71, 122–123, 126; true work, leisure as 117, 123; unmet leisure needs as potential threat 74, 121; walking 71, 90, 91, 122, 126

Levitas, Ruth 1, 2, 62, 149, 164

London: as antithesis of Garden City 4; electrification of 87; hypothetical reconstruction after success of garden cities 102, 103, 120, 151, 155; planning control of railways 90; population increase 100; underground railway 86

*Looking Backward*: basic faith in altruism 151; centralized system of production for common good 53, 63; communal utilities 52–53; direct critique of society 36; early retirement 75; equal distribution of basic goods 52; inherited investments as basis of inequality 50; international peace and cooperation 53; Howard influenced by 64; natural superiority of wealthy, as delusion 50–51; reasoned argument and cooperation, poverty resolvable by 53; unthinkability of alternatives to status quo, as delusion 50

Louv, Richard 34

Lyson, Thomas 26

MacKaye, Benton 22–23

Mann, Tom 66

Marris, Emma 34, 35

Marx, Karl *see Capital*

Mill, J.S. 4, 42

More, Thomas *see Utopia*

*Mutual Aid*: *see* Kropotkin, Peter

nature and human nature in Broadacre City: cave-dweller vs. nomad parable (Wright) 153, 154, 157; embedding in natural world, essential to good life in 154; human nature as humane growth of individuality 152–153; inter-relatedness and fitness between people as path to richer communal life 153–154

nature and human nature in Garden City: basic faith in altruism, GC based on 150–151; experimental negotiation of good life, GC as 150; individualistic wealth-seeking, condemned by Howard 150; natural world and society both essential to good life 150; socialist neglect of independence and initiative, condemned by Howard 150

nature and human nature in Radiant City: collective order and discipline of nature 151–152; individualistic wealth-seeking, condemned by Le Corbusier 152; nature's impulse toward organization 151–152, 161; returning human nature to nature 151–152

neoliberalism 26, 41, 55; *see also* capitalism

New Urbanism 25

New York City: Central Park 20; electrification 87; flows of people and goods 22; first radio broadcast 87; High Line 34; population growth 100; Times Square 22; *Wheatfield, Battery Park City* 30

Nolen, John 24, 29

Nordahl, Darrin 26

Olmsted, Frederick Law 20, 23, 24, 33

Oudolf, Piet 34

Papago Trail 26

Paracelsus 109

Paris: electrification 87; Le Corbusier's criticisms of and proposed replacement with RC 156; population growth 100

pedestrian vehicle-free areas 26, 27

politics: as partisanship 18, 19; as relations between people 17, 18–19, 32, 35; shared social space, access to 18; as statecraft 18, 19; zero-sum vs. cooperative and value-generating 19; *see also* landscapes as political media

*Progress and Poverty* (George): capital, definition of 47; class antagonism, no reason for 46, 47, 53; equal moral right to use of land 47, 49; Howard influenced by 64; inverse capital–wages relationship, refutation of 46; labor, definition of 47; labor controlled by landowners 49, 62–63; labor not subordinate to capital 47–48, 62–63; land, expansive definition of 46–47; land ownership as violent expropriation 48, 62, 63; poverty, concern with 46; publication of 45–46; Single Tax on use of land 49, 63, 75; unearned increment of land speculation 36, 49; violent solutions, concern to avoid 46; wealth, definition of 47; Wright influenced by 76

Radburn 26
Radiant City *see* agency required for implementation of Utopia; agency required as precondition for Utopia; agriculture and food in Radiant City; authority, freedom, and cooperation in Radiant City; building technology; capital in Radiant City; electricity; history, Radiant City in; labor in Radiant City; land in Radiant City; leisure in Radiant City; nature and human nature in Radiant City; transportation; urban growth; war technology
Reed, Chris 25–26
regional planning 22–23
Resettlement Authority (US) 36
*Rethinking Urban Parks* 29–30
Ricardo, David 42
Rich, Sarah 26
Rowe, Peter 29

Schwartz, Marth 30
*Second Nature Urban Agriculture* 26
Shaw, Albert 134
Single Tax Movement 49; *see also Progress and Poverty*
Sitwell, George 32–33
Smith, Adam 22, 42, 55
Smithson, Robert 31
Souter-Brown, Gayle 33–34
Spence, Thomas 68–69
Spencer, Herbert 68–69
Stein, Clarence 26–27
Stevens, Wallace 30–31
suburbs: as commuter dormitory towns 90, 121, 139; increased accessibility with steam power 21–22; modern pastoralism 29

technology: advances in lifetimes of Howard, Le Corbusier, and Wright 84, 86–87; distributing benefits of 84–85, 154; first and second machine ages (Le Corbusier) 85, 136, 151, 156; inequality exacerbated by 84, 85; potential to improve human condition 84, 85; labor and skills degraded by 44, 84; pollution

86, 87; *see also* building technology; electricity; transportation
transportation: automobiles, liberating function in BC 92; automobile infrastructure in RC 91; elevated highways in RC 91; elevators in RC 88, 90–91; freight network in RC 90; highly developed network in GC; interconnected garden cities 90; proximity as efficiency factor in GC 89; publicly owned system in BC 143; railroad rights-of-way expanded in BC 92, 143, 161; railroads in GC 89, 90; separation of transport modes in RC 90, 91; streetcars in RC 91; subsidized transport in BC 92, 141; trolleys in RC 90; walking in GC 89; walking in RC 90, 91

urban food production 26
urban growth: cities increasingly divorced from countryside 101; as consequence of expropriation of land 101; decentralized BC, as radical abolition of rural–urban distinction 103; equality of rural and urban life, as ideal (Le Corbusier) 102; GC as reintegration of rural and urban 102; rapid rural–urban migration as social problem 45, 100, 101, 154
*Utopia* (More): authoritarian character of 130; communal dining 13, 52–53; criminal justice 10; distribution of cities 12; equal distribution of basic goods 11, 14, 52–53; family-based trades 12–13; hierarchy 13–14, 130; houses and gardens 13; impoverishment of the laboring poor 10–12; inequality 11–12; markets 12; militarism of 13; money, antipathy toward 11–12; patriarchal domination of women 14; property, absence of 13; sheep-farming and enclosure, detrimental effects of 11, 44, 48, 63; slavery 13, 14, 130; travel restriction 13–14; urbal–rural relationships 12
utopian thinking: concerns about authoritarianism in 130–131; as critique of current policy limitations 1–2; discrediting of 2, 131; as holistic re-imagining of global problems 1, 62, 164; inspiring the future as critical task 169; land ownership as central issue 58; as method 1–2, 149; provisional answers to guide explorations 162; as radical

176 *Index*

structural change 23; time ripe for 1; utopian writings on landscape 9–10; utopias as states of the world vs. utopian action in the world 164; *see also* agency

*Values in Landscape Architecture and Environmental Design* 32

Wakefield, Edward 68
Waldheim, Charles 25, 26

Wall, Alex 25, 26
Walpole, Horace 28, 33
war: aerial attack, decentralization as advantageous in BC 95–96; aerial attack, RC relatively invulnerable to 95; wartime industrial mobilization, as demonstration of feasibility for large-scale peacetime projects 96, 142
Wright, Frank Lloyd *see* Broadacre City